Fostering Learning Versatility in Business Schools

Wolfgang Amann

INDIA • UK • USA

Copyright © Wolfgang Amann, 2021

All rights reserved. No part of this publication may be reproduced, stored in a retrieval system, or transmitted in any form or by any means, electronic, mechanical, recording or otherwise, without the prior written permission of the author.

This book has been published with all reasonable efforts taken to make the material error-free after the consent of the author. The author of this book is solely responsible and liable for its content including but not limited to the views, representations, descriptions, statements, information, opinions and references ["Content"]. The publisher does not endorse or approve the Content of this book or guarantee the reliability, accuracy or completeness of the Content published herein. The publisher and the author make no representations or warranties of any kind with respect to this book or its contents. The author and the publisher disclaim all such representations and warranties, including for example warranties of merchantability and educational or medical advice for a particular purpose. In addition, the author and the publisher do not represent or warrant that the information accessible via this book is accurate, complete or current.

Paperback ISBN: 978-1-954399-00-6

Hardback ISBN: 978-1-954399-02-0

eBook ISBN: 978-1-954399-01-3

First Published in January 2021

Published by Walnut Publication (an imprint of Vyusta Ventures LLP)

www.walnutpublication.com

USA

6834 Cantrell Road #2096, Little Rock, AR 72207, USA

India

#722, Esplanade One, Rasulgarh, Bhubaneswar – 751010, India

#55 S/F, Panchkuian Marg, Connaught Place, New Delhi - 110001, India

UK

International House, 12 Constance Street, London E16 2DQ, United Kingdom

Table of contents

Table of contents i
List of figures iv
List of tables v
Acknowledgements vi
Summary vii

Chapter 1: Overview of the research project 1
1.1 Introduction 1
1.2 Background of the research – innovating business schools by overcoming fossilisation 2
1.3 Research objectives 5
1.4 The analysis structure 6
1.5 Conclusions 7

Chapter 2: Why leadership style versatility (LSV) matters: linking the concept to learning outcomes 8
2.1 Introduction 8
2.2 Overview of the challenges 9
2.3 Literature review 10
2.4 Conceptual framework 18
2.5 Methodology and method 22
2.6 Empirical results 25
2.7 Analysis and interpretation 27
2.8 Implications, limitations, and suggestions for future research 28
2.9 Conclusions 31

Chapter 3: Reflections on study 1 and building the case for study 2 32

3.1 Introduction..32

3.2 The Indian business school landscape's potential to benefit from LSV research 32

3.3 Enlarging the philosophical paradigms to further explore LSV 34

Chapter 4: Exploring the faculty view on LSV – Insights from the second empirical study..... 38

4.1 Introduction..38

4.2 Review of the challenges 38

4.3 Literature review 39

4.4 Methodology and method..53

4.5 Empirical results 56

4.6 Bridging data, framework, theory and hypotheses...63

4.7 Implications, limitations, and suggestions for future research..64

4.8 Conclusions 69

Chapter 5: Reflections on study 2 and building the case for study 3 71

5.1 Reflections on learning more about LSV as a construct...71

5.2 Reflections on applying grounded theory..72

Chapter 6: Exploring the student view on LSV – insights from the third empirical study 76

6.1 Introduction..76

6.2 Elements of an initial literature review 77

6.3 Methodology and method..90

6.4 Empirical results producing the grounded theory of 'emergence' for a student-oriented view on LSV 103

6.5 Discussion of results and second literature review on the student-oriented grounded theory and emerging hypotheses 112

6.6 Limitations and implications for research and practice 116

6.7 Conclusions 122

Chapter 7: Implications for theory and practice 124
7.1 Overview of the findings in light of the research projects 124
7.2 Limitations 125
7.3 Implications for theory – towards a future research agenda for learning styles versatility 127
7.4 Implications for practice – students, faculty and business school leadership 129
7.5 Implications for grounded theory researchers 132
7.6 Summary 132

Chapter 8: Conclusions 133
8.1 Complying with the Principles of Responsible Management Education 133
8.2 The strong case for Ashby's law of requisite variety 133
8.3 The case for a self-structured leadership pipeline for business schools 134
8.4 Effectively addressing a research gap 134

Reference list 135
About the author 172

List of figures

Figure 1: Generic business model for business schools 3
Figure 2: Flow of the analysis – moving towards an integrated view of LSV 6
Figure 3: Nomological approach to the field of LSV and structure of the literature review 12
Figure 4: Visualisation of a requisite variety view on learning challenges and learning style versatility 18
Figure 5: Conceptual framework of the analysis 21
Figure 6: Distribution of learners across versatility categories 26
Figure 7: Generic business model for business schools 35
Figure 8: Key shift in philosophical paradigms across the included LSV studies 36
Figure 9: Examples of lowest, limited, and higher LSV based on the Honey and Mumford (2009) framework 45
Figure 10: Overview of the various relationships between metacognition and LSV 47
Figure 11: Emerging outside-in grounded theory on LSV leveraging at the study partner institution . 61
Figure 12: Positionality effects 74
Figure 13: Comparison of developmental phases in leadership versatility research versus LSV research 85
Figure 14: Insights on how to grow leadership versatility based on selected frameworks 89
Figure 15: Emergence framework as grounded theory for student-oriented LSV dynamics 111
Figure 16: Divergent educational philosophies of students versus faculty members encountered in this study 118
Figure 17: Change model towards more LSV as value added in a competitive world 121
Figure 18: Categorising research efforts and showing a path for research related to LSV 128
Figure 19: Periods in gender studies 129

List of tables

Table 1: Overview of learners based on LSV 23
Table 2: Descriptive statistics of key variables 25
Table 3: Selected elements of a larger learning quotient conceptualisation 43
Table 4: Overview of the logic of mapping and comparing codes 57
Table 5: Selected options for coding in (A) traditional, (B) evolved, and (C) constructivist grounded theory 72
Table 6: Timeline of selected educational taxonomies 78
Table 7: Opposing schools of thoughts in the learning style literature and their implications for LSV ... 81
Table 8: The development of the leadership and learning style field 85
Table 9: Constructivist versus objectivist grounded theory 92
Table 10: Exemplified ambiguity in Charmaz's constructive grounded theory 93
Table 11: Critical self-assessment of the chosen method 99
Table 12: Sample coding and emerging categories in student-external factors 104
Table 13: Codes and categories of the learners 105
Table 14: Excerpt 1 from memo writing 106
Table 15: Excerpt 2 from memo writing 107
Table 16: Overview of outcomes based on research objectives 125
Table 17: Summary of limitations across the three empirical studies on LSV 126
Table 23: Overview of the evolution of categories based on iterative comparisons of codes in the ongoing interview process 161

Acknowledgements

Supported by two faculty members and experts in the field of learning from the University of Dundee, I decided to work towards an innovation in business schools. Both Dr Elizabeth Lakin and Dr Richard Ingram helped advance this project with their expertise and constructive feedback. Our much-appreciated discussions of emerging thoughts were invaluable for the success of this initiative. I want to acknowledge, equally, the support I received from my anonymous research partner in India's school leadership team, along with the much-appreciated availability and insights the faculty and student interviewees shared.

Summary

Business schools operate in a highly dynamic environment and regularly need to reassess the value they add to a given context. The following research presents a critical analysis of the concept of 'learning style versatility' (LSV) and further substantiates it, relying on three related studies. The concept captures the degree to which a learner can effectively apply different learning styles in the process of learning. In this study, it is presented as an emerging construct. By boosting learning skills business schools increase the value they offer and the quality of the courses participants receive. Recognizing and appropriately responding to LSV can potentially add tremendous value to business schools as well as to individual learners' skills and knowledge.

The first of three studies represents a 'proof of concept', thus the research project starts by substantiating the hypothesis that LSV is an important construct. Offering a first and aligned conceptualisation and operationalisation of the construct, the initial study answers the research question on how LSV impacts learning outcomes, and it confirms a positive, statistically significant impact. Seemingly, the higher the LSV, the better the students' grades. This first study also provides an initial working definition of LSV which will recur in the subsequent two empirical and qualitative studies.

Next, two qualitative studies follow, which develop grounded theories on how the faculty and students experience the phenomenon. As for the faculty, a four-level framework explains hygiene factors – in allusion to early motivation theory – to be managed if LSV should deploy more of its potential. Study three complements the analysis by interviewing students on matters that disclose how they perceive LSV-related dynamics. There is an interesting student-driven emergent approach to altering the learning experience and exceeding what the limited classroom setting offers. In order to arrive at a context-rich understanding of the phenomenon, I conducted all three studies at the same private business school in one of India's main cities. The research closes with a future research agenda mapped for this still nascent construct that hitherto has been dealt with in a rather fragmented way.

"Developing the flexibility to respond productively to all sorts of instructional situations would be a laudable goal... How best to encourage this flexibility is yet to be determined" (Bhagat et al., 2015, p. 59).

Chapter 1: Overview of the research project

1.1 Introduction

Research has to be rigorous but eventually but we should not ignore the importance of actionable knowledge (Pandey, 2017). This actionable knowledge can foster process improvements (Arumugam & Christy, 2018). Because of my desire to help improve real-world conditions while rigorously carrying out research, I started to wonder what innovations we really need in business schools. Having worked in higher education and the business school context for more than two decade, I noticed the need amongst program participants to not only learn knowledge and skills in the field of business but also to grow their learning acumen as such.

As outlined in the more detailed literature reviews provided in this study, the business school context and management education in general have recently become particularly dynamic, showing a clear need to innovate and differentiate. Iñiguez de Onzoño and Carmona (2012) characterise the situation of business schools as one haunted by the Red Queen effect. In evolutionary theory, the Red Queen effect prescribes perpetual change and adaptation for survival. Evolution and triggered organisational change enable institutions to stay in their game competitively, as the fight for survival continues to intensify.

However, what happens if a new generation of aspiring business school leaders do not wait until they are in senior leadership positions to develop next generation ideas? What if they take a few years to generate actionable knowledge that is conceptually reasonably substantiated and empirically grounded, so that when the opportunity for promotion arises, the candidate is ready? Such candidates could then innovate without losing valuable time. For that logic to work, though, a newly generated idea should potentially be able to represent a major redirection of the logic guiding business schools, or as Keller (2013) puts it, should redirect "the one thing" (p. 1) that can add above average value when it receives dedicated attention. This research and resulting book aspire in such a way to help business schools leap, as Yu (2018) has suggested for organisations, to improve over time.

The following section (1.2) outlines further why this is necessary. Section 1.3 details the research objectives, which I shall critically review towards the end of the research project, in section 8.5. Section

1.4 provides an overview of the research structure. Chapters two to seven, which form the core of the research project, show how the study is made up of three empirical studies. These chapters report on and unify the various projects by introducing them, linking them, and reflecting on them.

1.2 Background of the research – innovating business schools by overcoming fossilisation

The rationale for presenting learning style versatility (LSV) not as a panacea, but as one constructive idea for the future of business schools, lies in the increasing complexity business schools are facing. As a working definition I propose, LSV refers to the degree to which a learner can effectively apply different learning styles in the process of learning. This would be a very useful kind of competence for stakeholders in business environments that are becoming increasingly challenging. Reflecting on whether this is actually happening, Amann, Nedopil, and Steger (2011) present a framework for complexity with four factors that drive complexity, namely diversity, interdependence, rapid flux and ambiguity, which they define as meta-challenges driving organisational performance or explaining organisational adversity as well as failure. Complexity characterises the business school environment and management education industry, as the following description sets out.

Regarding diversity, stakeholders have become more pluralistic than the focus on recruiters in place before. In a higher education context increasingly characterised by commercialisation, a growing number of participants voice concerns regarding ethical shortcomings and conceptual flaws. Such concern finds that the entire orientation towards the functionalist paradigm pursuing efficiency and effectiveness needs to be dissolved in order to foster a new paradigm in management education which centralizes human dignity (Pirson et al., 2016).

Besides individual researchers, larger institutions also call for a system change, or at least more diversity in current systems, in the discussions on value, theory and purpose in business schools. The United Nations Global Compact initiative on Principles of Responsible Management Education (PRME) issued six clear principles on how to revamp business schools, as well as an addendum principle determining that these institutions should be role models which themselves apply the logic they convey in teaching, i.e. to students in the classroom or to corporate partnerships, and in research. In an interim evaluation, Perry and Win (2013) conclude that PRME indeed does have a system-wide impact, yet an even deeper and more far-reaching impact can be expected in sustainability terms. Diversity on the mission, vision, values, teaching, research, or partnering levels, to name but a few, therefore challenges established solutions. The main topic of the research submitted in this document equally enhances complexity by asking how we should deal with the diversity of learners.

Increasing diversity has an effect on interdependence, a second complexity driver. As figure 1 (below) shows, system elements in a business school show strong interdependencies. Durand and Dameron (2017) illustrate this in their overview of an integrated and aligned, though still generic, business model for business schools. Ivory et al. (2006) and Lorange (2008) explain how diverse the business school landscape is. Various institutions' business models designed to generate value and pursue a strategic direction, show considerable disparity. This requires school leaders to find an idiosyncratic alignment of all key factors in their particular situation.

Figure 1 below, shows how various interdependencies materialise, for example, when suitably talented candidates join the school and thereby support the reputation and funding opportunities given at the centre of this visualisation and conceptualisation. Such candidates, in turn, potentially attract recruiters. Both factors, i.e., talented students and visible recruiters, positively impact the programme's potential to attract donations. Regarding research, a solid Ph.D. programme, well-qualified faculty, and the corresponding research output (either showing research rigour in accredited journals or showing thought leadership in practitioners' outlets) create a virtuous circle which fosters the attraction of talented students, recruiters and donations.

Further, such interdependency helps to attract postgraduate programme participants as well as executives, and it supports them in their lifelong learning endeavours. The right quality and quantity of components generate desired revenues, which in turn fosters the desired research output and reputational gains.

Figure 1: Generic business model for business schools

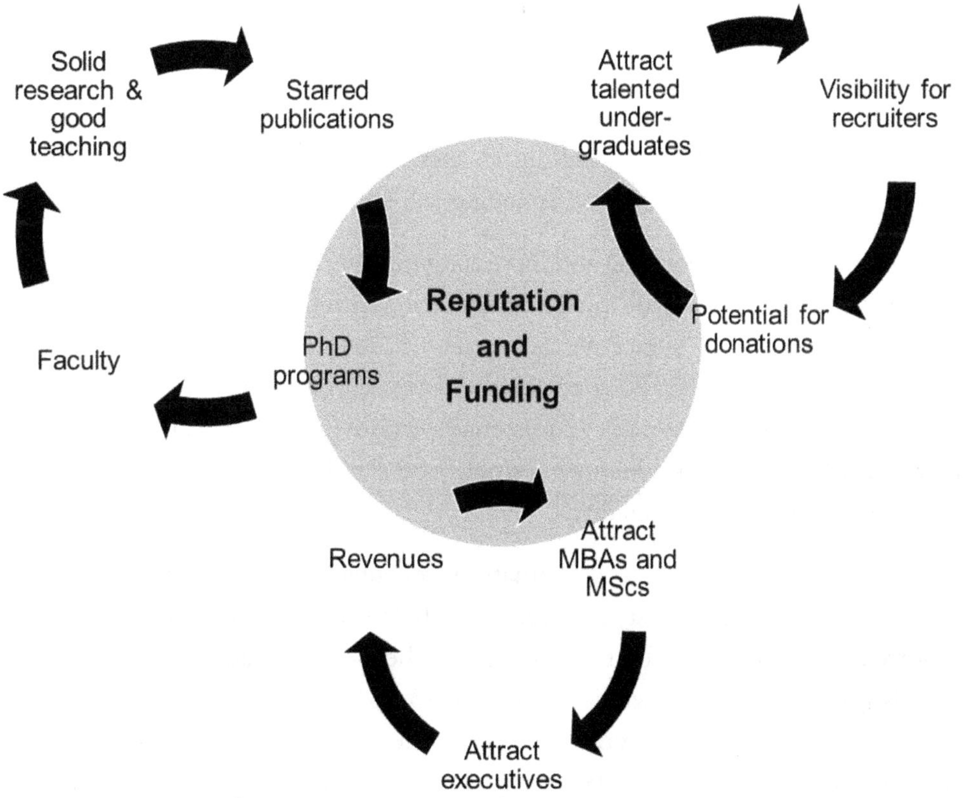

Source: Based on Durand and Dameron, 2017, p. 9

Achieving this alignment is not an easy task. It becomes even more challenging when the additional two complexity drivers materialise. Fast flux forces business schools to adapt more rapidly than before. Factors such as technological change, e.g. in the form of massive open online courses (MOOCs) (Burd et al., 2015) or new partnering strategies as existing funding sources, are falling away. Thus, more value needs to be created swiftly (Nikitina & Lapina, 2017), questions need solutions at an ever-faster pace. Lastly, ambiguous future development visions do not support clear, reliable planning which means that institutional leaders can expect more complexity in future internationalisation processes (Andreff, 2017).

Dealing with a controversial construct and managing a rather fossilized construct

The literature review sections in the three studies reported below, will elaborate on the available body of knowledge – what is known and what unknown – in order to clarify the research gap this project addresses, and how it will be done. From the very beginning, however, I acknowledge that the field of learning styles is controversial, and therefore one that has been polarizing. Figure 3, given in the literature review of the first empirical study, maps a nomological net of the very many major questions the literature addresses. Some learning experts, such as Kirschner (2017), call learning styles a myth. He reviews the field holistically and condenses the main arguments, evaluating them on three levels. First, he doubts that a single optimal learning style exists, even if one considers the actually effective learning mode and not a mere preference. Second, he finds the empirical foundations, especially those concerning validity, too weak to justify any further propagation of the concept. Empirical studies on reliable and valid approaches to operationalization during measurement and linking practices to outcomes, prove to be weak. Third, he is critical of pigeon-holing learners, which he finds ethically improper, but also undesirable in terms of consequences, such as having self-fulfilling prophecy effects.

Coffield et al. (2004) add that the existing and increasing number of dichotomies causes confusion. Thus, practical applicability is yet another problem. In addition, Knoll et al. (2016) doubt learners' ability to report accurately, finding their subjective accounts of their preferences disconnected from what objectively would be best for them. Poor correlation between preferences and best practices limits the predictive power regarding how past test scores enable improved future learning. Coffield et al. (2004) reviewed instruments and could not identify a single one simultaneously fulfilling test-retest reliability, consistency, construct or predictive validity.

The question how to best deal with such a situation, remains. This research project suggests a radical shift from learning styles to learning style versatility to help the field overcome the current impasse and associated controversies that are only too familiar in the field of leadership styles, which eventually matured towards leadership style versatility, as Figure 13 and the corresponding theoretical discussions show. Schnitker and Emmons (2013) critically review the German dialectic model of thesis, antithesis and subsequent synthesis attributed to Hegel, who in turn admits to relying on Kant in searching for a framework to progress beyond a stalemate.

An argument can be made for the following thesis, antithesis and synthesis train of thought. The thesis states that learning style represents a contested field, yet has potential in the larger effort to optimize learning.

The antithesis states that hitherto the learning style fields has failed to mature. In a way, past studies could not see the wood for the trees because their focus was too narrow. The antithesis prompts a shift away from mere learning styles to learning style versatility as a more useful concept, which can overcome past shortcomings such as pigeon-holing and poor empirical results' insufficient explanations. To support this research project's antithesis, the field of leadership can serve as a source of inspiration. As I shall soon demonstrate, the field progressed to include versatility instead of mere typologies. The three studies on which this project reports – all within the boundaries of their limitations and consciously chosen positions – shed more light on learning style versatility and in doing so substantiate the antithesis; considered against the thesis, a new synthesis will emerge which could proclaim 1) the importance for researchers to work towards maturing a field, and 2) the interest and relevance of learning styles which through the study has been given a broader and more solid foundation. It is not, as some have suggested, just a myth. The field should not be abandoned, but taken further to achieve a better understanding. Therefore, it is necessary to explicate the research objectives as clearly as possible, as will be done in the next section.

1.3 Research objectives

In light of the introduction above, the research objectives are:

- firstly, to establish whether learning versatility is in fact a construct that has, to date, been under-researched;

- secondly, if so, to trigger the process of operationalising LSV in order to commence the crucial process of measuring and building proxies for it;

- thirdly, to show the construct's importance by investigating whether LSV impacts study performance, e.g. in the form of grades as representative of study outcomes;

- fourthly, to review how LSV relates to other key learning related constructs;

- fifthly, to gather additional qualitative insight, by means of interviews, on how faculty perceives LSV;

- finally, to gather complementing qualitative, empirical insight on how students perceive LSV.

In the following figure, I summarise and visualise the flow of the research to provide an integrative view on LSV in a business school context. In an introduction, I link the three studies, after which various sections show the connections as well as transitions between them. In closing I reflect on and also acknowledge the study's limitations, give its implications for theory and practice, and draw a number of final conclusions.

The working definition of LSV proposed in study 1 remains, and therefore is repeated in studies 2 and 3. By the end of this research, there are answers to whether there is a case for more LSV orientation and how to really understand the construct better, specifically considering the growing adversity with which business school graduates have to cope. Such adversity requires students to become better learners. Equally, the need for business schools to pay more attention to individuality in terms of learner profiles, and to pursue more added value, is emphasized.

Figure 2: Flow of the analysis – moving towards an integrated view of LSV

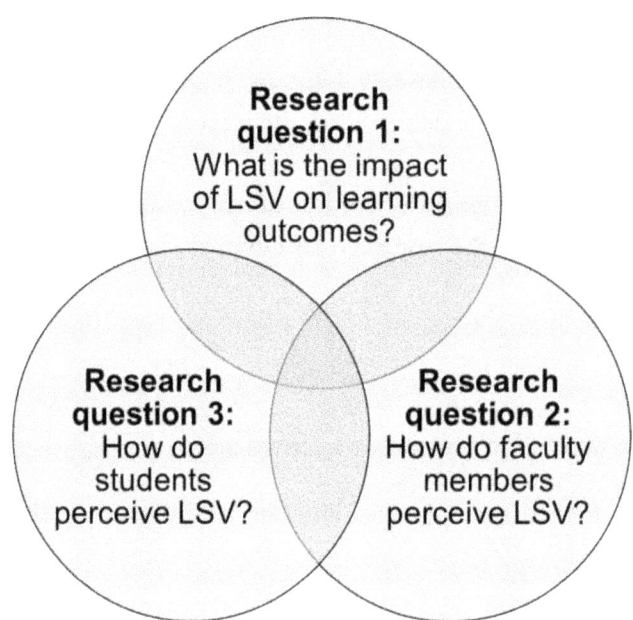

1.4 The analysis structure

The aforementioned research objectives already indicate the flow of the analysis as a journey of discovery. The first chapter introduces the personal motivation for pursuing this tripartite research project in the field of educational psychology. Chapter 1 further points to the meta-challenge complexity poses for business schools, before outlining the research objectives. In reviewing the literature, LSV emerges as a promising way forward.

Chapter 2 aims to empirically test whether LSV as a hitherto under-researched topic can actually explain study performance in terms of grades and of other potential outcome variables. If so, further research can shed more light on how better to understand this emergent construct in context. Also, this chapter will give a more thorough understanding of two key stakeholder groups, faculty and students.

Chapter 3 links the results of the first study to the second empirical study. This chapter reviews the status quo, considering learning styles within the research project, and shows why there is a need to shift the perspective of research questions, methodology and methods.

Chapter 4 presents the first qualitative study in this research initiative and focuses on the faculty perspective. It describes how faculty members perceive the construct, explains which factors matter from their point of view, and explicates how faculty believe the construct should be comprehended.

Chapter 5 provides a critical reflection that links this first qualitative study, which is the second pillar of the tripartite study, to the third empirical endeavour. The chapter connects this integrated submission to chapter 6, where the focus of attention and empirical effort shifts once again. Here, the students' view is in the spotlight as I address the research question on how students perceive LSV.

Chapter 7 outlines the limitations of the entire research project, and then derives critical implications for theory and practice. The reflections and analysis in this chapter link the research results to the original research objectives and provide answers to the questions about the next critical steps researchers and practitioners need to take. Chapter 8 provides final conclusions and closes this research project which is devoted to an integrative research initiative on LSV in a business school context.

As outlined, the directly following chapter forms the foundation of this research initiative on learning style versatility. A first empirical study adopting a positivist methodology conceptualises, then operationalises, and subsequently measures the impact of learning style versatility. It will shed light on whether there is a link to learning outcomes measured by grades. Once confirmed, this warrants further research into how teachers as well as students perceive the phenomenon.

1.5 Conclusions

Three interconnected studies on learning style versatility explore the learning style versatility concept, showing how it could serve as qualifying feature for future roles in higher education generally, and business schools specifically. The study also addresses a gap identified in the literature. Insights from all three studies are foundational in drawing the implications for theory and practice, along with the overall conclusions presented at the end of the research project. Thereby, as will be detailed, based on lateral thinking, I address the research gap. There are shortcomings in the learning styles literature; to attend to them a connection to a type of progress in the field of leadership has been helpful. To conclude, the benefit of this study is threefold: it contributes to personal learning, the available academic body of knowledge, and business school educational practice.

Chapter 2: Why leadership style versatility (LSV) matters: linking the concept to learning outcomes

2.1 Introduction

This study investigates the link between LSV and learning outcomes, and paves the way to a better understanding of an LSV ergo-ecology. LSV refers to a learner's ability to effectively apply different learning styles in the process of learning. The research presented here forms part of the discourse on the larger responsibilities of business schools, which scholars have increasingly criticised as lacking relevance and an ethics orientation regarding their programmes' content. The research draws a parallel between the fields of learning styles and leadership. In explaining performance, leadership studies have shifted attention from capturing and categorising the variety of leadership styles that could generally or situationally be most effective, to leadership versatility. In comparison to the leadership literature, the rich literature on learning styles has, due to being in an early maturity stage, not yet fully embraced versatility. Addressing this research gap as an opportunity, the study initially tests the hypothesis that LSV positively impacts learning outcomes in the form of grades.

Based on a proposed new LSV proxy, this study provides statistically significant empirical evidence based on 121 survey responses from a private university in India. LSV indeed impacts learning outcomes in terms of the more objective cumulated grade average, yet evidence suggests this is not the case for the more subjective perceptions of learning success which include learners' satisfaction. Linear regression functions were calculated with age, gender and programme level (undergraduate versus graduated programme status) as control variables. While results are independent of students' age, gender mattered.

Eventually, I conclude this study's report by building a trajectory for the field of LSV, which I suggest represents the route to the next maturity level regarding the debates on the rich, fragmented, and yet still inconclusive learning styles field. Understanding LSV as part of a learner's individuality can improve the performance of both a business school and its learners. In conclusion, further, the study affirms the call for orientating towards the individuality of a learner and thus emphasizing human dignity over shareholder value. Thereby the project contributes to a key debate within responsible management education.

2.2 Overview of the challenges

This study deals with two challenges. Firstly, it addresses the fact that business school graduates have to cope with business environments that are increasingly volatile, uncertain, complex and ambiguous (VUCA) as has been detailed by Betof et al. (2014), Codreanu (2016), and Fassinger et al., (2017).

Assuming this to be true, the study has to consider a business environment that requires leaders who adopt a lifelong learning approach to managing these complex conditions. Thus we view leaders as learners for such a VUCA environment (Mikkelsen & Jarche, 2015). In line with the authors named here, this study assumes that future leaders and managers can benefit from understanding the best way in which they learn so that they can better prepare for the demands lying ahead for them.

Secondly, this study addresses an issue which is related to how business schools have evolved over time. According to Lorange (2012), business schools have to innovate and overcome outdated structures. There is fierce competition for them to improve their position in terms of rigour and relevance, as well as to differentiate themselves from others (Fragueiro & Thomas, 2011). However, if faculty members are caught up in a publish-or-perish framework that determines their selection, promotion and retention as staff members, this can inhibit their creativity in terms of selecting and delivering classroom content (Smeyers et al., 2014) or of innovating their schools.

This becomes more challenging and complex as learning demands increase. Today's learning has to be multi-levelled to include elements pointed out by Thaker (2015) on (1) the level of *knowing* (knowledge, models and facts), (2) the level of *doing* (actual problem-solving skills), (3) the level of *being* (clarifying which values count), and (4) the level of *becoming* (key development stages over time). Business schools thus need to retain learning as a meta-responsibility as part of their full focus, and should ongoingly review what aspects of their program they can improve.

The research presented in this study investigates a central piece of the puzzle by attempting to understand learners in business schools in such depth that they can meet the increasing demands of a VUCA world innovatively. The study moves beyond the frequently encountered learning style (LS) discussions to introduce the concept of 'LSV'. It provides original, empirical support for LSV's relevance in achieving a better understanding of learning processes and in subsequently optimising learning outcomes.

The following analysis shows the connection between LSV and the field of leadership styles. The latter field was the first to seek and acknowledge the existence of different styles and went on to investigate the circumstances in which each style would be more conducive to success in leading. As outlined below, the literature in the leadership field, as Kaplan and Kaiser (2003a) have shown empirically, concluded that leadership style versatility makes all the difference in a leader's performance.

Individual style is, of course, easy to distinguish and then to study. Yet, according to these authors productivity, engagement and overall organisational results only become superior across the board when a leader is versatile. In the field of learning styles, research has not yet taken the step from focussing on individual styles to exploring whether a learner's flexibility, and therefore his/her actual LSV, could explain and account for better outcomes. To my best knowledge, and based on results from the literature review, no explicit study on LSV and study outcomes could be traced in key journals and databases. This study aims to contribute to the existing body of literature on learning as well as learning styles.

2.3 Literature review

There literature search for this study proceeded incrementally, therefore differently to the way the overall results will be presented. In line with Wohlin's (2014) explanation of the 'snowballing' approach to searching for literature, the first step in this study was to clarify the key term, namely "learning styles". In practice, the starting point was a topic-related search in academic databases, followed by a corresponding search on Google Scholar via https://scholar.google.com/, as different search engines deliver different results. Such a structured approach was needed because an online database search for learning styles had initially created a list of 728,160 hits. Following Wohlin (2014), the searches relied on:

- "Backward snowballing" (Wohlin, 2014, p. 3) involves screening reference lists to identify published articles for further scrutiny. The type of publication and year could provide context. I gave special attention to peer-reviewed journals which count as an indication of high quality. More recent articles were prioritised, as they would include literature reviews of key accomplishments in the literature over the years. The abstracts and conclusion sections of shortlisted articles were then examined for relevance. If deemed informative, the entire article was sourced.

- "Forward snowballing" (Wohlin, 2014, p. 3) could, in addition to library databases, assist in finding details of citations as precisely as possible via Google Scholar in particular, to assess relevance. In this way the citations can also be traced easily. Abstracts of the follow-up articles that cited the originally identified papers were evaluated. Once the abstract was assessed to be promising in terms of shedding additional light on the phenomenon, I would read the conclusion, and if relevant, the entire paper.

A process of repeated divergence (looking for more papers) and convergence (distilling the most relevant elements of ongoing debates) followed. This distillation enabled a map of relevant themes. The ensuing nomological approach I depict in figure 3 helps with the visualisation. First it gives an overview of the logical steps taken in framing the concept. A nomological approach depicts key pieces, variables and topics which jointly shape a field and its relevance (Ziegler et al., 2013). Next, the represented topics are logically selected and ordered from 1a and 1b on the left of the following figure to topic 7 on the right. They are explained further in the sections below. The two factors of ethical responsibility generally, and societal trends specifically, account for the sensitivity of the topic.

Topic 1a: Attention to individuality as an ethical responsibility

The importance of learning styles can be derived from taking ethics into account. All three elements of ethical consideration, namely value, process and outcome are applicable in this context. Various studies, for example, Kosower and Berman (1996), confirm that there are indeed different learning styles.

The question that emerges is whether from a value perspective, the individuality and uniqueness of learning styles should be respected or ignored. Faculty and course directors need to consider whether in the process of curriculum development and teaching they should leverage (or ignore) individual learning styles – as suggested and illustrated by Labib et al. (2017). From an outcome perspective they need to consider whether, as suggested by Wieland et al. (2018), it matters how institutions reach their targets.

It is important to note the considerable tuition fees business school students pay (Thomas & Peters, 2012). On this basis, in principle, a considerable degree of customer orientation could be expected. In these circumstances I would suggest as part of a general customer orientation, the ever-growing commercialisation of higher education (Bok, 2003) should include particular attention to the LSV of a learner as customer. This should go beyond customer satisfaction surveys at the end of courses or programmes to acknowledge truly value-adding transformative learning interventions.

Amann, Pirson, et al. (2011) present a concept for the future of business schools, referring to humanistic business schools (HUBs) in which they call for a considerable increase in respect for human dignity and thus also in respect for the aforementioned individuality. Human dignity should represent the end of doing business in and for itself; this would challenge the strong orientation many have towards shareholder value. Respect for individuality can be made visible in an improved well-being orientation and strong ethical values, thus replacing the prominence of mere financial value that exists in short-sighted views on business. Business schools have been criticised in the past for contributing to fostering insufficiently sustainable solutions in business (Muff et al., 2017).

Until recently, business schools largely gave very little attention to ethical education, and a number of schools even lost their way completely (Bennis & O'Toole, 2005) due to being overly focussed on shareholder value (Matten & Moon, 2004). In a predominantly shareholder value-oriented setting, business takes a very reductionist view, largely serving the shareholders, while ignoring the demands that would be legitimate according to a stakeholder view. In a more ethically sensitive setting society in general, or staff members specifically, can make demands on businesses as well. The UN's initiative on the Principles of Responsible Management Education (PRME) was launched precisely to counter these dynamics.

Further, institutions should go further than researching or teaching sustainability. The addendum principle encourages business schools to "walk the talk" and become role models in order to serve their students. They need to understand that "our own organisational practices should serve as example of the values and attitudes we convey to our students" (Godemann et al., 2014, p. 19). Still, Godemann et al. conclude that to date "little attention is paid to the addendum/additional principle" (p. 20).

Figure 3: Nomological approach to the field of LSV and structure of the literature review

To take research to a higher level as prescribed by the PRME, as part of a more sustainable process, the individuality of each learner should be integrated and not ignored. A preferred approach to teaching in business school classrooms respects the existence of different learning styles and at least will start an exploration of how potentially to build better learning processes. Besides just taking a value and process view of ethics, managers can, by respecting different learning styles, generate more ethical, considerate and equity-oriented institutions with higher credibility levels.

Topic 1b: Societal trends

Pashler et al. (2008) link the growing academic interest in learning styles as a topic to institutions' extensive marketing efforts associated with commercialising the measurement of learning styles. These authors are not the only ones to criticise commercialisation trends in learning and development initiatives. Actual empirical tests of claims that have been made are weak if not contradictory (see, for example, Kellerman, 2012). Consequently, proprietary commercial tools, certification programmes, and accompanying literature have emerged.

As outlined below, Pashler et al. (2008) indicate that rigorous empirical studies could not substantiate the hype and widespread belief in learning styles as a tool. According to these authors the basic assumption that everyone has the potential to be a good learner, if only he or she is better understood, is easily marketable. If someone is alleged not to learn well or enough, those who are involved can shift the responsibility, and thus also the blame, to the learning institution.

Such institutions can then be blamed for not paying sufficient attention to heterogeneity in the classroom or for ineffectively tailoring their teaching to the course participants. Students are then perceived as victims of practices that do not attend to individuality; the blame for poor learning outcomes then goes to a lack of faculty skills or motivation, or to the commercial learning institution being unwilling to invest more in quality to secure profits. Self-esteem discussions (Tenge, 2006) that were *en vogue* when the learning style concept started to gain traction, catalysed the development of learning style instruments. Yet, as mentioned, this is mostly not supported by sufficient reliable evidence that performance empirically improves the link between learning styles and tailoring instruction methods.

Topics 2 and 3: Aptitude differences and ability to express learning style preferences

Notably the tools available for student learning support might not recognize learning complexity, nor depict it holistically when scholars attempt to conceptualise and operationalise learning. Learning theories are extremely rich and at times complicated. Definitions of 'learning' range from focussing on an increase in knowledge to focussing on the social settings of knowledge creation. The latter contrasts with a transmission model of learning (Cox, 2017).

Other definitions of learning style view the aim of gaining knowledge as insufficient or less relevant and prefer to emphasize "an increase, through experience, of problem-solving ability" (Washburne, 1936, p. 611). Thus, there are fragmented theoretical foundations, and the assumption that people fit into distinct boxes regarding how they learn best, is only weakly supported (e.g. Druckman & Porter, 1991; Strieker & Ross, 1964). This study suggests a new perspective, one that has enriched the field of leadership in education. In this study, I posit that the learning style debate should be revisited, expanded, reframed and re-conceptualised from a versatility perspective and not only from a simplistic categorisation perspective.

Therefore, this study aims to start the related academic debate, modestly acknowledging that more research will be necessary to conclude whether a versatility assessment of learning styles can be more effective than placing learners in abstract categories of learning styles. The field of leadership has already taken this step, as Kaplan and Kaiser (2003a) has detailed.

Topic 4: Definitions of learning styles and LSV

There is a need to clarify the terms of learning styles and the emerging construct of LSV. Firstly, for Rolfe and Cheek (2012) the term learning style "refers to the concept that individuals differ in regard to what mode of instruction or study is most effective for them" (p. 105). Such a definition is open regarding whether it refers to knowledge development or problem-solving abilities. Alternatively, Curry (1981) focused on behaviour, and views learning styles as the "characteristic cognitive, effective, and psychosocial behaviours that serve as relatively stable indicators of how learners perceive, interact with, and respond to the learning environment" (p. 535) without specifying whether learning styles should focus on mere knowledge gains or on more aspects of learning.

Secondly, if a process view on learning is important, some definitions are narrower and some broader. Hayes and Allinson (1993) define a learning style as a person's preference for a distinct way of processing new information and subsequently organising a given learnt piece of insight or information. Similarly, Whetten and Cameron (2002) not only include the processing of information in their understanding of learning styles, but also emphasize the information gathering phase as well as the phase in which individuals act upon the received information.

Thirdly, when it comes to the quiddity of learning styles, Claxton and Ralston (1978) emphasize that a person's learning style should be defined as something constant. Fourthly, if learning styles are constant, a question arises as to how best a potential diversity of styles represented in a group of learners should be dealt with. According to Sánchez-Prieto et al. (2016), it has become important to move beyond the strong focus on the teacher in order to adapt learning journeys and to embrace technology. In this view learning styles represent a construct that should be optimised from a contingency perspective. Thus, from a teleological viewpoint and definition of learning styles, claims cannot be made regarding which one is more effective. The evaluation of effectiveness is contingent on a more or less enabling context.

Moving beyond learning styles towards LSV

Reviewing the literature disclosed a major gap in past studies in that they overemphasize individual learning styles, while LSV is neglected. Research simply has not yet advanced to the next possible level, because parallels to other fields and how constructs mature over time have not been drawn. Past studies remain limited to exploring which styles exist and when a particular style might be more conducive to a good learning outcome, or not.

LSV is the central emerging construct of this study. The following gives a preliminary working definition of LSV as a concept articulating the degree to which a learner can effectively apply different learning styles in the process of learning, contingent upon the learning challenge at hand. It is not congruent with learning agility, which addresses mental agility, as well as people agility, change agility, or results agility. Thus 'LSV' and 'learning agility' (Lombardo & Eichinger, 2000) represent different constructs.

This study agrees with Robinson (2016) that learning versatility is a rare and valuable feature which functions as a determinant in leadership development programmes. She argues that learning flexibility correlates with leadership versatility, which is a feature that equips leaders to deal with diverse situations more effectively. Prioritising such flexible learners as candidates for programmes in admission policies can be one way of integrating newly gained insights.

Emphasizing learning flexibility along with leadership flexibility can also enhance the overall programme's success because more versatile learners can create a different learning environment and classroom atmosphere. Honey and Mumford (2009) substantiate the claim that versatile learners are rare by calculating that groups of learners are typically more uniform in learning style than versatile. Their study did not directly work with an index nor had versatility as its purpose; rather, they interpreted their secondary data of thousands of collected surveys, finding that only roughly 29% of their respondents are versatile. The research project proposed here also assumes that groups in general consist of diverse individuals with diverse learning styles, that creating transparency on individual styles is beneficial, and that subsequently addressing these styles in a differentiated way is a promising way forward. Nevertheless, most empirical studies focus on distinct individual learning styles, not on LSV.

Topic 5: Measuring learning styles and LSV

Business schools have often been criticised for their focus on shareholder value, their one-dimensional understanding of performance, and for drilling graduates to be more efficient and effective, while they do not focus enough on sustainability with a triple-bottom line (i.e. by simultaneously fostering financial, environmental and social sustainability) or human dignity (Amann, Pirson, et al. 2011).

The criticism includes that these schools pay poor attention to the individuality of the learner, i.e. they do not attend to the 'being' and 'becoming' levels of learning. Interestingly enough, the school types interested in fostering either the big P (for profits) or the big D (for human dignity) would create more enabling learning environments if they were to pay more attention to learning styles. The importance of learning styles stems from them being a pre-condition for effective classroom sessions. In exploring possible options, there are numerous studies on measuring learning styles; however, quantity does not necessarily indicate the maturity of the field or the quality of gained insights. The major gap this study identified is that in the field of learning styles a conceptual step forward and maturation of the field that includes versatility aspects, has been overlooked.

This study starts with the basics. Certain types of learners have higher class attendance rates than others (Brennenstuhl & Catalanello, 1979). In different classrooms at different levels, there is a statistically significant difference when it comes to social anxiety levels, which is based on learning style heterogeneity (Kutay, 2006). Also, when and where faculty expect learning to happen is not necessarily naturally aligned with when and where students actually do learn (White & Anderson, 1995).

Developing sensitivity regarding when learning occurs and who learns in which ways can help boost effectiveness in developing both the big P and the big D. There is a fine distinction between a functionalist view and a symbolic understanding of what constitutes a great school. The former attends to learning styles and versatility from a means-end perspective, while the latter more big D-oriented understanding attends to respect for learners' individuality and their related dignity which represents a value and an end in itself.

Even merely learning more about one's own learning style can have an impact. It is part of adaptive learning – a process which saw the students perform better in academic terms merely by them reflecting on and acknowledging their learning style preferences (Hwang et al., 2014). The positive effect of explicit discussion and reflection on the diverse learning styles present in a classroom is not limited to the students; active system elements, i.e. endogenous variables or stakeholders with the right to experience that their individuality and thus human dignity, are also given reasonable consideration.

Haar et al. (2002) have explained that teachers who proactively deal with learning style diversity they encounter in their classrooms, also adapt and perform better. "[B]y getting into the habit of reflecting on their teaching and on their students' learning, the teachers … developed a means of almost automatically doing what is considered 'good teaching'. They utilised whatever strategies, techniques or methods were needed to ensure that their students were learning" (Haar et al., 2002, p. 16). The explicit inverse holds as well, in that diverging learning and teaching styles caused the usefulness of the learning intervention to deteriorate.

Thus, Cameron et al. (2015) conclude that to maximise benefit "student learning styles should be assessed before designing appropriate teaching methodologies" (p. 218). This pattern and the explicit core of effectiveness considerations together have been labelled the 'meshing hypothesis' (Pashler et al., 2008), which posits that "instruction is best provided in a format that matches the preferences of the learner" (p. 105). Mismatches between preferred styles and encountered teaching approaches can be obstacles to learning (De Vita, 2001; Cook, 2005).

Interim summary: 'Learning style' – a concept not perfectly understood, mastered or well operationalised yet

This section deals with the 'learning style' concept which currently is not fully understood, mastered or operationalised. In the past, Bennet (1995) remarked that 'learning styles' represent an idea which needs to be understood better. Numerous studies followed and the idea of exploring learning styles to optimise learning experience has spread internationally, across diverse countries, in (e.g.) north and south America, Europe and Asia (Milgram et al., 1993). Yet, the field of learning styles has not escaped criticism, as the following points will illustrate.

Firstly, Pashler et al. (2008) warn that too many studies are flawed by methodological weakness and that, overall, they reveal partly weak, partly contradictory results in terms of the meshing hypothesis. To name just one of the examples they reviewed, Sternberg et al. (1999) omitted crucial information about the extent to which they eliminated outliers in the study, also neglecting attention to what caused the outliers, and not reporting important mean scores of final assessments. Thus, they did not mention learning outcomes as consequences of matching or mismatching learning styles and study tasks.

Further, even a selection of extreme learner archetypes, individuals whose styles were matched and perfectly tailored to fit them personally, did not consistently outscore their counterparts across all assessments. Moreover, Sternberg et al. (1999) questioned the link between learners expressing mere preferences and others with actual aptitudes for learning in an explicitly preferred way.

Secondly, one has to note that the available body of knowledge as well as the range of concepts of learning and related styles are quite comprehensive and complex, which leads to numerous different conceptualisations and empirical operationalisations. At times, the boundaries between various constructs, such as between 'learning style' and 'personality type', become blurred. To illustrate, Coffield et al. (2004) review 71 instruments, but warn that their list is by no means exhaustive. They classify the constructs according to (1) constitutionally-based learning styles and preferences (e.g. the 'big five' as being agreeable, conscientious, extroverted, neurotic, and open to experience), (2) cognitive structure (e.g. the Rod and Frame Test), (3) stable personality type (e.g. the Myers-Briggs Type Indicator (MBTI), and (4) 'flexibly stable' learning preferences (e.g. Herrmann's 'whole brain' model) and overall learning approaches orstrategies (e.g. Inventory of Learning Styles or ILS). This divergence of approaches makes it difficult to advance the field, because individual researchers and practitioners could start from vastly different starting points.

Thirdly, the field covering learning outcomes' measurement has not been truly mastered yet. Measuring learning outcomes is a challenge, as multiple levels need to be considered. For example, Kirkpatrick (1976) suggests a four-level pyramid of learning outcomes, ranking outcomes like a learner's initial reaction to a learning intervention, e.g., reactions of satisfaction, gained knowledge, perceived behavioural change, and perceived value according to their relevance to employers. Philips (1996) adds an additional, fifth level to the pyramid in which explicit efforts are made to measure educational efforts' return on investment towards becoming more holistic.

Relatedly, Amann et al. (2017) call for adding a sixth layer to these outcomes, considering how the learning experience has exceeded expectations, has created additional value beyond the narrow definition, and has to a greater or lesser degree driven the humanistic growth of learners. Amann et al. (2017), thus, call for connecting holistic assessment of learning outcomes to the previously identified need to integrate the 'being' and 'becoming' level of learning. In this context, Kolb and Kolb (2006) state "the current evaluation methods favored by most institutions of higher education are not only deficient in responding to the experiential learning pedagogy, they are inadequate in measuring learning outcomes of any educational pedagogy currently in practice" (p. 81).

Once these topics are better understood and initial empirical insights have been gathered, it will become easier for school leaders to justify allocating or shifting more resources to LSV. Equally, more insight on the construct can help optimise its deployment over time, which addresses specifically topics 6 and 7, given on the right side in figure 3 above.

2.4 Conceptual framework

LSV represents a new perspective in the field of business school development as well as the field of learning. It responds to a call for an orientation towards more human dignity in business science education. The concept has more potential than 'learning style' to offer innovative and unique value to the learner and other stakeholders, thus it addresses items 6 and 7 in the nomological net presented above. It is based on the logic and emerging conceptual framework to be described here.

Theoretically, Ashby's (2011) law of requisite variety influences this conceptualisation. It posits that in order to succeed, agents in a system ought to mirror the complexity they face, internally. The more they comply with this line of thought, the higher their likelihood of good performance. Learners and graduates would then perform better in a VUCA world as outlined in the introduction above. Figure 4 depicts the proposed link between learning demands and LSV. The logic of requisite variety posits that the higher the LSV, the better off learners and schools are in handling increased demands they will face as graduates.

Figure 4: Visualisation of a requisite variety view on learning challenges and learning style versatility

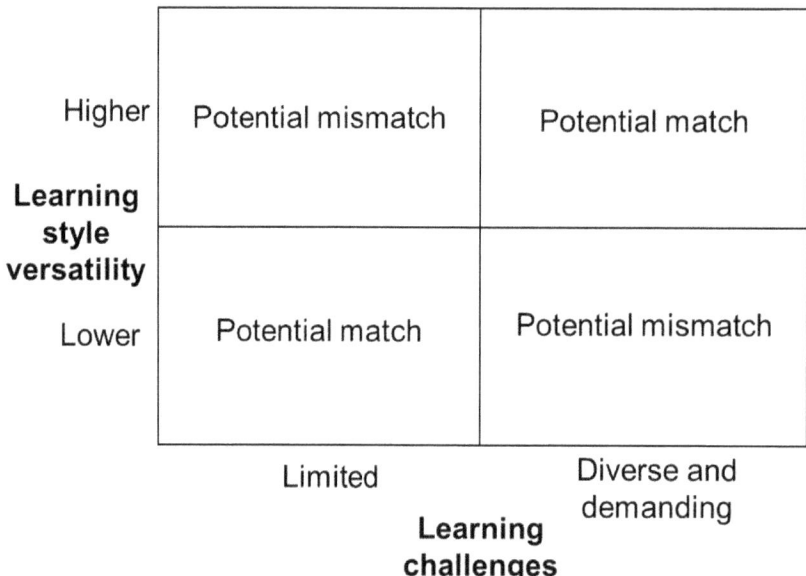

Also, interesting theoretical and conceptual insights could emerge from answers to the research question: *What is the impact of LSV on learning outcomes?* If a positive link can be established, then the development of prescriptive knowledge can impact both a learning journey's design and a school's selection and admission processes, i.e. item 7 in figure 3 above.

All circumstances being equal, Ashby's (2011) suggestion to mirror demands internally and build up complexity, e.g. in the form of LSV, contrasts starkly with Luhmann's (1991) idea of coping with challenges and complexity by focusing on simplicity. The study at hand could present a unique opportunity to theoretically combine the two views, e.g. in questioning what foci education should pursue. Instead of paying attention primarily to functional knowledge taught in business schools about, e.g., procurement, operations or marketing, one could focus on LSV, revisiting the assumption of it being an exogenous variable and a constant construct. As an endogenous variable in learning and life journeys, it could foster performance and dignity, and therefore holistic success.

From a different perspective, such as one taken by a faculty member or course director, integrating reflection on LSV in the curriculum can assure that it becomes a more pronounced topic, thus emphasizing its relevance to a learner's but also a business school's success. This would require moving beyond a perspective of LSV as a mere exogenous variable. The latter perspective rather fatalistically presents LSV as a construct assumed to be constant, as mentioned above, while it should rather be aligned with multi-level learning as Datar et al. (2010) suggest. These authors view a school's teaching and a student's learning responsibilities holistically and demand that business schools emphasize processes of knowing, doing and becoming. In this context 'becoming' could also refer to growing into a more versatile learner.

In leadership development there is a school of thought which initially assumed the existence of a dominant leadership style, and which eventually gained the insight that there are different leadership styles relevant to different occasions. Thus, the notion of 'situational leadership' emerged.

Finally, this way of thinking, outlined by Kaplan and Kaiser (2003a), ended up emphasizing the meta-skill which determines success, namely true leadership versatility. These authors substantiate their claim about leadership versatility with truly large-scale studies that show the positive impact of leadership style versatility on numerous organisational factors, such as employee engagement, business unit productivity, and overall effectiveness. If a learner can benefit from currently available insights, exercises and tools to become a more versatile leader, the same readiness to grow and become a more versatile learner should be possible.

Other streams of learning, for example, view absorptive capacity as a dynamic variable (Zahra & George, 2002). Absorptive capacity includes learning how to learn. Numerous other scholars have proposed the idea of learning new ways of thinking, as well. For example, Gröschl and Gabaldon (2018) advocate the adoption of Morin's transdisciplinary approach, which is more systemic, humanistic, dialogical and translogical than many that went before, and which embraces both complexity and ambidexterity, while also developing critical thinking, creativity and self-awareness skills.

Kegan and Lahey (2009) not only foresee the opportunity and desirability of such changes in mind-set, they advocate transitions of the adult mind-set from a socialised mind to a self-authoring mind, and eventually to a self-transforming mind. The latter would encourage learners not only to rewrite their mental software (Hofstede & Minkov, 2010) once, but repeatedly, if needs be. Learning style preference could thus become the object of further research of such new mental software updates and self-transforming minds. A key insight participants in education would need to gain first, however, would be to determine whether besides being potentially desirable, learning versatility is in fact more effective in enabling success. This is the core question of the study at hand.

The figure below gives a visual representation of this study's conceptual framework, differentiating four distinct cases which jointly create the foundation of a learning style ergo-ecology view. In more general terms, according to García-Acosta et al. (2014), ergo-ecology aims "to provide tools for confronting twenty-first century challenges" (p. 111). It is multidisciplinary and emphasizes human aspects in interaction with its ecosystem. More precisely, and as understood in this study, it embeds the ergonomics of LSV in its ecosystem, allowing us to differentiate four different scenarios which each portray divergent degrees of fit, efficiency and effectiveness.

The bottom-left quadrant has been labelled eco-sufficiency. Limited LSV suffices when learners encounter not necessarily simplistic, yet also not overly complicated or complex learning challenges. Such a learning constellation is eco-sufficient. Fostering higher versatility levels, e.g. by attracting higher quality students through sign-up bonuses or scholarships, can raise expectations of returns on education in time, energy and possibly also financial terms. The learner in this system is sufficiently equipped for the situation he/she encounters.

The top-left quadrant refers to a case in which the learner's limited LSV does not meet the diversity of learning challenges and stimuli provided. The learner might find some of the learning interventions, such as exercises, role play, or stakeholder dialoguing odd, as (e.g.) in the case of a pronounced theorist who is not an activist. Designing a tremendously rich learning journey (top left corner) would overwhelm the limited learner. Due to the school's resources not being allocated well, the offer cannot be taken up, thus the learning system is eco-ineffective. It easily overwhelms the learner. Although this case represents a school that puts effort into rich learning experiences, the emotional reaction among limited learners could be a negative one.

At the current stage of the analysis this, of course, assumes a constant LSV and not a dynamic absorptive capacity. The literature does point to the human brain showing degrees of plasticity in the learning context, though (Ebernacer et al., 2015).

Figure 5: Conceptual framework of the analysis

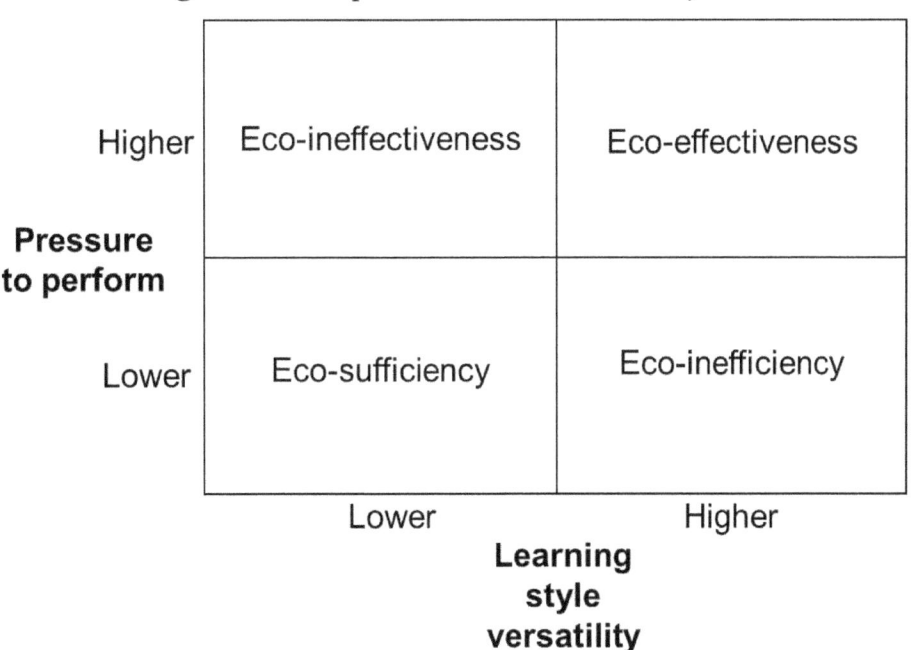

The bottom-right quadrant represents a similar kind of inadequacy. A highly versatile learner with diverse learning preferences might find a one-dimensional teaching strategy too limiting, and will question the andragogic skills of a faculty member. The system is eco-inefficient as the learner's ability or more accurately, his/her versatility, is underutilised and thus even wasted. The learner might feel that their skills and resources are not properly taken into account. In turn, this could lead to disengagement and negative evaluations of the study programme's efficacy.

The top right quadrant represents an ideal scenario in the list of possible situations. In this eco-effective situation, all resources including the versatile learner and capable surrounding ecosystem match and are fully utilised. The learner encounters a programme with heterogeneous faculty members and rich, diverging teaching strategies. Such a programme might entail Excel-based financial modelling in finance classes, lectures in other courses, a service project in a sustainability course, hands-on communication training, and alternatively, a reflection-based business philosophy course coupled with a professional thesis in which, after a literature review that identifies research gaps, data has to be gathered for finding answers to specific research questions. In order to work towards an initial and partial empirical test of the conceptualised programme, the following hypothesis emerges. For simplicity reasons, it assumes that the learning environment is more or less the same for all programme participants.

H1: In a given learning environment, the higher the LSV, the higher the cumulative grade average of a student.

The following sections describe how this hypothesis was tested, and therefore, how the research question was answered. To our best knowledge this study is the first to explicitly start out giving LSV a central position, defining this construct, and then showing its parallel to leadership style versatility. In such a context, this study attempts to operationalise and run a first test on LSV.

2.5 Methodology and method

The research objective to identify the impact of LSV and the nature of the research question, jointly direct the use of a positivist methodology and a quantitative research design (Cohen et al., 2007). A quantitative online survey follows, based on the established learning style tool, the Honey and Mumford Learning Style Questionnaire (LSQ) (Duff & Duffy, 2002).

Although the LSQ was clearly developed to measure learning styles, not LSV, De Vita (2001) points out that it is widely used, thoroughly reviewed in the literature, and thus understood as a tool with higher validity and predictive accuracy than, e.g. the Learning Style Instrument.

The LSQ identifies four learning archetypes, namely the activist, who learns through experience, the reflector, who learns through reflective observation, the theorist, who benefits most from frameworks and concepts, and finally, the pragmatist, who prefers to learn from active experimentation. Based on 80 items to be rated, an individual receives raw scores, which can then be categorised into very low, low, moderate, strong or very strong results for each of the individual learning styles.

Towards the first proxy for LSV

With special attention to the independent variable, several options were possible. A decision was taken in favour of a proxy categorising various levels, which were compiled and calculated based on the logic outlined in table 1, leading to a 10-point scale. Variable operationalisation represents a crucial task for researchers. Any first-generation operationalisation will reflect the nascent state by lacking rich two-sided evaluations and thick descriptions of observations until thorough tests and discussions have been done.

Honey and Mumford (2009) distinguish between learning style preferences and actual skills. However, skills could be harder to test with surveys than preferences. This study contributes to this task by suggesting a first generation of LSV indicators, which will have to mature further over time. This is in line with other attempts to operationalise multidimensional constructs longitudinally, such as corporate performance or internationalisation – fields where congruent and divergent alternatives emerged over decades (Amann & Khan, 2017).

Table 1: Overview of learners based on LSV

Description of category	Included case per category	Style versatility index score
Perfect	All four learning styles rated as very strong	10
Extreme	3 rated very strong, 1 rated strong	9
Very high	2 rated very strong and 2 rated strong, 1 rated very strong with 3 remaining rated as strong	8
High	3 rated at least as strong, 1 medium	7
Higher	3 rated as strong, 1 as weak	6
Medium	2 clearly strong and 2 medium scores, i.e. no clear weaknesses	5
Lower	2 rated as strong, at least 1 as weak	4
Low	Neither any strengths, nor extreme weaknesses – all rated as medium or a maximum of 2 lows	3
Very low	1 clearly strong and 2 or 3 maximum scores at medium level	2
Lowest	1 clearly strong and a maximum of 1 medium score	1

Operationalising learning outcomes as dependent variables and control variables

Regarding the dependent variable, this study builds on past research. In the literature, quantitative research provided evidence that particular learning styles positively impact classroom success as well as learners' satisfaction (Dunn et al., 1989; Griggs, 1992, Thomson & Mascazine, 1997). This study is built on the assumption that a clear focus and primary analysis of students' grades is the main way of operationalising learning success. Learning outcomes will be operationalised quantitatively with the help of achieved grades (GPA), which can range from 1 as the lowest to 10 as the highest. While there are multiple different grading scales, the particular one used in this study is influenced by the established practice of the school chosen as research partner.

For further exploratory analysis, I added a more refined view on learning outcomes, which operationalises learning outcomes based on a learner and programme participant's subjective perceptions regarding the Kirkpatrick (1976) model of learning levels. According to this model, such subjective perceptions refer to a learner's initial reaction to a learning intervention, e.g. a reaction of satisfaction, gained knowledge, perceived behavioural change, and perceived value which is relevant to employers. The reactions are phrased in easy-to-score, subjective perceptions and corresponding statements: "I am very happy with my programme at institution X", "I feel I get a very good return on investment", "I learn on multiple levels, such as knowing, doing, being", "I learn a lot of new knowledge", "The programme positively changes my behaviour", "What I learn in the programme will most likely lead to a measurable positive impact at my (future) employer's organisation", "I am very satisfied with my learning progress". The Likert-scale goes from 1 to 5, where 1 = strongly agree, 2 = agree, 3 = neither agree nor disagree, 4 = disagree, and 5 = strongly disagree.

Taking the analysis further, the cumulative grade point average (GPA) ranges from 1 as the lowest, to 10 as the highest possible value at the institution where the study was carried out (see below). Satisfaction is measured on a five-point Likert scale as an answer to the question whether a student is satisfied with the programme (1 = not at all, 5 = very much). Both types of dependent variables, the GPA as well as the agreement scores and perceptions, were treated as pseudo-metric variables in the multivariate analysis.

Regarding control variables, previous research identified a deteriorating grade success with age (Peiperl & Trevelyan, 1997). This study wanted to ensure that any age impact would be controlled for and therefore entered age as a metric variable. While Peiperl and Trevelyan (1997) found no evidence for gender impacting grades, other studies, such as Yeung (2011) point to the potential impact of gender on grades in education. As India continues to be a country with gender inequality (Sharma, 2016), female students could feel obliged to study harder to ensure social mobility and career success.

This does not mean, however, that their grades are better. They might on average be lower in business schools or at least similar to men's in social aspects of business, such as organisational behaviour or change, but worse in more technical courses, such as corporate finance and decision modelling (Markman, 2017). This study controlled for such a gender effect as well. Finally, as outlined below, study participants came from the bachelor and MBA levels, and empirical analysis controlled for whether the track or study level had an impact on overall learning outcomes. These control variables were entered into the regression in dummy variable form.

Additionally, Cameron et al. (2015) reason that achieving learning outcomes can be a complex assignment, covering the impact of demographic factors, including culture and age, as well as more internal factors, such as course content and teaching styles. In order to at least partially consider factors additional to age, additional survey questions integrate a student's perception of the variety of teaching styles applied, based on a 5-point Likert scale ("Programme faculty use a variety of teaching methods"). They form part of a further exploratory analysis.

Study participants and data collection

A private business school in one of India's main cities was chosen as a cooperation partner for this study. I have omitted its name in this description to assure anonymity. India represents an interesting study ground for learning innovations as it has the largest number of business schools of any country in the world. Roughly a third of the 17000 business degree awarding institutions worldwide, are situated in India. Innovations there could easily be scaled up elsewhere and can benefit a larger audience and community.

All 99 undergraduate students currently enrolled in its Bachelor of Business Administration (BBA) and all its 107 Master of Business Administration (MBA) students were invited to participate in the survey. The study was conducted in the spring of 2019 via an online survey, which is a modern, timesaving, environmentally friendly method which simultaneously minimises mistakes that could otherwise occur if data is entered manually from filled out paper surveys. Participation was voluntary and implementation adhered to the principle of informed consent (Christians, 2000), having reminded participants of the opportunity to withdraw from the study at any time without having to give reasons or face consequences. I analysed the data only after it had been anonymised according to the guidelines for best practices in learning-style-related research (Pashler et al., 2008).

2.6 Empirical results

Table 2 below summarises the descriptive statistics. Overall, the survey yielded 120 fully completed responses out of a total of 206 enrolled students (58%). The majority of both study levels participated and a sample selection bias test revealed no significant biases in terms of gender for the entirety of the study. The research partner institution's student body is 66% male; no gender bias was identified in the responses. The average ages of undergraduate and graduate students are in close range of one another, indicating that individuals pursue graduate studies at an early age.

The average age overall might also explain why all students were single, so that the impact of marital status on learning outcomes could not be measured. On average, grades are better at the graduate level, as probably more is at stake when graduating from a master's programme, and graduate admission requirements favour individuals who perform better at undergraduate level. Consequently, the level of studies (undergraduate versus graduate) entered the ensuing analysis as an additional dummy variable.

Table 2: Descriptive statistics of key variables

Criteria	BBA	MBA	Total
Response rate	62 out of 99 (63%)	58 out of 107 (54%)	120 out of 206 (58%)
Gender split	71% male, 29% female	61% male, 39% female	66% male, 44% female
Age min./max./average/std. deviation	19, 25, 20.03, 1.11	20, 25, 22.31, 1.22	19, 25, 21.14, 1.62
Independent variable: LSV (LSV), min./max./average/std. deviation	1, 10, 5.85, 2.36	1, 10, 6.64, 2.38	1, 10, 6.24, 2.39
Dependent variable: GPA, min./max./average/std. deviation	1, 8.67, 6.99, 1.8	5.9, 9.50, 7.93, 1.02	1, 9.5, 7.45, 1.54

Figure 6 provides an overview of participants' distribution across the categories identified in the LSV index given in table 1. Learners represented in this study cover all conceptualised categories: perfect

(5.8%), extreme (14.9%), very high (2.5%), high (21.5%), higher (5.8%), medium (17.4%), lower (5%), low (11%), very low (4.1%), and lowest (11.6%). Some segments are obviously smaller. Future studies could cluster groups, if this phenomenon persists.

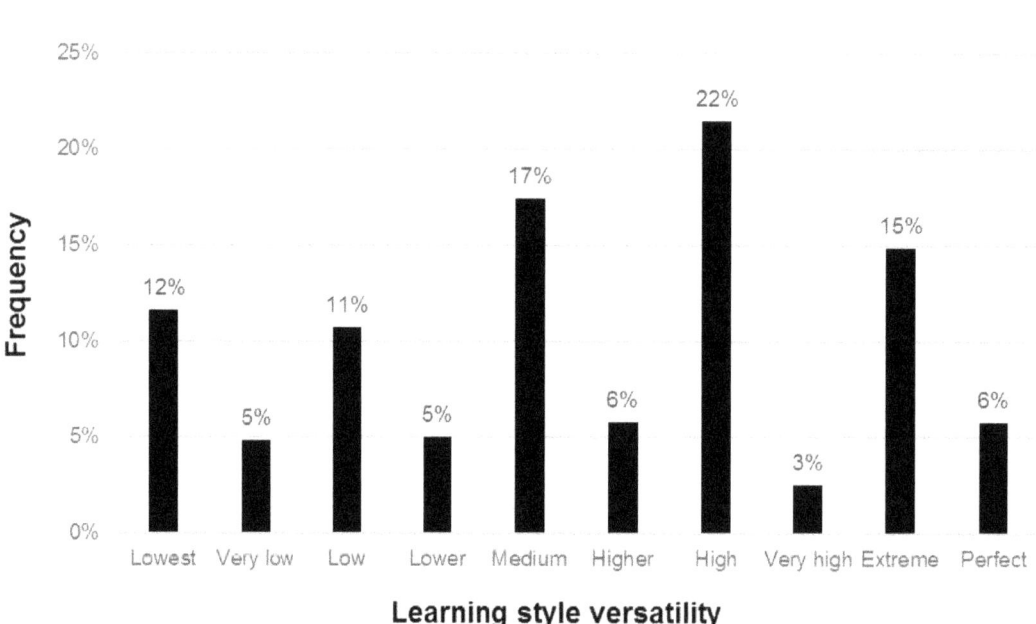

Figure 6: Distribution of learners across versatility categories

Contrasting these percentages with those Honey and Mumford (2009) reported, several idiosyncrasies of this study emerge. The percentage of less versatile learners in the form of individuals with one or two strong preferences are reported to amount to 55% in general, versus 38.1% in this study. The segment of 'strength-free' learners without clear preferences has been reported as amounting to 38% in general, versus 10.7% in this study.

To conclude, while relying on the same measurement tool to depict individual learning style preferences, this study includes a higher percentage of learners who claim that they prefer and effectively apply more than just one or two learning styles. This could possibly be explained by the tremendous competition programme participants and graduates face in the Indian job market. Future studies should explore more and divergent contexts to confirm this finding.

I carried out a linear regression, with age and gender as control variables as the literature suggests, to determine LSV's impact on learning outcomes in general, and on the GPA specifically. This rendered the following results:

- Regarding the overall model summary: While the R of .463 indicates a rather low correlation, the R squared of .187 indicates that the model can explain 18.7% of the grade variation.

- Based on the analysis of variation (ANOVA), the F value of 7.891 is an indication of the overall significance of the model (df = 4). At a very significant level of $p<.000$, the model is a good fit for the data.

- As for the coefficients, LSV as a variable with a standardised coefficient Beta of .247 is significant at $p<.01$ (with the standardised coefficient beta values for age .119 and its $p<.307$, gender .211 with a significance level of $p<.0123$, and the study level dummy .321 with $p<.01$). If one differentiates further between the undergraduate and graduate level, the results are confirmed, which could be interpreted as corroborating a parallel test reliability.

In this context, an additional exploratory data analysis using a separate t-test shows that women outperform men in terms of achieving better grades in a statistically significant way (significance level .003), based on an independent samples test with a significance level of $p<.00$. Female students have a grade average of 8.02 versus 7.16 of their male counterparts. However, male students with an LVSI average of 6.10 had lower LSV than the female students with an LVSI average of 6.56, yet the t-test was not significant at established levels ($p>.33$) in Levene's Test for Equality of Variance. The data analysis and reporting on the dataset as well as the analysis, the ANOVA, t-tests, and linear regression in general do not assume that variables have to follow a normal distribution. A Shapiro-Wilk test, which is recommended for smaller datasets, did not confirm their normal distribution at standard levels of statistical significance.

In contrast, and taking the exploratory analysis further than the confirmed hypothesis H1, I could detect no significant impact for LSV on overall satisfaction with the programme or with the learning progress, perceived return on investment, perceived learning opportunities on multiple levels, perceived learning of new knowledge, the perceived positive impact on behavioural changes, or perceived potential benefit of the learning for employers. None of the linear regressions yielded statistically significant positive, or for that matter, negative impact. The following section discusses these results further.

2.7 Analysis and interpretation

To my best knowledge, based on scrutinising the literature on learning styles through searching available academic literature databases, as well as consulting fellow researchers at various conferences on learning, such as the Academy of Management's Teaching and Learning Conference (TLC), this is the first study that has quantitatively attempted to evidence the positive impact of LSV on grades. If a learner is more versatile, he or she is able to benefit from the diversity of approaches to learning that different faculty members apply. This is in line with the eco-effectiveness logic outlined in figure 3 above. Its underlying logic based on Ashby's (2011) concept of requisite variety law fosters LSV as a key variable and coping mechanism for learners confronted with learning challenges in their education environment.

A key insight acquired by delving deeper, is that women perform better than their male counterparts. As there are no other studies measuring learning style versatility among business students in this explicit form, and the literature does not (yet) cover the topic either, there is an opportunity for future research to confirm this observation and potentially generalise it in a gender-focused study. Women's grades are better, yet the reason for their superior performance might not be a different level of LSV. Filtering gender out of the variance by modelling it as a control variable, differences in LSV exist in the form of women showing a higher average LSV but not at statistically significant levels. The results are in line with Wallen et al. (2017) who find that women might "respond to gender norms by reducing public assertiveness but not private effort" (p. 1). It therefore could be that not female students' similar LSV, but rather the more dedicated effort they invested, explains their better performance. This should be considered in gender equality debates and therefore represents an opportunity for further research.

This study also reveals that there is a need to distinguish between various ways of measuring learning outcomes. A variety of authors have called for a richer view on this inarguably multi-dimensional construct. Kirkpatrick (1976) suggests a four-layer pyramid. Philips (1996) added a fifth layer. Amann et al. (2017) subsequently offered a sixth layer. This study shows that while multiple layers mirror the multidimensionality of the learning construct, such emerging insight on LSV makes the analysis and discussion of learning outcomes a more challenging enterprise. What is actually meant when we refer to learning outcomes, or learning? Teacher-rated learning in the form of grades are affected, and can be boosted by a learner's LSV.

Yet, even a less versatile learner can perceive his/her learning journey as satisfying in that they gain new knowledge or change their behaviour in response to the learning intervention, have more to offer an employer, or receive a return on education/investment. Conversely, there is a plethora of factors that can invert such perceptions, e.g. when a private business school is over-commercialised (Bok, 2003), if faculty seem lost or distracted by (e.g.) ever more aggressive publish-or-perish pressures (Smeyers et al., 2014), or if the type of business school is simply not right for the learner due to it being (e.g.) too conservative, reactive, uninspiring, or out of touch with practical relevance. Not all schools are created equally (Lorange, 2012), and regardless of a given LSV, the context must be a fit or enabling, too.

Grades are important in business schools because as outlined by Robles and Roberson (2014), they impact both study efforts as well as perceived future success. Yet, the same authors also warn that overemphasising grades can distract from more holistic learning, long-term retention, and effective scholarship in general. This insight links the tangible results of this study to implications outlined in the next section.

2.8 Implications, limitations, and suggestions for future research

Better understanding learning styles and LSV offers several insights that would be useful to business school deans, programme directors, and individual faculty members, but also to business schools as institutions. Business school rankings are linked to projected future success, e.g. in terms of executive education income. IMD Business School's MBA dean, Seán Meehan, attributed a short-term boost of 63% more MBA applications to its no. 1 ranking in the Forbes business school ranking (Schwertfeger, 2018). A number of established ranking criteria are directly linked to learning success. Köksalan et al. (2010), for example, list the salary increase, the perceived value for money, or career progress as relevant standard business school ranking criteria.

Obviously, if students learn a great deal or perceive to have gained in having learnt valuable new content in a particular programme, their feedback in ranking surveys will be more positive than otherwise. Such feedback in turn boosts the school's rankings. A virtuous cycle can be triggered, which then sees secondary positive effects, such as attracting better students and faculty, rendering the overall learning environment more conducive to shaping students' knowledge, skills and careers.

Besides this functionalist view, a symbolic and broader value aspect is emerging. Knefelkamp (2003) emphasizes that reaching all students and providing curricula that cover the needs of all can be a problem in a democratic and pluralistic environment. Equally, the United Nations Principles of Responsible Management education call for more responsible innovations in business schools (Godemann et al., 2014). Respecting and preserving human dignity in all its facets, including a learner's individuality and very own LSV, is one important way responsible management education should proceed. We need more research on how better to integrate and endogenize LSV in a holistic approach to ergo-ecology, as defined by García-Acosta et al. (2014) above. This indicates a need for outlining limitations, suggestions for future research, and trajectory building in the field of LSV.

This study addresses a specific gap in the literature when it comes to learning styles. Firstly, while the field of leadership styles has evolved into emphasizing leadership style versatility, a similar development has not yet taken place regarding learning styles. There is a potential opportunity. One of the study's aims is to build a learning styles versatility trajectory, believing that disseminating such a versatility view is a crucial next step. However, the scope of each research project has to be clearly defined. Thus the study simultaneously calls for continued evolution of leadership style-oriented research to a field that will more fully embrace an ergo-ecology view in which the ergonomics of leadership styles in the larger systems are investigated further.

Now that the importance of leadership style versatility has been established at least with initial evidence, it intuitively makes sense to pursue three avenues in future research. As the study was clearly limited to one institution in one city in a particular cultural context, other vicinities, cultures, or strategic positions of schools could not be explored. Other schools might well attract different types of students and learners based on their brand, strategy, marketing budget, admission guidelines, and last, but not least their cultural context. Further research should shed light on such other contexts to confirm or detail the analysis.

Secondly, more qualitative research is needed to establish why the identified empirical results materialise in the first place, and how meshing various components occurs or does not. This study started with a hypothesised linear link between LSV and GPA. In light of the limited literature on LSV, more sophisticated hypotheses could not easily be derived from the literature. This research into the identified link between LSV and grades can provide them.

The study has provided a foundation for future prescriptive research mentioned in the nomological approach represented in figure 3 above. Regarding the nature of research we require, less positivist and more phenomenological research should ensue. Honey and Mumford (2009) had difficulties in finding extreme and perfect levels of learning versatility, e.g. in the form of learners who prefer and apply three or four learning styles effectively. Their published data dates back to 2009; it is conceivable that a VUCA world demands more from current programme participants than was required ten years ago.

Grounded theory is suggested to advance the theorising process, as well as to promote the inquiry targeting practical improvements, as next steps. For example, cases should be explored for all four quadrants in figure 3, investigating a holistic learning versatility ergo-ecology including in-depth case studies on eco-effectiveness, eco-sufficiency, eco-inefficiency, and eco-ineffectiveness. It is also advisable to further break down the 2x2 matrix as, especially in the middle of the LSV and GPA link, there might be more dynamics.

Defining a trajectory for the LSV field should not stop there. The third key limitation of this study resides in finding a pragmatic way to operationalise LSV. It builds on an established learning style tool, which has been field-tested. Yet, future studies are encouraged to generate different ways of conceptualising and operationalising LSV so as to have a phase of divergence before organized conferences on dominant, promising proxies. Such a development to widen the scope and revisit assumptions should also review ways to overcome the view that learning styles and versatility are constant, i.e. it should show that versatile learners are not only born, but often are made.

In the learning style debate, Engels and De Gara (2010) identify migrations, while Compton and Compton (2017) speak of progression. Business school graduates are likely to experience such transitions, migrations and progressions as well when their classroom learning involves various formats of lectures and case discussions that can shift practices towards training and learning on the job.

Revisiting assumptions in this way represents a normal development concerning the nascent state of the field of LSV. The study could not rely on a rich choice of available tools that are thoroughly reviewed in the literature and empirically tested in previous studies, as has been done in cases where there are only learning styles to work with. In contrast, other fields, such as international management, in which measuring the degree of internationalisation and financial performance of international operations is a core topic, could rely on 40 years of history, studies, experience, single-item or composite indices, in order to thoroughly understand variable operationalisations and concrete proxies (Glaum & Oesterle, 2007).

2.9 Conclusions

This study extends the field of learning styles by positing and empirically substantiating (in one distinct setting) that LSV can help us understand learning outcomes, at least ones that relate to grades. LSV refers to an individual preference for applying more than one learning style effectively, contingent upon the learning challenge to hand. This could represent the start of a development we have seen in the leadership field and literature, where first different leadership styles were acknowledged, but the real performance of the concept became evident in the behaviour of versatile leaders themselves.

This study provides the first empirical substantiation that, within the study's limits and the project's analysis, LSV matters. The study continues by working with the first proxy-level measure for leadership style versatility. This allows for first experiences with variable operationalisations to build on in future studies. The next contribution this study makes, lies in its trajectory building. It suggests switching attention away from merely looking into learning styles as in, for example, Cameron et al. (2015), to focus on versatility in learning styles.

Simultaneously, I call for additional quantitative replication studies in other contexts, as well as for in-depth grounded theory, doing qualitative research to better understand the patterns and dynamics at work. Once progress has been made, the final part of the originally presented nomological net in figure 3 can be targeted. A phase of prescriptive research, pragmatically following appreciative inquiry can then help optimise reality with actionable knowledge as part of a holistic ergo-ecology view on LSV specifically, and on learning in business schools more generally. In a time where business schools are criticised for not meeting expectations regarding relevance or ethics, this study strongly encourages more attention to a learner's individuality. This can be done either as a means to an end (better graduates, better career prospects), or more ideally as an end in itself to increase dignity orientation in business schools and to implement the promising United Nations Global Compact PRME.

Chapter 3: Reflections on study 1 and building the case for study 2

3.1 Introduction

"Research is the art of the feasible" (Blaxter et al., 2006, p. 157). Finding a cooperation partner for three related studies is not easy. Yet, through my personal contact with the Dean of a particular business school, this research initiative on LSV become feasible. At the same time, this opportunistic and pragmatic approach to partnering for research coincided with a research environment that Kumar and Dash (2011) have identified as "haunted" by significant quality issues. They argue that there is a need to find constructive answers to a plethora of questions and show that there is a gap in the literature in addressing them successfully. Going beyond their analysis on a meta-level across numerous topics, by zooming in on one construct, namely that of LSV, this study provides additional, concrete and constructive answers. The following sections of chapter 3 shed more light on the Indian educational sector (section 3.2.) and outline why the Indian context represents a meaningful environment for this research. Section 3.3 presents considerations in favour of extending the philosophical paradigms to be applied in the next two parts of this integrative study on LSV. Added reflections link chapter 2 which presents a first study, to the subsequent research.

3.2 The Indian business school landscape's potential to benefit from LSV research

Originally, business education in the South Asian sub-continent focused strongly on trade and commerce. The very earliest establishment of a school of commerce was in Chennai in 1886 (Singh et al., 2015). Shetty (2014) explains that until India's independence in 1947, management education did not form an essential part of the country's education system. This was co-determined by the caste system that designated the societal, social and employment roles of most. In those circumstances, business was traditionally reserved for specific castes – the requisite insights passed on from generation to generation.

The first management school opened in 1954 in Kolkatta (Philip, 1992). During the following decades business education gradually started to include management alongside commerce (Dey, 1999). Traditionally, management education comes from a highly centralised tradition, with centralised curricula and dependency on either governmental or other cross-institutional accreditation agencies (Sarangapani, 2014). Currently, India hosts the second largest number of business schools in the world (Khatun & Dar, 2019); however, highly commercially oriented institutions have recently, in the terms these authors use, "mushroomed", thus showing rapid growth, and driving up competition among institutions, while they largely perceive quality to be driven down. Similar issues to those in Western institutions have affected Indian business schools, such as the challenges of internationalisation, Western views on management, technology integration, the role of government subsidies over time, introducing courses of varying duration, and networking. This is evidenced not only at the increasingly prestigious Institutes of Management (IIMs) founded in the 1960s but also beyond (Philip, 1992). Over time, these IIMs have set the benchmarks for other institutions across practically all quality dimensions (Shetty, 2014).

As Sarangapani (2014) explains, the number of business schools approved by the All India Council for Technical Education (AICTE) between 2010 and 2018 alone, have grown by almost 30% to 3267. AICTE officially recognises management schools not affiliated with universities (Kumar & Dash, 2017). Shetty (2014) characterises the Indian business school landscape with a statement that the clear and vast majority of newly opened institutions "are not exhibiting any significant initiative to improve the quality of education. They are lacking requisite institutional structure for a transformative classroom delivery process" (p. 141).

Key additional malaises that substantiate this claim are a lack of interdisciplinary thinking, no institutional exchanges to add quality or facilitate peer learning, passive faculty members who, in comparison to peers from the global north, avoid public discourses on quality, excessive teaching with inordinately high teaching-loads that prevent faculty from innovating and students from reflecting on and properly absorbing critical content; also they are assessed to present irrelevant content from abroad which is unsuitable for application in the Indian context.

Often faculty have very little or no background in industry, thus relevance to the marketplace is not assured. Students fail to distinguish between preparing for and passing exams and learning for life by getting an education. This frequently results in graduates being unemployable as there is a huge gap between taught skills and content and what the recruiters need. Considering the financial side of these operations, such quality issues are not surprising. In terms of revenue and expenditure, most colleges allocate less than 10% of their resources to delivering the academic side of their operation (Kumar & Dash, 2011). Jagadeesh (2000) draws attention to the pattern that in spite of clear AICTE standards, institutions stop complying with set guidelines after approval and accreditation.

Bhattacharya (2010) adds to this analysis that a typical Indian business school teaches almost double the number of courses that a Western counterpart of high reputation does, yet neglects soft skills or experiential learning opportunities. This has repercussions for the value created: the benefits these schools offer are mostly of lesser value. Due to higher student numbers and a less advantageous student-teacher ratio, the overall learning experience might also suffer. As India is now one of the largest producers (Saikia, 2011) of MBAs, innovations in teaching and learning could help a large number of learners.

As a researcher, I do not view these quality issues fatalistically. Focusing on LSV has potential. In positive scenarios, it could help institutions make forward strides, thus they could stand out when competing, deliver greater impact, and add more value. However, the LSV phenomenon has to be better understood, which is the purpose and research objective of chapter 4 (emphasizing the faculty view) and chapter 6 (exploring the students' view).

3.3 Enlarging the philosophical paradigms to further explore LSV

The first of three studies, as reported in chapter 2, examined why one should pay attention to LSV in the first place. The impact of LSV on students' grades is statistically significant or, put differently, is accepted as statistically significant based on established decision criteria of significance levels. After establishing that LSV matters, more research is needed to advance towards an integrative view of the construct. According to Eyisi (2016), there are advantages and disadvantages to a quantitative research design as I applied it in the first study. Now, the larger research project continues with compensating studies that complement ontological and epistemological views. Robson (2002) escalates the semantics on these main alternatives by pointing out that there has been a "paradigm war between constructivists and positivists" (p. 43). Bryman (2008) is more reconciliatory, merely pointing to fundamentally different epistemological and ontological assumptions.

Quantitative research as carried out in study 1 is based on the ontological assumption that "reality exists independently from human conceptions and interpretations" (Ormston et al., 2014, p. 4). Whether LSV is important and has an impact can of course also be examined on an individual, subjective, and interpretative level. Yet, learning and knowing that this is the case, also applying a more objective frame and research design, represents an insight that is more valuable. It can substantiate more organisational and cross-organisational change. It is a largely value-free inquiry as Snape and Spencer (2003) already called for in the context of quantitative, positivist research.

Epistemologically, or regarding how to actually find out more about this reality, actually measuring and quantifying the impact of LSV fits the research question and research objective of substantiating the claim that the construct matters. It should matter without or outside the consciousness of the researcher (Crotty, 1998). The tested insight should be generalisable and replicable (Wellington, 2000).

Going forward and working towards an integrative view of LSV in a business school setting, this research is very much in line with Ormston et al. (2014). They argue that in grasping a given situation, multiple realities are likely to exist. Figure 7 reminds one of the reasonably complicated, highly interdependent generic business models that institutions frequently operate. They do so in the context of an increasingly complex environment, as set out in section 1.2.

Figure 7: Generic business model for business schools

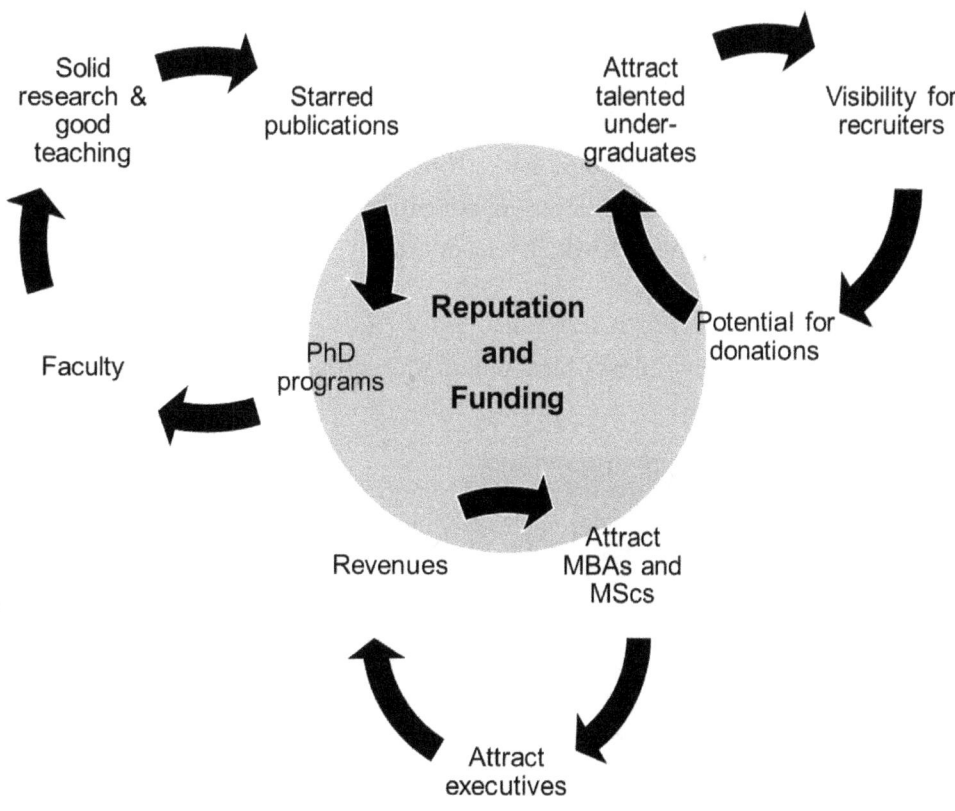

Source: Based on Durand and Dameron, 2017, p. 9.

Trying to analyse multiple stakeholders' views does not serve a postmodern view of approximately knowing the dynamics that determine the cause-and-effect relationship. As outlined in figure 8 below, we witness a fundamental shift in philosophical paradigms underlying the research when we move from study 1 to study 2, and later on also to study 3. This enables a more integrative perspective on LSV in a business school context.

Ontologically, it is almost impossible to gain knowledge of the world of business schools from direct observation and precise measurement of objective facts in a single reality. I assume that institutions, their local or cultural contexts, the business models they adopt over time and stakeholder perceptions frequently diverge. To name just one example, an investor or owner could view a profitable business school as a success, while students or faculty members might rate its success differently as they expect more resources in terms of technology in the classroom, faculty training or career services. These factors would add cost and lower profit, yet could improve the perceived success from a different stakeholder view.

This reflects a bias for more qualitative research to gain more analytical depth and context-rich information. Subjectivism can add further and richer views than objectivism would. Epistemologically, a thorough understanding of the dynamics at work originate from perceptions combined with interpretations. This requires a highly focused research objective – one that is firstly aimed at understanding. There aren't any detailed models to derive from the literature yet, nor from past qualitative research. In view of the aforementioned ethical issues in business schools, a value-free analysis is not desirable, because these issues matter in education and research, as the UN Principles of Responsible Management Education (PRME) have set out.

Figure 8: Key shift in philosophical paradigms across the included LSV studies

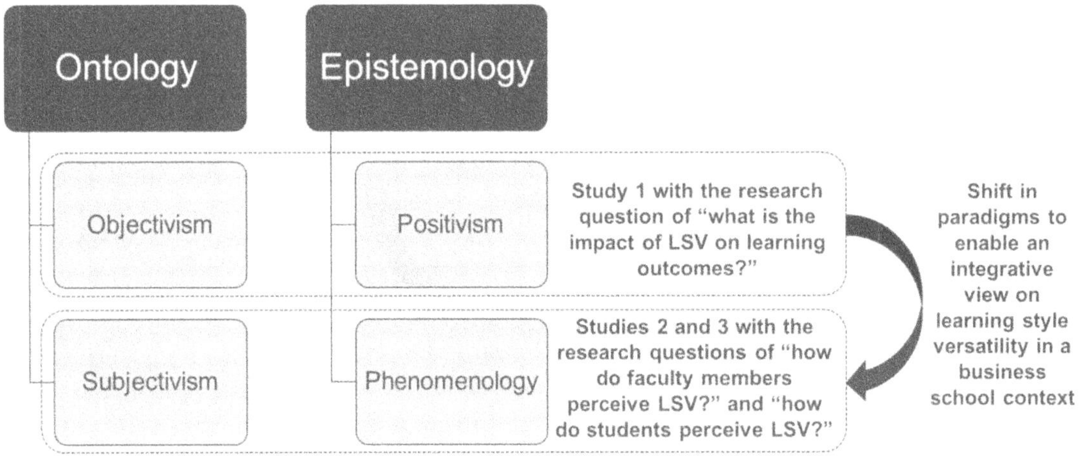

```
Ontology        Epistemology

Objectivism ─── Positivism      Study 1 with the research        Shift in
                                question of "what is the         paradigms to
                                impact of LSV on learning        enable an
                                outcomes?"                       integrative
                                                                 view on
                                                                 learning style
Subjectivism ── Phenomenology   Studies 2 and 3 with the         versatility in a
                                research questions of "how       business
                                do faculty members               school context
                                perceive LSV?" and "how
                                do students perceive LSV?"
```

Source: Author, based on Al-Saadi, 2014, p. 5.

Potential biases (orientation towards and preference for humanism, continuous improvement, strategic differentiation, or customer satisfaction, to name but a few) emanating from positionality prompted me to recognize substantial room for improvement. We would have missed such insight if research were really to be value-free and independent of the idealist kind of research as is outlined above in section 1.1. For this reason, researchers like me endeavour to construct meaning in unique ways, adopting their own perspectives, which is acceptable qualitative research (Wellington, 2000) and in this case carries interesting benefits.

Reality is experienced subjectively, which is particularly relevant in a stakeholder analysis aiming to find a stakeholder-specific view. Stakeholders themselves have diverse interpretations of reality. Therefore, the type of research questions for the next two steps shift from a "what" question to a "how" question, along with the corresponding ontological and epistemological assumptions about the phenomenon of

LSV. The research objective is no longer to substantiate the importance of the construct, as this has already been done in chapter 2.

In this chapter, the research initiative on LSV pursues a better understanding of the phenomenon in a given context, which is the very same context in which the quantitative study reported in chapter 2 was carried out. This can help us gain a better understanding of one context, and will demonstrate how the dynamics of the LSV phenomenon materialise in the interviewees' perception. In contrast to the first study, the goal here is no longer to generalise, but to understand. The following chapter, chapter 4, presents this qualitative study carried out on the basis of interviews with faculty members.

Chapter 4: Exploring the faculty view on LSV – Insights from the second empirical study

4.1 Introduction

The first empirical study presented in chapter 2 empirically established a positive impact the emerging concept of LSV has on grades – within the constraints of this particular study. Thereby I perpetuated the foundational assumption of this research project that fostering LSV could, if better understood, be a desirable learning goal. This second empirical study aims to enrich the emerging body of knowledge in this nascent field by addressing a logically linked question on how we can improve our understanding of the institutional factors which account for faculty's stance towards learning styles and LSV. Several stakeholders contribute to optimising learning in a given ecosystem. This study attends specifically to the faculty view on awareness of LSV, considering learners' and instructors' responsibilities, practically observing potential drivers and noting the dominant barriers to optimised learning journeys.

This study presents the cornerstones of a faculty-oriented grounded theory on understanding the factors explicitly and implicitly related to using LSV in a private business school that offers undergraduate and graduate programmes in a major city in India. There are, of course, further stakeholders, such as the institution's governance bodies, state-level or country-level government entities dealing with educational equality, or non-governmental associations, instructors are most directly involved in classroom or overall learning processes. Any institutional or external influence would at least partially materialise through them. Based on the same logic, this study did not focus on non-teaching staff. To develop new insights, I conducted in-depth, qualitative interviews with faculty members at the same institution as was engaged in study 1. The results show that although LSV can have conceptual and practical advantages, there are persistent barriers related to national culture, institutional factors, and individual faculty features. They explain the limited use of learning styles and versatility initiatives in the school's learning ecosystem.

The study continues by developing hypotheses for further testing the grounded theory across different settings. It serves as preparatory work for further studies, e.g. for gauging students' perspectives and their experience as system elements in a learning environment to be better understood and optimised from an LSV point of view.

4.2 Review of the challenges

The United Nations Global Compact PRME initiative has recently added a seventh, so-called addendum principle to the six prime principles already established (Godemann et al., 2014). The PRME demands that sustainability should be an integral part of the curriculum, and also integrated with graduates' values and their pursued purpose. Going forward, PRME values should penetrate teaching and research, but also business schools' partnerships and public dialogues. Additionally, the addendum principle requires that in the current context, these institutions should not merely teach or research sustainability, or otherwise maintain the *status quo* in their organisations without fully embracing broader responsibilities; rather, they should "walk the talk" and evolve into credible role models.

This should trigger policies, strategies, and a variety of initiatives towards progress on which business schools then regularly report. Godemann et al. (2014) explained that until around 2014 "little attention [had been] paid to the addendum/additional principle" (p. 20). Progress can materialise in two crucial ways. One is to implement an organisational philosophy of constant and sustained improvement (Lepage, 1991). The other envisages business schools as not only delivering courses on successful organisational change and publishing books that support the change, but also as transforming into credible, authentic role models that demonstrate successful change.

The study at hand intends to advance research on LSV as the concept has the potential to significantly enhance students' learning within the business school context. Business schools have been criticised for being trapped in old paradigms (Thomas, Lorange, & Sheth, 2013); developing new insights on increased LSV can support much needed change. As such, this study is part of the debate on what business schools actually do themselves in response to major challenges and an ever-changing context, such as one characterised by globalisation. Scholars such as Ghemawat (2011) have raised questions in this regard.

A related area of progress focuses on fostering human dignity as part of a larger orientation towards more sustainability and responsible management education. In view of ongoing criticism directed at schools for their persistent lack of relevance and ethics, as well as their far-reaching commercialisation and elitism, Amann, Pirson, et al. (2011) propose the concept of humanistic business schools, or HUBS, as the way forward (Spender & Locke, 2011).

Business schools should not only teach about sustainability and the crucial aspect of human dignity in business and society, but should also apply these matters in their own organisations. There are numerous stakeholders and groups of individuals within business schools to which this logic applies, such as the school leadership, the board or other governance entities, faculty, administrators, support groups in IT or sales, and last but not least, the programme participants and learners.

4.3 Literature review

Introduction to the role of literature reviews in grounded theory studies

The role of the literature review in a grounded theory study is contested. Glaser (2001) views the literature review as potentially harmful as it tempts researchers to fit data into existing theories instead of being innovative. Put differently, "the researcher is enjoined not to read the literature before data analysis, in order to encourage the researcher to be open to the concepts as he or she identifies them" Scott (2007, p. 9).

In stark contrast, Charmaz (2006) refuses to underestimate researchers' ability to respond appropriately to existing theories: she believes they are capable of more than merely being informed by what is already there, and that they can avoid succumbing to harmful preconceptions. She views researchers as people who approach data with an open mind, who can be sensitive to the need of letting theories emerge from the data, who can actively engage with other researchers and study participants and work intensively with the data. This section is based on Charmaz's (2006) view that it is worthwhile to be informed on two aspects which can only be achieved by consulting and reviewing the literature.

Firstly, her position is that "sensitizing concepts can help you start to code your data" (Charmaz, 2014, p. 117) as it endows the researcher with an overview of available concepts and the respective semantics. This especially holds true for the rich and fragmented field of learning where researchers explored a number of related concepts. Delineating concepts helps shape studies and clarify what they ought to be looking for. Secondly, at least initially reviewing the literature is crucial to learn whether or not LSV is already established in a given field of research or is still a novel concept in a more original field. Researchers need to know the status quo in order to produce original research. Thus, the literature review for this study started out with LSV as key word, and with terms used in learning styles-oriented research, as well as related ones entered into established academic literature databases.

For this study, the forward and backward snowballing approach based on Wohlin (2014) and described in Chapter 2, unfolded. From there onwards, the scope widened to include related areas on learning outcomes as detailed in the actual literature review section below. This culminated in the overviews in table 3 and figure 9 in the following sections. The literature review also includes a search for characteristics of business environments for business school graduates and what a compelling logic might be to cope with them. As outlined below, two approaches emerge when we attempt to cope with an ever more complex environment. They include simplification or complication as part of a logic introduced in the following sections (cf. Amann et al., 2012).

Thirdly, the literature acknowledges the possibility that fields mature over time. As explained below, the leadership field has progressed towards a versatility view which can benefit the learning style literature that currently has conceptual and empirical flaws. Reviewing these two elements critically need not create or sustain dominant preconceptions. Therefore, while acknowledging the risk voiced by Glaser (2001), the ensuing literature review follows Charmaz (2006) by framing researchers as capable and reflexive in their work.

LSV and related constructs

LSV has been defined in section 2 and continues to represent the central construct of this study. The following section highlights the unique focus of LSV, which is based on a review of central notions and constructs. LSV is clearly distinguishable and differentiated from several related constructs as I shall outline below. The construct adds a unique focus. Yet together these constructs form the foundation of an integrated view on learning quotient (LQ) that captures the ability to learn effectively. As the following overview shows, LSV complements these other constructs, while also addressing a crucial aspect of learning that is not otherwise emphasized.

Such an integrated view of an LQ can benefit from including the importance of enduring interest and consistent effort (Tyumeneva et al., 2017). The power of an ability to focus single-mindedly, has been outlined in the literature repeatedly, e.g. by Canfield et al. (2015), as has the value of enduring interest. Thus, an individual who is able to focus and remains interested in the material, achieves better (learning) outcomes than one without these qualities.

Grit and growth mind-sets versus LSV

Perseverance, which forms the second driver of successful learning, is also identified as 'grit'. This is in line with a growth-oriented mind-set. Individuals who adopt the philosophy of a 'growth mind-set', would be ones who "believe that their most basic abilities can be developed through dedication and hard work – brains and talent are just the starting point. This view creates a love of learning and a resilience that is essential for great accomplishment" (Dweck, 2015).

A variation of the growth mind-set, is introduced by the notion of 'definitely unfinished' (Clark & Sousa, 2018). Designating current states as 'unfinished', signals plasticity, i.e. a dynamic, evolutionary, non-fatalistic view of the human mind and assumes intentional flexibility; 'unfinished' in this context also indicates that more interesting and relevant potential might hitherto have remained untapped. Recognising what is unfinished, signals the potential to improve and that the best could yet be to come.

Absorptive capacity versus LSV

This line of thought that distinguishes potential from actually realised capacity to grow, evolve and transform is also inherent in the construct of 'absorptive capacity' (Zahra & George, 2002). Having emerged from an organisational theory and development view, the concept enriches the learning field by differentiating a resource, such as a powerful brain, from other dynamic capabilities, thus identifying the ability to adapt via learning. Absorptive capacity adds a perspective the defines learning as a broad process, which moves beyond simply acquiring new knowledge and reconfiguring existing mind-sets, to transforming and exploiting the acquired knowledge by applying it effectively in order to gain an advantage in competitive settings.

This increased awareness of the context and the teleological view on outperforming others in competitive settings is relevant for business schools and their graduates, because competition is an essential feature of business. From the individual learner's view, competition is evident in the selective admission to better schools, the quest for higher grades, in requirements for achieving distinctions, and also in landing the best job offers. Learning institutions have been confronted with ever more fierce competition, as well as with commercialisation (Bok, 2003).

Learning agility versus LSV

Another related concept, 'learning agility', refers to individuals who possess openness, willingness to learn, flexibility, curiosity, tolerance of ambiguity, people skills, vision and innovation (Eichinger & Lombardo, 2004). However, such a broad definition is less able to delineate what is included and what excluded from the construct's scope.

As table 3 below shows, Gravett and Caldwell (2016) add clarity by defining learning agility more narrowly as adaptability and willingness to confront the unknown. They identify four types of learning agility, namely mental agility, people agility, agility to change, and agility to achieve results. Mental agility describes the capacity to handle complexity and lateral thinking. People agility requires self-awareness and the ability to readily deal with different people and situations. Change agility deals with an individual's ability to cope with discomfort emerging from rapid change or failure, thus pushing boundaries and showing resilience. Results agility, to close this four-dimensional conceptualisation of learning agility, depicts the ability to deliver results on first attempts due to a person's inspiration and impact. Such a definition of results agility, which Gravett and Caldwell (2016) draw from Korn Ferry (2015), however, could be at odds with the learning school of strategizing and problem-solving which requires and recognises no negative aspects in proceeding iteratively, in trying again and again until one succeeds. The latter procedure assures learning from feedback given shortly after experiences which can be labelled as "failure" (Mintzberg et al., 2009).

Other modern, more tolerant approaches to failure include the "fake-it-until-you-make-it" (Gunder, 2011) line of thought. Gunder even praises situations characterised by learners with insufficiently developed skills who cope by relying on their courage, pragmatism and fast learning. As it is, the necessity to learn is no new phenomenon. Averbook (2014) explains that in pre-Socratic ancient Greece Heraclitus already mentioned that "the only thing that is constant is change". This emphasizes that the constructs of change and learning are closely entwined, that learning is a necessary component of this change process (Aramburu et al., 2006).

Other voices, such as Argyris (1977, p. 117) who argued that learning is related to "detection and correction of errors", can enrich the debate. With such a perspective the learning definition put forward by Gravett and Caldwell (2016) and Korn Ferry (2015) is not a suitable one in characterising learning agility as they emphasize first-time success, which is hardly possible if no errors are recognised and corrected. The following table summarises and describes these key learning-related constructs.

Table 3: Selected elements of a larger learning quotient conceptualisation

Construct	Main emphasis
Grit	Addresses the consistency of interests and perseverance of effort (Tyumeneva et al., 2017).
Growth mind-set	Emphasizes the plasticity of the mind and flexibility which allows formation of new ideas through dedication plus hard work; however, effort alone does not equal learning (Dweck, 2015).
'Definitely unfinished'	Motivates further learning by positing that highly attractive learning potential might not have been tapped yet (Clark & Sousa, 2018).
Absorptive capacity	Provides a measure for effectively tapping into learning potential (Zahra & George, 2002).
Learning agility	Underlines the importance of adaptability and willingness to confront the unknown, relying on four dimensions: mental, people, change and results agility (Gravett & Caldwell, 2016).
Learning styles	Acknowledges learners' features influencing ways of learning more effectively (Rolfe & Cheek, 2012).
LSV	Distinguishes different degrees of the ability to apply more than one learning style effectively (Amann, 2019).
Multiple intelligences	Refers to computational power in the field of logical-mathematical versus linguistic versus musical versus bodily-kinaesthetic versus a spatial or interpersonal, and even intrapersonal, tasks (Gardner, 1983).
Metacognition	Monitors and controls own thought processes while learning (Nelson & Narens, 1994).
Self-system	Examines importance, efficacy, emotional response, and overall motivation at the beginning of a potential learning process (Marzano & Kendall, 2007)

Further, although definitions of learning agility emphasize openness to the unknown, curiosity and readiness to confront the unknown, I would suggest that a clearer distinction between various learning fields (engaging the four agilities mentioned above) would have been helpful. In addition, it would be useful to delineate the various explanations of how the mechanisms function at work. According to Örtenblad (2001), the field of learning needs greater conceptual clarity. This is where the concept of LSV can add value. As outlined above, LSV refers to the degree to which a learner can effectively apply different learning styles in the process of learning.

Illustrations of learning styles and LSV

Figure 9 below illustrates three learner profiles. Learner A has one clear strength in terms of being an activist learner. Filling out the Honey and Mumford survey on learning styles, this learner receives raw scores for each of the four main learning styles the model considers. At the same time, there is a percentile score shedding light on the learner's position relative to others participating in the study. Learner A at the bottom of the following figure is a clear pragmatist, and a pragmatist only. Such a learner would dislike being taught by many different lecturers, and object to passive learning approaches or long pre-reading lists. S/he would reject mere class discussion in which three main to-do's would be deducted pragmatically.

Learner A tends to be flexible, moderately open minded, and would enjoy experimenting. Further, this learner would easily get involved in group activities and participate with others. S/he likes short and concise 'here and now' activities, classes full of drama, excitement or crises. Learner A prefers to be in the limelight, and would choose new ideas rather than one dogma. S/he does not shy away from challenges and draws special benefit from operating in a team due to appreciating the plurality of voices and thoughts that can be shared and exchanged. However, Learner A has qualities that are opposite to those of a versatile learner, described as Learner B.

Learner B is different in being less inclined than learner A to enjoy a variety of different activities in class. S/he would need time for reflection, where insights can emerge and be put in order. Learner B expects pragmatic, hands-on assignments shared at the end of a presented framework, without which the learning experience would be experienced as incomplete. This learner's LSV is not as low as in the case of learner A. Finally, learner C would benefit from highly diverse classes that present a complete set of learning pedagogies or andragogies, depending on the age group.

As per Rolfe and Cheek (2012), learning styles and LSV are thus based on the initial assumption that each learner has personal characteristics "that influence the way in which that person learns" (p. 176). These authors find that adjusting teaching styles can improve learning outcomes.

It should be noted that the original definition of learning styles, understands the concept as a set of behaviours clearly identifiable on several levels, namely the cognitive, the affective, and the psychosocial level, as outlined by Curry (1981). This author states that the various styles remain relatively stable and can be used to characterise how learners are positioned regarding their perceptions, interactions and responses to their learning context.

However, an identification of distinct learning styles differs from learning style versatility; to date the latter has not been sufficiently attended to. Hayes and Allinson's (1993) definition of learning style as a person's preference for a distinct way of processing and subsequently organising a given piece of information while learning, is conceptually open to focusing on not only one style, although a learner's reliance on just one style is usually assumed.

Figure 9: Examples of lowest, limited, and higher LSV based on the Honey and Mumford (2009) framework

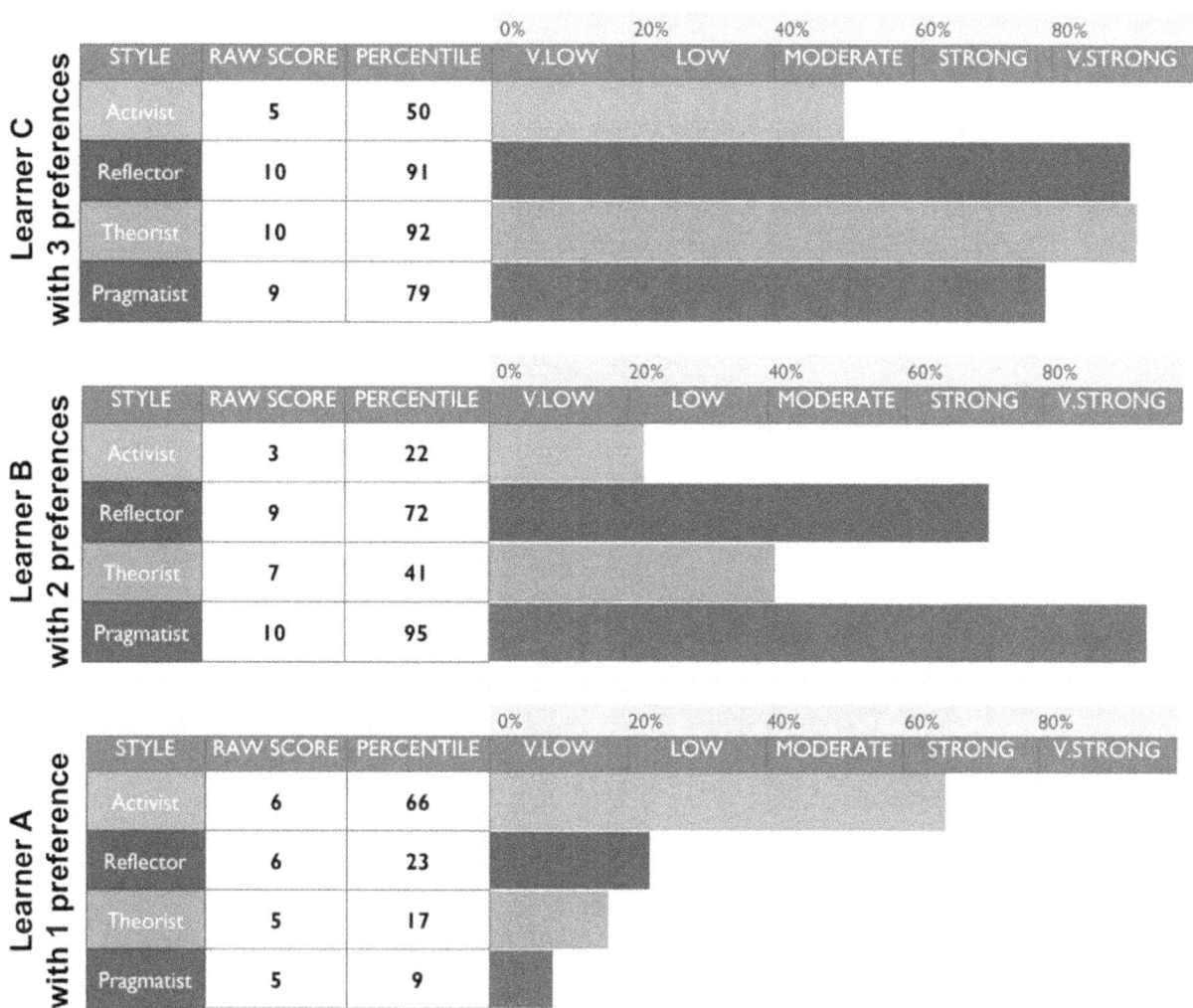

Multiple intelligences versus LSV

Table 3 on learning related constructs given above, also contains the construct of multiple intelligences. In differentiating LSV from multiple intelligences we gain a better understanding of how each construct is positioned. Gardner's (1983) seminal book on multiple intelligences and frames of mind encourages a view of human intelligence that goes beyond one single way of conceptualising and operationalising intelligence as, for example, a binary of linguistic versus a logical-mathematical capacity.

Gardner (1983) suggests distinguishing musical and bodily-kinaesthetic capacities, spatial or interpersonal senses, and even intrapersonal aspects of intelligence. Updating his original views over time and adding a link to the digital age and context, Gardner and Davis' (2013) once more focus on other constructs than learning styles or LSV in learning success. As Strauss (2013) interprets Gardner's work, the construct of multiple intelligences or 'MI theory' refers to noteworthy computational power to perform well in a field. Learning styles, in contrast, focus on how learners approach materials; thus they address a different process.

Metacognition versus LSV

Five different perspectives can characterise the relationship between the two constructs metacognition and LSV. For Nelson and Narens (1994), the construct of metacognition addresses a learner's ability to monitor and control his/her own thought processes. Concurrently, Turner-Walker (2016) views metacognition as the "ability to think about what one is thinking about" (p. 3). There are divergent definitions of the term metacognition, though. For example, Tempelaar (2006) views metacognition as critical thinking, giving considerably less attention to self-awareness. From a definition point of view, metacognition thus stands for a divergent construct. No matter whether it is about critical thinking or self-awareness, the focus is not in the first place on how versatile a learner is when it comes to learning styles. Figure 10 visualises this lack of construct overlap in the top left corner.

The second potential relationship between the two constructs emerges from the following. The underlying line of thought within metacognition is that such awareness and monitoring enhance performance (see e.g. Kinnunen & Vauras, 1995). According to Schmidt & Ford (2003), besides developing awareness, creating transparency about additional learning goals can make actual learning more effective. There is a key difference between metacognition and the nascent field of LSV. The diverging definitions of metacognition are not helpful in delineating these differences. The question as to whether or not learners have to be aware of their own thought processes, and of the need to monitor and control them as Nelson and Narens (1994) suggested in the field of metacognition, still has to be answered for LSV.

Questions regarding awareness represent an unaddressed research gap in the LSV field. There are two options. Faculty can attempt to hone LSV with or without a learner being aware of this process, thus with or without applying the logic assigned to this awareness within metacognition. Applying Turner-Walker's (2016) view, however, makes it easier to juxtapose metacognition and LSV. One does not have be able to "think about what one is thinking about" (p. 3) in order to be a versatile learner, especially if a mere descriptive view is applied in talent management or an admission and selection process.

Figure 10: Overview of the various relationships between metacognition and LSV

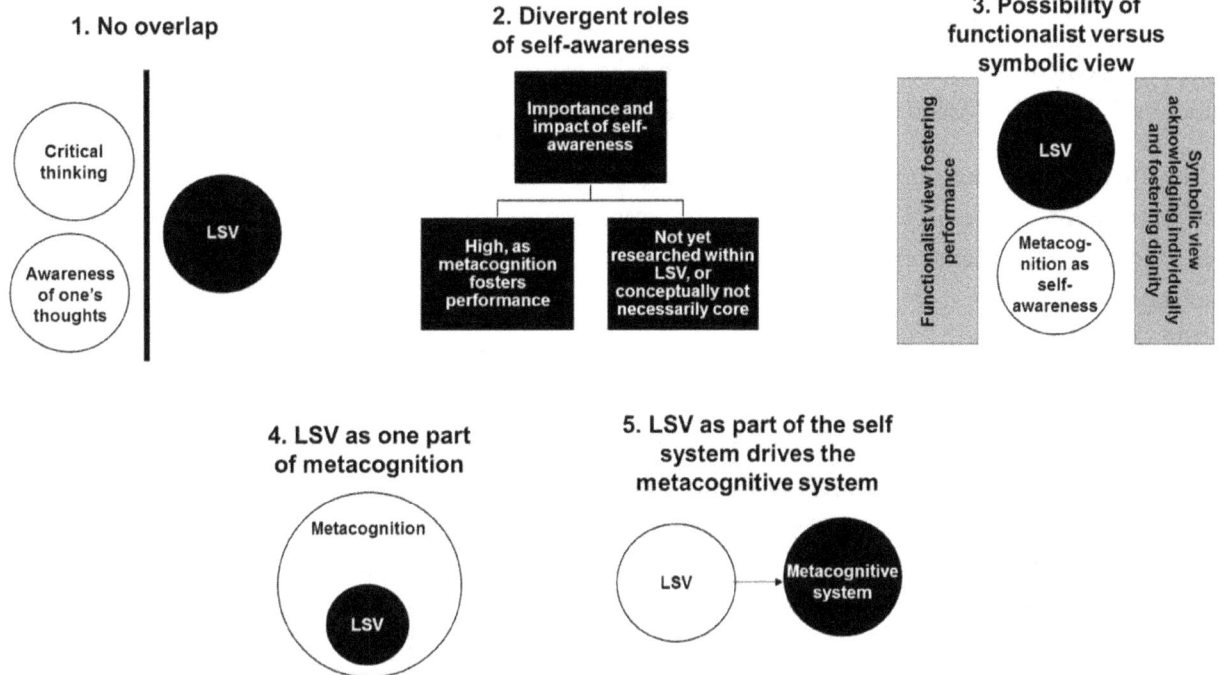

A learner with high LSV simply is more open to different modes of learning – with or without awareness of it. Actual strategies to hone this versatility warrant further research, too. It would be premature to conclude that being aware of one's LSV is equal to LSV itself. This is portrayed in figure 10 below in the top right-hand corner.

The third view characterising the relationship between metacognition and LSV is one that identifies metacognition and LSV as distinct constructs, yet acknowledges a parallel between the two fields they represent. Morris et al. (2019) state that when researchers who study performance recognise and focus on individual differences, researching metacognition opens a promising avenue.

The same logic applies for LSV, as recognising such versatility can assist us in understanding and enhancing performance, while it can also be studied as part of focusing on human dignity and individuality as an end in itself. Studying this individuality does not have to occur as a means to an end; it can be an end in itself. This resembles the discussion on another construct in academic research – organisational culture. One could approach the latter from a functionalist view as a means to the end of boosting performance (cf. Denison, 1984). Alternatively, the symbolic value emphasizes dignity as an end in itself as this individuality has meaning. This is visualised in the bottom righthand corner in figure 10 below.

Fourthly, there is a possibility to view LSV as part of metacognition as shown in the bottom, middle part of figure 10. Jans and Leclerq (1997) define metacognition as active judgement in the learning process. More versatile learners would be able to process new material more effectively, which can enable better judgement. A more versatile learner can take more charge of the learning process as different modes of embracing subjects are more possible than would otherwise be the case.

Also, the revised Bloom taxonomy of learning goals or RBT (Anderson, Krathwohl, et al., 2001) sees self-knowledge, which could include insight or awareness regarding one's LSV as part of metacognition. More directly and explicitly, the authors see beliefs about self-efficacy as being included in metacognition.

Having had experience of either portraying substantial self-efficacy or not, is likely to shape learners' beliefs about self-efficacy. There is at least one more potential view of the link between metacognition and LSV. It emanates from once more revisiting definitions and the evolution of learning constructs over time. 'Marzano's new learning taxonomy' (MNT) (Marzano & Kendall, 2001, 2007) conceptualises learning as a process which first engages the self-system. It decides whether to embrace a task or not. This takes place before the subsequent metacognitive system takes the learning process further creating clarity on learning goals and strategies, which then in turn relies on the cognitive system for implementation.

The self-system is thus separate and has primacy over the other systems. It helps examine the importance of presented learning subjects. It sheds light on efficacy, a learner's emotional response, and motivation. In contrast, the metacognitive system only specifies goals and monitors progress, clarity and accuracy. Assessments of one's LSV would be placed on the self-system level, not the metacognitive sub-level. According to this logic, awareness of a strong LSV as part of the self-system would entail a higher perceived self-efficacy, a more enabling emotional response, and arguably more motivation to embrace a presented topic. This argument can be made interpreting MNT within an LSV discussion, yet MNT does not rely on the semantics of LSV. This still allows for the conclusion that LSV, if understood as being part of and positioned on the self-system level, drives the metacognitive system and the further learning process. This case is illustrated in figure 10's bottom left part.

Emerging insights on LSV

The main conceptual evolution of learning styles and LSV is two-pronged. Firstly, acknowledging versatility emphasizes that the quest is no longer to identify the one main learning mode deemed most effective for an individual, as this can create ambiguity and confusion if a learner does not necessarily adhere to such a single style (Honey & Mumford, 2009). Secondly, as outlined in chapter 2, the field of learning styles currently needs innovation. In line with what others have argued (e.g. Coffield et al., 2004), the field has been controversial in having produced more than 70 conceptualisations based on limited and empirically unconvincing evidence.

More importantly, the field of learning styles has not made a crucial next step in its conceptual maturation process. The field of leadership, for example, has moved from definitions and various conceptualisations to identifying leadership types, and has now reached the insight that it is not one effective leadership style that matters the most, but rather leadership style versatility that enables leaders to cope situationally with a given scenario (Kaplan & Kaiser, 2003a).

In contrast, the field of learning styles is only now starting to 'unfreeze' and move forward. Chapter 2 presents a first and statistically significant study demonstrating that – very much in line with leadership versatility studies – more LSV leads to better outcomes. In the case of LSV, there is a positive link between more versatility and better grades within the constraints of this study. This move towards a versatility orientation can, based on arguments outlined below, help overcome the doubts one segment of researchers continues to have, even criticising the concept of learning style as a myth (see e.g. Newton & Miah, 2017).

The literature underpinning the faculty view on dealing with LSV

As the field of LSV is in an early stage, the literature covering this concept is limited. Besides the first quantitative study on the impact LSV has on grades presented in chapter 2, this study continues the research by addressing the research question regarding how faculty members perceive LSV. The following three sections discuss pillars of further exploration for LSV. Firstly, to ensure good progress, the analysis starts by suggesting we transfer, i.e. copy-and-past, several trains of thought from the learning style field, which are presented and perceived as increasingly dated, to the emerging field of LSV.

Secondly, I reflect on how LSV can overcome past flaws in the learning style discussions. Thirdly, a brief discussion follows on how the requisite variety rule can provide a solid foundation for the benefit of an 'LSV related meshing hypothesis' (LSVRMH). Type A and B will be introduced below.

'Copy-and-pasting' the arguments advocated in the learning style literature

There are several theoretical and empirical insights in the field of learning styles that work effectively and therefore can be transferred into the field of LSV – a construct, which has been explored for decades. Firstly, according to Hwang et al. (2014), the general awareness of one's learning style can boost academic performance. A similar argument can be made regarding self-awareness helping a learner to overcome blind spots. Being aware of gaps can help trigger learning to close the gaps, or at least narrow them down (Lanz, 2013).

Self-awareness alone provides an incomplete understanding of the learning system, though. Cameron et al. (2015) argue that an explicit evaluation of learners' preferred modes of learning can help in designing more appropriate teaching methodologies. Pashler et al. (2008) refer to this as a 'meshing hypothesis', which they further discuss in exploring learning ecosystems. For Eudy (2018), the term 'learning ecosystem' seems to have become trendier in the learning community. According to him, it helps people think more strategically about their learning system, which consists of the involved individuals, the content to convey, the applied technologies, learning cultures and strategies. Pashler et al. (2008) explain that instruction ought to be provided in a format sensitive to the learners' preferences as they are encountered in the classroom. A mismatch between learning styles and teaching approaches can pose obstacles to learning (De Vita, 2001; Cook, 2005). The discussion on meshing goes even further, and becomes more complex.

Merrill (2000) distinguishes between content-by-strategy and learning-style-by-strategy interactions, explaining that how to convey content rather than teach learning styles, should dominate reflection on how to teach. Yet, the meshing hypothesis with its argument of congruence can be developed further to serve as a new 'LSV-related meshing hypothesis' (LSVRMH Type A; for more details on type B, see below). The question is that if the LSV in a given group is limited or unknown, why diversify existing solutions by investing in new forms of learning technology, pedagogy or andragogy?

Regardless of any cost consideration, Amann, Pirson, et al. (2011) argue that business schools should become more dignity-oriented. Institutions should counter the strong commercialisation trend currently characterising higher education (Bok, 2003). Attention to the LSVRMH can constitute a new and concrete form of paying attention to and fostering human dignity in business schools and institutions of higher education more generally.

Overcoming past flaws in the learning style discussions

Reviewing the literature, it becomes clear that a lack of progress in the field of learning styles has long been overlooked. As the following exposition will show, there is an opportunity to trigger progress towards understanding learning versatility by considering how the term 'versatility' applies in the leadership field. Opportunities to overcome specific criticism of the learning style literature have arisen to alleviate or even overcome the criticism as the field advances.

Initially, Pashler et al. (2008) pointed out numerous studies flawed by methodological weakness. For example, studies measure preferences, but not concrete abilities. They depict engaging and at times congenial topics, but not styles linked to learning effectiveness. The authors also criticise an overreliance on an unquestioned meshing hypothesis even considering that a learner can still acquire new knowledge or skills if exposed to a less preferred learning experience. These authors continue their critique by pointing to the excessive commercialisation and emergence of a learning style industry, while scientific, empirical evidence to support alleged benefits is not necessarily strong.

Hence, there is a need to reconceptualise and re-operationalise. Possibly, similar to the early-stage understanding of leadership styles, some of the methodological weaknesses stem from a poor understanding of the learning styles field. Innovative approaches can help. Understanding that not a single style, but rather style versatility can help in diverse and dynamic environments can open up new avenues for teaching, programme design, strategizing on value in education, or advancing research. It could change the view on (1) what the focus should be if one is to explain learning success in the exploratory phase of research, and (2) what should be measured and subsequently managed and improved when scholars continue with prescriptive research.

Inherently, the learning style debate as it was conducted in the past seems to foster a certain degree of inertia, which goes against the strong need for business schools to evolve (Lorange, 2012). As Thaker (2015) indicates, modern learning is a multi-level process which should include elements on the levels of knowing, doing, being and becoming. Besides the symbolic and ethical lens, the past learning style debate had a dominant means-to-an-end perspective. It focused on the question of how to optimise learning of established content and skills. The question was not how to create more versatile learners, nor to concretise the debate on learning-to-learn (Stephens, 2013) or on the 'becoming' idea (Thaker, 2015).

Rather, modern learning adopted a transformative view referred to as the 'LSV related meshing hypothesis' Type B. This hypothesis would aim first to explore how LSV-related dynamics work before going on to provide prescriptive, actionable knowledge. LSVRMH Type B would then pursue the goal of addressing the question as to how learning ecosystems and learning interventions should be actively shaped in order to leverage and develop LSV to create more versatile learners in the process. For highly competitive business schools, this would lead to a new meta-learning goal with an impact on school or programme visions and learning goals in line with the previously defined construct of metacognition. Shifting value away from what others do, provides institutions with a temporary advantage in an industry haunted by the Red Queen effect, as outlined in chapter 1.1 (Iñiguez de Onzoño & Carmona, 2012).

This would simultaneously ensure that schools prioritise the interests of the learners, helping them to differentiate themselves and foster lifelong learning. There have been previous calls for more critical thinking and thus development of metacognition in business schools and management education (see e.g. Tempelaar, 2006). Yet, for Tempelaar (2006), metacognition defined as mere critical thinking in a narrow view, or more broadly understood as self-awareness, monitoring, and controlling of learners' thought processes could be incongruent with the LSV construct. Figure 10 maps the main conceptual ways towards clarifying the relationship between metacognition and LSV.

In the context of learning, a related question is whether learning styles are a given and constant as early research on the construct by Claxton and Ralston (1978) posits, or whether there is room for development and growth over time. If the latter applies, a learner's LSV could evolve over time. The question whether this is possible once again shows a parallel to the field of leadership development. Piaw and Ting (2014) ask whether leaders are born or made. Their answer is neither a full acceptance nor rejection of either stance. They find that a number of factors contribute to the effectiveness of a leadership development intervention. The same logic represents a promising avenue for analysis in the learning field in general, as well as in the field of LSV in particular. The more the available body of knowledge on LSV grows, the more clarity there will be on what antecedents exist and how to evolve them effectively over time, and the more the assumption will hold that not only are leaders at least partly made, but they are also versatile learners.

Learning today must be multi-levelled to include Thaker's (2015) elements on (1) the level of knowing (knowledge, models and facts), (2) the level of doing (actual problem-solving skills), (3) the level of being (clarifying which values count), and (4) the level of becoming (key development stages over time). Business schools, thus, need to retain learning as a meta-responsibility as part of their full focus, and as an ongoing effort, they should review aspects that can be improved.

Requisite variety as the core theoretical foundation for the benefit of LSV-related meshing hypothesis type A and B

Continuing to learn from the field of leadership development in developing the field of LSV development, the insight emerges that in today's dynamic and complex business environments, a modern way of understanding leaders as learners (Mikkelsen & Jarche, 2015) represents a promising avenue forward. Learning and viewing leaders as learners can ensure a match between the challenges of external environments. Learning is an adequate coping mechanism to survive and strive in such contexts.

Ashby's (2011) law of requisite variety posits that complexity in external environments can best be addressed by matching degrees of internal complexity. External complexity refers to more adversity in VUCA business environments (Betof et al., 2014) in which business school graduates have to survive; it also refers to the diversity of courses and learning opportunities graduates encounter in their degree programmes. Learning can indeed be a coping mechanism and can represent internal complexity to match the external complexity. "Internal" can refer to both the individual ability to perform and interact in a given content, but also to the organisation-internal learning and corresponding support factors.

Robinson (2016) claims that learning versatility is a valuable determinant of successful leadership development programmes. Also, Lombardo and Eichinger (2000) argue that students with high potential are necessarily highly successful learners. Conceptually, leadership and learning can thus be linked.

The posited programme diversity can include professor-led courses on any of the core business functions and student-led applied work, as in capstone modules, internships, consulting projects or research-based master theses. This diversity can also grow when different faculty members either consciously or merely by personality, find diverging ways to understand and deliver learning experiences. Alternatively, by nature of the subjects they teach, some faculty create very distinct and divergent courses. For example, subjects vary, ranging from the largely fact based statistics or finance courses on the one hand, to qualitative, discussion-oriented courses on leadership and governance on the other.

If students pursue higher LSV, they learn via more and diverse modes that indisputably deliver more pronounced, elaborate and complex learning abilities. Building learning environments that hone the LSV of groups of learners, will include ensuring sound evidence, or at least qualitative insight, frameworks, or theories. This calls for adapting budgets, faculty skill profiles, programmes and school-level programme priorities. Possibly such adaptation will have repercussions on the admissions team, its policies and practices, which could possibly pre-screen for signs of a higher LSV.

Interim summary and implications for the emerging study

Some of the arguments put forward do show the benefits of learning styles as a relevant concept applicable to the field of LSV as well. Business schools and institutions of higher education should become more dignity-oriented and thus acknowledge individual differences more than they currently do. New types of meshing hypotheses could emerge if learning ecosystems are designed with awareness of learning style differences and by adapting learning interventions, particularly with LSV as a dynamic concept in mind. Thus, this study substantiates the view that LSV should not be viewed from a fatalistic perspective that sees it as a static, exogenous concept only. It suggests replacing the inflexible concept as applied in study 1 in chapter 2 with a relevant, dynamic one, as it can potentially impact study outcomes.

Schools ought to stand out and survive in an industry characterised by the Red Queen effect (Iñiguez de Onzoño & Carmona, 2012). Graduates need help to differentiate themselves and grow their chances in the competitive labour market. Disruption will require them to embark on lifelong learning (Christensen et al., 2010). Therefore, business schools would greatly benefit from developing learning systems with a focus on meta-learning outcomes and opportunities for individuals, programmes and schools in mind. In this way changing conceptualisations can help repair past flaws on the conceptual side and help revisit weak empirical evidence regarding the importance of learning styles. It is possible that LSV counts for more than an individual learning style, in very much the same way as leadership versatility rather than individual leadership style has proven to be the more mature, next level, empirically backed construct in boosting leadership effectiveness.

The requisite variety law provides a solid theoretical foundation for further inquiry into the very dynamics of LSVRMH Types A and B. Considering the nascent nature of the field, this study presents a grounded theory study on LSVRMH, in order to start growing the available body of knowledge on how LSV can be better understood.

We need to clarify how much innovation or augmentation a single study can contribute without losing focus. There are some fundamental challenges, e.g. differentiating between a learner's ability to express a concrete preference for a mode of learning and an actual, proven aptitude in this preferred way of learning (Sternberg et al., 1999). Several conceptualisation and operationalisation challenges might persist until further studies have devoted special research projects to them. Beyond research, the commercial nature of the learning style field (Pashler et al., 2008) should be balanced by more rigorous research to substantiate claims of the beneficial nature of the field. This study aims to contribute a small, qualitative effort to this substantiation quest.

4.4 Methodology and method

The nature of the research question, a typical 'how' question – "How do faculty members perceive LSV?" – requires a qualitative research methodology (Cohen et al., 2007) to capture the richer insights on the phenomenon of LSV. The goal is no longer to measure and quantify any kind of impact, but to understand faculty's reception of a given concept.

Creswell (2014) argues in favour of a qualitative, constructivist approach if the research goal is not only to understand a phenomenon, but also to generate theory (rather than testing various theories) based on the analysis of how a particular phenomenon materialises. Grounded theory is particularly suitable for analysing concepts grounded in data and, as Starks and Trinidad (2007) argue, for preparing an explanatory theory regarding complex social processes. According to these authors, grounded theory can shed light on and clarify research questions dealing with phenomena, such as how a fundamental social process X (in this research project the degree of awareness, acknowledgement, leveraging and potentially honing LSV) can unfold in a specific environment. In studying this versatility, I opted for a modern, iterative and flexible approach to grounded theory, as Charmaz (2006) suggested, based on a number of reasons.

In addition to encouraging more methodological self-consciousness among researchers, Charmaz and Belgrave (2019) question as well as balance the logic-deductive research which is becoming more dominant, yet could stifle creativity in qualitative research. According to them, neo-liberalism has downsides, such as focussing on quantification, more conventional research, externally imposed excellence criteria, or reduced sensitivity to contexts in which data is generated. They argue that researchers have an alternative: they can pursue truly interesting puzzles which are explored with new data, shaking off restrictions that are too tight for the process and focusing on creating meaning instead of merely ensuring process compliance. In contrast to Straussian grounded theory, which emphasizes a story in the data, constructivist grounded theories pursue the development of an analysis-based story constructed from the data, which adds a different value. The grounded theorist's individuality is acknowledged, not questioned or deemed a potential disturbance. When reviewing grounded theory approaches for this research, this more recent, highly constructivist, phenomenon-focused, flexible version resonated best with me as a researcher. Learning style versatility is a creative addition to and maturation of the learning style field. Constructivist grounded theory provides a productive approach to address the research question.

I interviewed participants at a private business school in one of India's major cities. It was the same institution at which Amann (2019) found that LSV has a positive impact on grades. As a grounded theory-oriented study, I chose a school other than the researcher's employer as cooperation partner, to prevent the phenomenon of 'guilty knowledge' (Williams, 2009) and to lower the risk of preconceived answers.

Cohen et al. (2011) mention the long tradition of interviews in education research. The 18 faculty members at the research site were originally targeted as interviewees for confidential, anonymous (Christians, 2000), relatively open-ended interviews (Opdenakker, 2006). To ensure informed consent (Christians, 2000), and following best practice in learning style related research (Pashler et al., 2008), I informed faculty members of the study's purpose, as well as of the research process to be followed. They learnt *ex ante* that participation is voluntary, and that data would be dealt with anonymously. Participants did not receive compensation. The chosen constructivist grounded theory planned for these interviews to be carried out until theoretical sufficiency, as a better sampling criterion than theoretical saturation, had been achieved (Charmaz, 2014). Grounded theory does not define and limit sample sizes in advance. Yet, after eleven interviews, I had gained sufficient insight to produce an emerging framework. The interviews were carried out in person, excepting a few conducted via a video link, between May and July 2019. Research that enables practical efficiency simultaneously administers the art of what is feasible (Blaxter et al., 2006) and relies on technology.

Approach to determine the cut-off point for interviews

As mentioned, interviews continued until sufficient insight had been gained and all core questions were clarified. Thus, repeated interview sessions were not necessary in most cases, although one interview required eight sessions to ensure an active engagement with the interviewee, and to reach a critical level of understanding. 'Sufficient insight' in this context refers to a clear decision on how to determine the cut-off point at which interviewing would end (Charmaz, 2014). In grounded theory, there are two basic approaches to arrive at a decision when to stop interviewing. Theoretical sufficiency versus saturation represent core options. The former asks when sufficient interviews were conducted to start conceptualising and theorising. The latter suggests a continuation of interviews until no new information per category or category as such emerge.

Yet, according to Corbin and Strauss (1996) the exact cut-off point cannot be predetermined, as the data dictates the sample size situationally. Both Glaser and Strauss (1967) and Strauss and Corbin (1990) share that even smaller groups of interviewees can be very effective if interviewees are carefully chosen and the interviewing process is effective. Sample accuracy, not larger sample size, matters most in grounded theory (Bowen, 2008). Thomson (2001) substantiates this in pointing out grounded theory studies with as little as five and as many as 114 interviews. In the context of this study, theoretical sufficiency was reached after 11 out of the 18 originally envisaged, total number of faculty members. The patterns were clear, there was enough input to form categories and to position categories in relation to each other. Constructive grounded theory precisely allows for this subjective judgment call. Section 4.5 following here, will shed light on this process.

Regarding the two basic options of theoretical sufficiency versus saturation, Dey (1999) argues that theoretical sufficiency adequately describes approaches frequently used in grounded theory. In this option of theoretical sufficiency, the researcher diligently works towards a judgment call when sufficient depth in the data collection, i.e. the interviewing process, is reached in order to build a grounded theory. Dey (1999) illustrates how researchers applying grounded theory often use theoretical sufficiency. Saturation in contrast would foresee a continuation of interviews until emerging categories are saturated and the net benefit of additional interviews disappears.

The primary decision-making criteria for not adding new interviews was indeed a subjective judgment call on whether sufficient insights had emerged to justify theorising. Regarding data integrity, selective coding and forming categories, which eventually lead to the grounded theory, ensured that they form an integrative part of the analysis-based story constructed from them. This is the goal and process of constructivist grounded theory Charmaz and Belgrave (2019) outlined, in contrast to Straussian grounded theory that pursues the one and only story in the data. The authors clarify that in objectivist grounded theory data is unproblematic, straightforward, uncontaminated and not preconceived, and researchers ought to deal with data in a direct and simple way, while epistemology does not matter. In contrast, in constructivist grounded theory, as the authors explain, data could be substantially more problematic, multi-layered and co-constructed, accepting the possibility of prior meaning while creating transparency on positionality and epistemology. Therefore, managing data is substantially more nuanced, but also complex (Charmaz and Belgrave, 2019).

Interviewees were all faculty members whose profession seemed to have honed their skill to explain their viewpoints in a very straightforward way. The interview process unfolded in highly effective manner, allowing the researcher to grasp the situation efficiently and effectively. There might have been additional knowledge gain with additional data, although probably minimal. Even so, saturation was not necessarily reached as additional examples could have emerged. Yet, a clear decision was taken in favour of theoretical sufficiency rather than saturation. The research objective was first to better understand and rapidly develop propositional knowledge in the form of a grounded theory.

The following section presents the emerging categories and emerging patterns as a foundation for designing a grounded theory on LSV in context. According to Starks and Trinidad (2007), grounded theory is appropriate for studying phenomena using those who have experienced them as participants. Faculty members represent a crucial stakeholder group as they can drive or impede an enabling participant-centred learning environment as outlined by Baeten et al. (2010). Faculty members were chosen for this study to ensure a critical level of analytic depth. There are of course also other crucial stakeholder groups, therefore I encourage further studies to explore the perceptions and prescriptive insights developed in other core stakeholder groups, e.g. among students.

4.5 Empirical results

This study followed Charmaz (2014) in starting an initial coding process after I transcribed all the text in Microsoft Excel. This transcription took place ongoingly so that information was easily available for follow-up interviews. The software allowed for sufficient text search and coding opportunities, and familiarity with it enabled immediate progress. An initial scrutiny of NVIVO and attending a workshop on its use as one option for qualitative research and text analysis identified the risk that it can distract from analysing the text, shifting too much attention to mastering the software. Initial text analysis commenced by coding first line by line, sentence by sentence, or smaller paragraphs, ideally using gerunds as "we gain a strong sense of action and sequence with gerunds" (Charmaz, 2014, p. 120).

Covering all ideas discussed with eleven interviewees was insightful, but eventually too voluminous to report in a study format.

Table 22 given in appendix 2 summarises the coding process based on the initial interview, along with sample quotes to substantiate them. Table 4 below presents its overall logic in summary form. Several trends become obvious in the data analysis.

Table 4: Overview of the logic of mapping and comparing codes

Sample quotes on initial codes from each interviewee →

Initial codes ↓

Additions ↓

Firstly, the focused codes that emerged in the first interview turned out to be quite robust in terms of recurring codes or categories; a limited number of relevant categories emerged as new ones once the first categories were identified. Most of the categories are substantiated considerably later in the process, after more interviews had taken place to probe and complement the original code sets.

Only a very few never or only partially recurred. Three additional codes emerged during the interviews when earlier quotes were compared with follow-up quotes and insights. I took extensive notes during the interview process. Participants did not like the idea of being recorded, which is why note-taking was discussed and agreed upon at the beginning of the interview. Transcribing the discussion during the interview process was quite energy-intensive, but necessary, because as many insights as possible had to be captured. I read key statements back to the interviewees right away to ensure their correctness.

During the coding process, the researcher's memo writing ensured that observations were captured. In this way the hierarchical differences the interviewer noticed when interviewees referred to school management and even to the foreign interviewer himself, were noted.

Also, the insight that the overall andragogic acumen of professors at the study partner institution seemed limited, was recorded, to name but a single example. Interviewees reiterated that lectures were rather traditional and conservative. Simulations and even case studies as a more interactive alternative to lecturing were only possible if sufficient resources were made available.

The first axis of an emerging grounded theory

The next step consisted of axial coding and aimed to relate core themes to each other. During this more in-depth analysis of the data, attending more precisely to the emerging categories, two main dimensions seem to align the captured comments most aptly.

On the one hand, the quotes and codes could be categorised along the axis of level of analysis, of which the levels were (1) society, (2) institution, and (3) individual faculty member. The following sections will refer specifically to features of the Indian institution that was the research site for this study.

On realm 1: national culture (society level)

There are societal forces in the form of the national culture, which shape behaviours in this educational institution in general, and in the classroom specifically. At this time no generalisations are made to account for institutions other than the research partner's set-up. Delving deeper into realm 1 shaped by national culture, the insight emerges that there is a national culture regarding the distribution of power. Following the culture anthropologists Hofstede and Minkov (2010), this is labelled as a high power distance index which ensures a structure according to which less powerful individuals align themselves with those in power, showing unequal distributions of power (Hofstede, 2011).

According to the Hofstede (2011) culture scores, India has one of the highest power distance scores, and a relatively low individualism score; the country ranks higher on the uncertainty avoidance index, and slightly lower on the long-term orientation index (Juhasz, 2014). In the educational context, this necessarily has repercussions, and the interviews clearly substantiated the impact of national culture on educational culture in this particular setting.

Our study noted that in the study partner organisation's classrooms Indian students and faculty members structure their expectations and relationships according to the Hofstede (2011) scores. Comments 2.8 ("we lecture, no questions allowed, then the exam"), 2.10 ("We do as told, we do not have tenure… the power is clearly distributed") or 10.7 ("I don't know if learners are born or made … students are immature") in the table in appendix 2 illustrate how national culture reduces the students' role considerably, as does comment 4.3: "Indian culture is there…. Teachers have the last word…".

In their perception, students feel comfortable taking lower positions in the student-faculty member hierarchy. A lower individualism score fosters alignment and compliance with the encountered social setting and the strong faculty role. National culture clarifies roles of students and faculty members from an uncertainty avoidance perspective.

The relevance of national culture lies in how it enriches the debate on what matters when learning ecosystems have to be explained. Thomas, Thomas and Wilson (2013), for example, do not include it in their overview of factors to prioritise. They focus on the overall mission and purpose, the university system, including faculty in promotion and tenure systems, leadership, accreditation and resources. Yet, factors related to learning style (versatility) seem to be at least partially culture-bound, not culture-free.

On realm 2: institutional level

The institutional level matters in considering LSV, as the business school model seems to understand faculty members as a resource to be used in securing financial returns for the organisation which is a private school, and in which the owner has a vested interest. Faculty explicitly mentioned that they work long hours and feel "milked like a cow", as comments 7.8 ("Faculty is too busy") or 8.9 ("We are milked as cows, not nurtured; we teach as much as possible … it is up to students to deal with it…") indicate. This school ownership setting diminishes the organisation's focus on innovation, faculty development, long-term organisational development plans for teaching and learning, budgets for experimentation, material, simulations, etc. Examples are comments 6.9 ("Institutional support and faculty development are not given, but much needed … faculty interest is not addressed, which really limits what we can do…"), 5.11 ("Lectures still dominate, very few experiments take place … new things make the professor stand out, which is not always positive among faculty or in the school in general"), 5.4 ("We teach so much … little time for training or innovating"), 5.3 ("We teach as told"), or 5.9 ("Ownership matters … our private set-up makes us think very short-term and on what they get out of it…"). This results in a high turnover of faculty members who feel largely disempowered.

On realm 3: individual faculty level

Next on this axis of analysis is the personal level of the individual faculty member. According to interviewee contributions, the body of faculty members have limited andragogy acumen and diverging degrees of idealism, caring and motivation. Although some of the interviewees showed idealism, overextension seemed to drain energy. Faculty members fulfilled students' cultural expectations if they merely lectured, or institutional expectations if they would superficially innovate. Generally, they attested to blindly adopting practices that one-directionally would diversify their teaching toolset. Comment 7.3 ("Postgraduate needs to be more practical … meshing will help learn more") suggests how energies could rise, or comment 7.5 ("More practical activities are always better… we use projects… ") emphasizes the value of practical application; however, these would merely address one of the four basic learning styles, and would hardly develop LSV. Comment 6.11 summarises it succinctly with "we do not talk about learning… we often lack the acumen". Before any positive change and professionalisation can take place, there must be progress regarding awareness, and wellness at Institutional level equally needs attention. The business model constrains investment, innovation or balanced workloads. Equally, individual faculty members do not drive their own learning, which considering today's free online resources' availability, could easily have been more pronounced. The next level would be considering how to create interest, desire and action, which will have its own challenges and requirements for healthy development.

The second axis on action readiness

The second axis for categorising participants' quotes and their codes will follow the action readiness scheme proposed by the AIDA sequence of constructs (Lee & Hoffman, 2015). This is a classical promotional theory from the marketing field which depicts action-readiness. Individuals must have the requisite awareness, interest, desire and eventual trigger action to get things started. Overworked faculty members who lack andragogic acumen or engagement would not be able to design and implement impactful LSV-oriented innovations.

As mentioned in comment 6.5 "each course is largely the same". Students reportedly lock themselves into the bathroom crying (comment 6.8) due to feeling unprepared for the challenges. Following Charmaz (2014), the action readiness framework should focus on the process related to the core phenomenon. Scrutinising the data, however, the overall situation at this study site resembles one where barriers to progress dominate. A number of interviewees were not even aware of the different learning styles concept. They merely deliver one-directional lecturing. Numerous comments came across as irrelevant when it came to addressing different learning styles or learning how to learn.

The next segment will discuss awareness paired with an interest in its relevance to high workload demands and the wish to comply with expectations that faculty should keep innovation costs low, not stand out, nor make colleagues look bad. Interviewee contributions affirm that the institutional structure discourages drastic divergences in various segments. A conclusion drawn from the interviewees is that faculty management can benefit from further alignment with innovative trends, preferably showing more idealism as expressed in comment 11.10 ("We need to talk more about how to learn to learn") and 11.11 ("I could do more … I probably would feel better if I did more for the students … in the future I aspire to do more").

Faculty members' desire to improve themselves is discouraged as they have to overcome the seemingly culturally imposed and organisationally reinforced understanding of students as immature. Examples are comments 10.7 ("I don't know if learners are born or made … students are immature") or 10.11 ("Students are not ready to listen to practical things … they need to learn and listen to more concepts first"). In contrast to what is expressed in comment 10.9 ("The student has no voice"), faculty members in general do not give students a voice. Also, considering that the literature pays a great deal of attention to learners' plasticity and the 'definitely unfinished' concept (Clark & Sousa, 2018) which determines that the best growth achievement is always yet to come, faculty members need to address scepticism, as pronounced in comment 10.10 ("Not all can adapt"), by heeding the literature in granting students more development opportunities.

In today's fast-moving world with a next generation that is substantially more technology-oriented than their predecessors, the professors do not always perceive themselves as 'superior', nor actually as the ultimate experts, as comment 9.2 ("Professor with actual experience is superior"... "has to have research too"... "active learning is always better") indicates.

This is very much in line with the latest globally available insights on learning and development which encourage learners to break out of highly socialised learning and move on to continuously self-authoring (Kegan & Lahey, 2009) their mental software (Hofstede & Minkov, 2010). To trigger efficient and effective action for launching efficient and effective initiatives in the field of LSV, the interviews reveal that faculty need either to receive more training in adult learning, or to drive their own learning, based on aligned incentives and workloads. To reiterate comment 9.5 ("A mix should be better"), a mix of being taught and self-education would indeed be better for LSVMH type A, and if embedded in the right transformational learning context, also for LSVMH type B.

The framework given in figure 11 below, presents the two identified axes for coding, and introduces four levels of hygiene factors which can explain the relatively poor orientation towards and implementation of LSV at this institution, while also emphasizing the faculty view.

Figure 11: Emerging outside-in grounded theory on LSV leveraging at the study partner institution

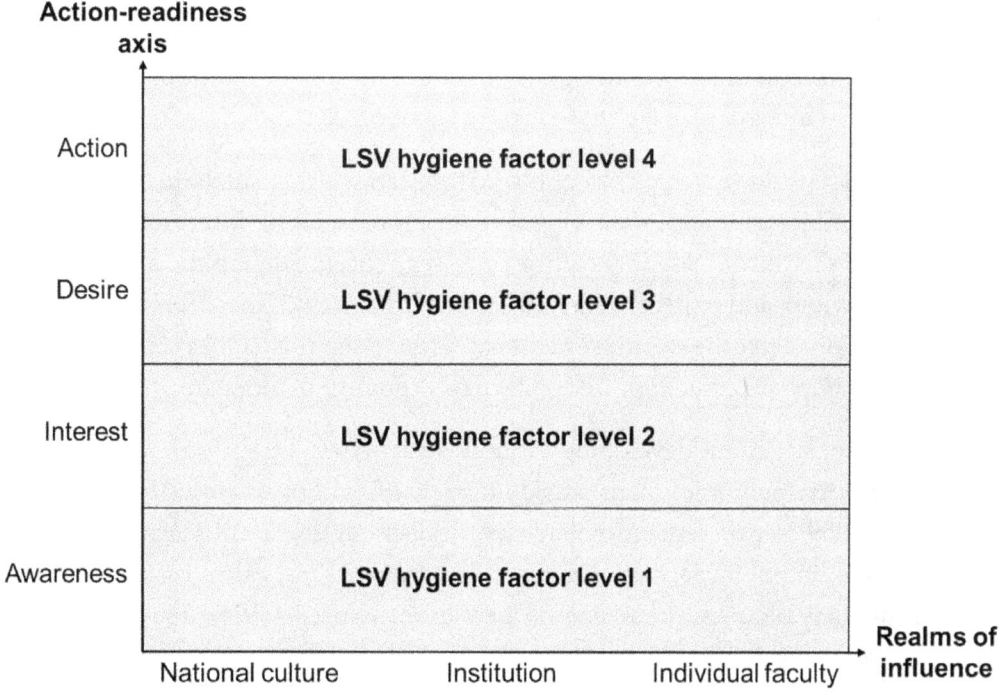

An additional observation regarding the individual faculty members, but also regarding the institution and the entire learning context refers to the general wellbeing of the institution. Considering the rather set national culture, the power distribution between faculty members and in the classroom, and the constraining business model in a highly competitive and commercialised business school education market, it appears that the nature of the learning context encountered at the study partner organisation is confined, and important factors for its wellbeing need to be attended to.

External factors or exogenous forces appear to pose barriers to an environment conducive to learning, so that more attention should be paid to learning styles and versatility. The overall situation, and the related grounded theory, is therefore one that is best described as an 'outside-in' model with stronger exogenous than endogenous factors enabling the institution to cope with and overcome their restrictions. Whatever happens in the classroom is shaped predominantly by external factors, such as national culture, the institution and its owners, the school's business model, short-term vision, limited faculty freedom and development, and harsh performance pressure on faculty in spite of tenure not being the norm.

The insight on action readiness can be linked to organisational theory, theory on motivation and organisational strategy. Contingency theory, as detailed and critically reviewed by Donaldson (2001), posits that there is no one best way to organise an institution. This applies to organising various structures in general, but can reasonably be assumed to hold for LSV as well. While it would have been interesting to study how to optimise existing approaches to LSV, I acknowledge that hygiene factors, which allude to Herzberg et al.'s (1959) semantics as already mentioned, must first be better understood from a conceptual and theoretical point of view and taken care of in practice, before higher levels of professionalism will be within reach. In sum, the grounded theory at hand is one of bottlenecks and critical hygiene factors. According to a contingency theoretical view on the emerging grounded theory, there is a need to understand and manage these factors situationally.

This is linked to theory on the strategic direction of organisations as Mintzberg et al. (2009) described it. Especially the environmental school seems highly relevant for a closer interpretation of the nature of the grounded theory in this study. National culture imposes substantially on the learning atmosphere in light of students' behaviour and expectations, but also of the faculty members' attitudes. Worsening external market conditions limit the business model and shape the owner's expectations, which in turn represent an externally imposed limitation on the faculty's room to manoeuvre.

To sum up, at this early stage, the developing grounded theory on LSV from a faculty perspective is strongly influenced by external forces in an outside-in view of factors at work. Intrinsic factors, to stay in Herzberg et al.'s (1959) set of semantics, such as idealism among faculty aspiring to be education specialists or a business school owner being active in the 'industry' for other values than financial gain, are not central in this early phase of theorising on LSV in the chosen setting. Faculty members react to institutional incentives, as well as to business model constraints and pressures from the encountered organisational culture.

4.6 Bridging data, framework, theory and hypotheses

Figure 8 given above, presents a framework based on the abductive reasoning process. This points to the need for clarifying what a theory is, and what this study's chosen approach to theorising is. Following Thornberg and Charmaz (2012), a positivist definition of 'theory' emphasizes statements on the relationship between abstract concepts which cover a wide range of observations captured in the data with the goal of explaining and predicting events, These authors explain that a more interpretive definition of theory centralises not explanation, but understanding.

The more pertinent teleological function of a theory is to help interpret the phenomenon being investigated, and not necessarily to articulate the causality links. According to Charmaz (2014) "grounded theory has had a long history of raising and answering 'why?' questions in addition to 'what?' and 'how?' questions. It is equally common for grounded theory to produce new and more relevant questions, such as on the actual 'why?'" (Charmaz, 2014, p. 245) that underlies a phenomenon, and not just the 'how'.

The data collected in the study partner organisation yields a strong 'why?' as the major question. Why is there so little progress towards applying learning style concepts? In a relatively small private school, one would expect more variables to be controllable compared to those in a larger school with a more rigid bureaucracy, as is often portrayed, e.g. by Thomas, Thomas and Wilson (2013).

Charmaz (2014) concludes that grounded theory can be considered "as theory that contains both positivist and interpretivist elements because it relies on empirical observations and depends on the researcher's constructions of them" (p. 231). While the constructivist nature of the abductive research process becomes clear in light of the aforementioned transition from focused data to axially coded categories and the grounded theory of wellness factors, the positivist nature of the theory needs more obvious strengthening. Considerable effort is needed to ensure this study's insight will be linked to a more objective external reality assumed to exist in parallel. The core question is therefore whether there are factors to be identified more generally which can explain institutions' lack of progress towards implementing more LSV.

Even granting that the concept is new in its explicit form, more latent learning efforts might have been triggered elsewhere. As Markovsky (2004) states, "a theorist attempts to convince readers that certain conclusions flow from a set of premises" (p. 831). I shall do this with a series of hypotheses given below, which cover national culture, institutional level constructs, as well as aspects situated on the individual faculty level emerging from figure 8 (in section 3.3 above) and the accompanying analysis. These hypotheses can be elaborated further, e.g. by delving deeper into other cultural dimensions, key institutional variables, as well as additional faculty features.

H1: National culture impacts the diffusion of LSV in a business school.

H2: The higher the power distance in a national culture, the more difficult the diffusion of LSV becomes.

H3: The business model of a school impacts the faculty's orientation towards LSV.

H4: The more an organisational culture fosters innovation, the easier it is to diffuse LSV as a new teaching priority.

H5: The higher the andragogic skills of faculty members, the easier it is to diffuse LSV as a new teaching priority.

H6: The more engaged a faculty member feels, the easier it is to diffuse LSV as a new teaching priority.

H7: The more a faculty member feels like a true educationist, the easier it is to diffuse LSV as a new teaching priority.

These hypotheses can be tested directly, which is the intention so as to enable subsequent research. This could, through multivariate analysis, quantitatively confirm (or reject) the aforementioned four levels of hygiene factors across three levels of abstraction, so that LSV initiatives are better understood and are more likely to succeed.

4.7 Implications, limitations, and suggestions for future research

Implications

This study is relevant to several research fields. Firstly, it aims to rejuvenate and help mature the field of learning styles. Willingham et al. (2015) conclude in their study on "The Scientific Status of Learning Styles Theories" that several reviews covering decades of research on learning styles failed to produce the posited positive empirical evidence the field claims there should be. Besides conceptual flaws, Coffield et al.'s (2004) review confirmed that construct operationalisation for measurement represents a weakness.

To conclude, however, Willingham et al. (2015) suggest that "educators' time and energy are better spent on other theories that might aid instruction" (p. 266). This represents an overly fatalistic view that could cause a loss of research opportunities due to obvious gaps. Paying attention to concepts such as learning styles along with impact yields insufficient results only, there is an opportunity to advance the field with a LSV view (Amann, 2019).

If ways to operationalise and measure concepts are found to be insufficient, rather than ceasing the research efforts, experimentation and innovation ought to follow. When Newton and Miah (2017) find that many teachers believe in variety of learning styles (58%), but significantly fewer teachers use any of them actively (33%), there is a knowing-doing gap. The barriers to attending to learning style as well as versatility considerations must be better understood to make progress. Only then will progress overcome this knowing-doing gap the authors have outlined.

The field of learning styles has been criticised for associated risks, such as those Newton and Miah (2017) mentioned, namely wasting resources, pigeonholing learners, creating unrealistic expectations of teachers, and undermining the credibility of education as a discipline due to conceptual flaws. Maturing the construct conceptually, improving the empirical evidence, understanding the wellness factors first before creating unreasonably high expectations, and working with a versatility view instead of a single-strength view, can help address concerns when researchers create new actionable and prescriptive knowledge.

Another factor obliges us to revisit the learning style field. This study can be understood as part of the field of adaptive education systems (AES), which aims to acknowledge that student abilities possibly diverge so that the value of personalising learning journeys, e.g. via learning style instruments, is foregrounded (Alzain et al., 2018). The latest technological innovations and their commodification enables tailoring different kinds of learning support at ever lower per unit cost. Numerous adaptive educational systems have been developed over many years, especially tapping into new technologies such as hypermedia, and they have considered so-called AES-CS (Adaptive Educational System based on Cognitive Styles) as outlined by Triantafillou et al. (2003).

Considering the technological opportunities, research on learning styles and learners' versatility ought to continue. Interestingly, to account for the (poor) status quo when it comes to acknowledging and leveraging LSV, the determinants seem not to be cost associated with newer technologies or the general availability of insights on cognitive or learning styles, because Google Scholar provides free access to many relevant articles; rather, established factors in organisational development and change are responsible. National culture, institutional limitations including the business model, organisational culture, and faculty-level factors represent barriers to properly exploiting LSV's potential as a concept. This is not a deterministic situation, as leadership can impact and evolve organisational culture (Denison, 1984).

This study, by and large, describes a business school with rather limited care regarding learning to learn or LSV. Lecturing is the dominant way of instruction. Innovations or faculty development initiatives are not encouraged. There is a one-dimensional view on active learning being superior to lecturing although the very concept of learning styles and LSV argue otherwise. The business model of profit orientation minimises teaching cost and maximises teaching loads, leaving faculty members' motivation low and their inclination to give up high.

Too many factors that determine the wellness of programmes and of faculty members appear to be ignored. Singh et al. (2014) describe the marked divergence of employers' and university instructors' priorities and their perceptions of graduates' readiness levels. Learning modes change drastically when graduates join their employers. Aalto et al. (2014) illustratively discuss challenges diverse teams experience at work, and Swedberg et al. (2015) accentuate how crucial on-the-job training is and how it resembles a different process to classroom instruction. Billet (2001) indicates the challenges of workplace learning. If LSV is too limited, difficulties at the personal level, such as burnout due to overly high demands and limited coping mechanisms, grow (Valcour, 2016).

This study is not the first to point out limited relevance of content presented in business schools. For example, Mintzberg (2004) criticised business schools heavily, asserting doubt about the value created in terms of LSV. Puempin and Amann (2005) discuss the strategic value potential of developing organisations. This study provides descriptions on how emerging versatility-oriented value potential is seriously inhibited. These wellness factors have to be better understood and managed before improvements can be set in motion. Tovstiga (2015) points to ever-shorter windows of opportunity to tap into these value potentials that could distinguish a particular organisation. Thus, schools are encouraged to rapidly reorient themselves towards more LSV, and to start by finding out how to remove the barriers to improve students' learning experience.

This study additionally can facilitate a better understanding of the debate between earlier grounded theory approaches (e.g. Glaser, 2001), and later ones (Charmaz, 2006, 2014). They have different stances on the role of the literature reviews. Being familiar with key concepts in organisational development, such as 'software of the mind', i.e. cultural orientation (Hofstede & Minkov, 2010), can help to inform researchers and sensitise them regarding such concepts in the interpretation phase. Applying the right semantics when coding, categorising, or coining the pillars and levels of an emerging grounded theory would necessarily be helpful. Even if particular concepts do not have to be included in an explicit literature review, to ensure that research stays properly focused or that a researcher keeps an open mind, familiarity with the concepts remains crucial. Thus, Charmaz (2006, 2014) offers more practical advice on applying grounded theory.

Limitations

There are several major limitations to the study at hand. Considering the true global patchwork of different cultures as cultural anthropologists have portrayed them (House et al., 2002), there are obvious limitations to a single-culture study in relation to national culture, as well as to a single-business model culture study. Other settings are likely to show how situational idiosyncrasies exert a major influence, which would necessitate further exploratory research.

Linked to the single-context background of this study, grounded theory has limitations. While the study acknowledges that the resulting theory is a mere interpretation, it cannot overcome the strong 'methodological ethnocentrism' of this approach (Fendt & Sachs, 2008, p. 447). Grounded theory reflects the researcher's personal background (Charmaz, 2014, p. 306) and interests (p. 244), rendering it a very fluid approach (p. 320), that disallows pure inductive reasoning (p. 306). Even an informed grounded theory approach (p. 306) could have de facto blind spots of which a researcher is not aware. Research such as this relies on the ability to imagine, induct, interpret and construct, risks having blind spots. Inductive reasoning, as Hamzah et al. (2016) have explained, has become established in, e.g. cognitive psychology and decision-making.

Thornberg (2006) recommends reflexivity as a means of addressing grounded theory's risks. Yet, if an early career researcher or a novice in the field attempts to apply grounded theory, the blind spots would possibly remain, even with a reflective stance. This could potentially double the risk of blind spots. Charmaz (2014) substantially invests in trusting the researcher and grants high levels of freedom in the theory construction process; however, she provides little with which researchers can question a 'bona fide' theory.

If the approach chosen for a particular study is likely to be questioned almost automatically due to the field being fragmented and polarised, that will inhibit efforts to build a cumulative body of knowledge by combining existing knowledge with developing new knowledge. This goes beyond epistemological and ontological assumptions that commonly emerge when qualitative and quantitative research compete. Scholars find it difficult to agree on what grounded theory is, what the role of a literature review is, whether to focus on theoretical sufficiency or on saturation, how to formalise the analysis and report, and when to stop efforts towards generalisation. This divergence of approaches should not impede applying them to learn more about them. Yet, over time and after strong divergence, the field of grounded theory could benefit from a phase of convergent approaches, as Charmaz (2014) suggested.

Finally, this study relies on faculty members' own depiction of their actions and experience in an educational setting in which the phenomenon of learning style and versatility aspects materialise. As is often the case in interview data, however, their contributions are at times given hesitantly and seemingly inhibited. Thus it is possible that the impressions I gained are partial and incomplete.

On positionality and reflexivity in this grounded theory research project

At this point in the research process, it is essential to create transparency on reflexivity. For Berger (2013), reflexivity refers to both an internal dialogue as well as an ongoing critical self-evaluation. As described by Finlay (2002) regarding the role of the researcher in qualitative projects, especially in grounded theory, the researcher occupies a central role actively influencing the emerging constructs in grounded theory. In similar vein, Watanabe (2017) encourages researchers to create transparency about positionality effects as part of reflexivity, reminding them to be alert to any noteworthy biases. I acknowledge that I carried out this research as an organisation-external researcher in agreement with the two research supervisors and with the ethics committee's approval. Necessarily, my bias enters the analysis in that I interviewed participants at one business school while working for another which is globally ranked more highly.

While certainly my employer institution has its strengths, it also has weaknesses. Yet, the overall role and quality of faculty, along with faculty management, the business model, the speed of adaptation, the international accreditation with corresponding peer reviews together create a system in which faculty in my position are likely to flourish. Teaching loads are lower than e.g. at the research site. Also, the non-profit status and quality orientation to optimise ranking positions together create a bias; in comparison, the research partner organisation could lag far behind what is known to me or would be ideal. It is, however, a bias which allows me to recognise the huge gap that could be closed if the business model in the partner organisation were to change. Therefore, I posit that the core bias in my positioned perspective does not necessarily have a negative impact. In fact, it would rather be the opposite. Personally experiencing a better environment for faculty and students develops empathy for colleagues who have to operate in a very different environment.

The second bias I perceive is my strong orientation towards human dignity as outlined throughout the analysis of this submission. Human dignity ought to replace, or at least complement, the one-dimensional functionalist goal system of businesses which too frequently is also that of business schools. Merely researching or teaching efficiency and effectiveness related topics from the perspective of dominant shareholder value and profit maximisation, is insufficient. Being strongly supportive of the addendum principle put forward in the Principles of Responsible Management Education which the United Nations Global Compact movement launched, gives me a strong bias towards business schools. These formalised principles prescribe that business schools should be role models and not merely teach students how to perform well or sustainably. They should indeed foster human dignity, and the absence of such a people orientation probably catches my attention more than would otherwise be the case. Once again, however, I conclude that such a bias is not a negative disposition as alignment with the Principles of Responsible Management Education, which include guidelines for responsible research, ought to foster a strong focus on sustainability and human dignity in research. The two key biases at work thus do not impede my research; rather, they enable me to recognize gaps that are important not only in my view, but also according to the research lens prescribed by the United Nations Global Compact Principles of Responsible Management Education.

An interesting addition or alternative to the chosen methodology could have been appreciative inquiry (Hung et al., 2018). Immediately linking exploration to the quest for creating prescriptive knowledge to improve a particular situation, could have provided additional insights, actionable knowledge, also ensuring equal, if not more practical relevance. This applies particularly to the LSVMH type B and the question on how to transform the learning environment at the study partner organisation.

Suggestions for future research

Quantitative research designs that test the aforementioned hypotheses across other similar and diverging cultures, various institutional set-ups, and different faculty members can help corroborate insights gained from this study. To improve the possibility of advancing the professionalism of instruction in business schools, we need concerted efforts towards a cumulative body of knowledge on the barriers that have to be overcome.

Subsequently, if these wellness factors are better understood, more research on taking ideas "from good to great" (Collins, 2001) can follow. Merely triggering and catalysing attempts to replicate this study in similar and divergent contexts would already be worthwhile. Gaining membership of the United Nations Global Compact initiative on Principles of Responsible Management Education (PRME) could materialise for the partner school, as this initiative strongly encourages institutions to report on the addendum principle and year-on-year progress. This adds to the business model-oriented factors explored in this study, and could create a holistic view, or enrich it. Such contributions are beyond the scope of a single study and should be tackled in subsequent research efforts.

Suggestions for future research further include revisiting the original understanding of the concepts learning style and LSV. In order to facilitate progress, this study, as well as Amann (2019), pragmatically converged on a definition which temporarily blocked out diverging ways of understanding learning styles. Acknowledging that learning styles are multidimensional (Cassidy, 2010), and having at least 70 tools in place (Coffield et al., 2004), will enable progress towards the LSV need to manage complexity.

Sadler-Smith (2010) originally defined learning styles as referring to one, several, or all of the following four elements: cognitive personality elements, information-processing style (the primary foundation for the study at hand), approaches to studying, and instructional preferences. He still finds that frameworks and instruments do not necessarily overlap. Further studies are therefore needed to elaborate on cognitive personality versatility, information processing style versatility, study style versatility, and instructional preference versatility. This is a normal process of conceptual divergence after a preceding phase of convergence.

Empirically, and as pointed out in discussing the methodological limitations of this study above, faculty members represent a crucial stakeholder group and agent in the learning ecosystem. This study extends Amann's (2019) quantitative research, presenting the first qualitative research on faculty members' perspectives. Future studies are encouraged to investigate the role students play.

4.8 Conclusions

Davies (2016) asks whether business school deans are in trouble due to the severe adversity both the graduates and their institutions encounter internationally. This study could count as a constructive answer to that question. There is room for improvement in the form of establishing LSV as a new meta-goal in reflecting on learning. This study suggests a new paradigm for anticipatory, opportunity-driven schools that can rapidly incorporate relevant, emerging insights to help schools overtake competitors stuck in old paradigms (see Thomas, Lorange & Sheth, 2013). While Romanelli et al.(2009) already identified learning styles as one of the crucial higher education success factors, Amann (2009) clearly linked the concept to enhanced study outcomes. Across several countries, Howard-Jones (2014) found that over 90% of instructors agree with the idea of the meshing hypothesis that states individuals would learn more efficiently and effectively if instruction is tailored to their learning styles. Yet, there is a belief-use gap (Newton & Miah, 2017) for a number of reasons, which a new wave of LSV-oriented research can address effectively.

As the field of learning styles finds new momentum and maturation towards LSV, a question arises on how to understand the faculty side of the organisational change and quality management process it entails. This study contributes in two ways. Firstly, it proposes a grounded theory on better understanding the context, specifically, the faculty view in a particular setting. The study has identified four levels of wellness factors in compiling an action-readiness stage-model for LSV in the learning process. Secondly, the study cautions that when contemplating LSV as a new meta-level learning goal for business schools, agents in the system should take care of wellness factors.

Lack of attention to these factors can impede progress in this early stage of the available body of knowledge on the construct. Thus, our ambitions have to be modest until further insights have been achieved on how to advance solutions identified earlier. The study closes with suggestions for future research and has given detailed, specific hypotheses for further testing (section 5 above), which represents the next step to developing more qualitative research on other system elements, such as the student body.

Chapter 5: Reflections on study 2 and building the case for study 3

5.1 Reflections on learning more about LSV as a construct

Study 1 in chapter 2 suggests that LSV has an impact on grades. The link between LSV and grades thus emerges as a factor that warrants further attention in research and practice. Within the parameters of the literature review for study 2 in chapter 4, it becomes more and more obvious that the LSV construct is under-researched. It focuses on an area different to that of related constructs in the field of learning. Yet, merely reasoning that an important construct has received little to no explicit attention so far in the literature on learning styles does not produce actionable knowledge. The results of the study presented in chapter 4 outline that the field of LSV is far removed from prescriptive frameworks of rich idealised states. Several factors identified on three levels seem possibly to impede progress in the context of the study partner organisation. Without managing and overcoming the wellness factors on these levels as outlined above, they remain desirable, but not feasible. Future research is encouraged to test the proposed hypotheses and therefore the extent to which these hygiene factors can be generalised within similar or different cultural contexts, the same or different ownership settings, and similar or different faculty bodies.

Study 2 in chapter 4 suggested new types of the meshing hypothesis with its LSVRMH type A and B. However, these emerging, still conceptual and not yet empirically tested LSV related hypotheses, need to be substantiated by further exploration, specifically concerning the second group of individuals, who (besides faculty) are essential for effective meshing – the students. Study 2 revealed that in the study partner organisation, the faculty are clearly not ready for peak performance when it comes to tapping into the potential of the LSV construct. Little is known about the student side of the equation. Are there similar cultural preferences in place that foster only one type of learning? Are there similar and observable bandwagon effects regarding what is considered as a modern andragogy? Are there wellness factors on the student side as well, such as misinterpreting the exam orientation as a measure of doing well in studies and preparing for their employability or for careers, as outlined in section 3.2 where I describe the Indian education system in the field of business? Further research ought to shed more light on the students as essential stakeholders in the learning environment. This is what study 3 in chapter 6 will cover.

5.2 Reflections on applying grounded theory

As detailed by Charmaz (2006), grounded theory allows for constructive, abductive research, which complements the potential of positivist research as outlined in section 3.3. Simultaneously, it demands a lot from the researcher – for three reasons.

Firstly, there is a multitude of approaches within grounded theory. Vollstedt and Rezat (2019), for example, delineate the development of grounded theory over time and show how various later schools of thought branched off. There is disagreement on whether researchers should review the literature in advance of interpreting data or not, as I have outlined in the rationale for the literature review given in section 4.3. Glaser (1992) insisted that "there is a need not to review any of the literature in the substantive area under study" (p. 31). However, he gives no directives that will ensure researchers are sufficiently sensitised to key variables and semantics.

Vollstedt and Rezat (2019) also illustrate that besides varying approaches to data collection and evaluation, even within one of these branches, the specific coding practices can evolve starkly over time. Glaser and Strauss (1967) base their work on the conviction that qualitative research can also be rigorous. Yet, we need clarity on what this rigorous process is. This question is justified in the light of fundamental arguments about the right approach. How rigorous a process is it when Strauss and Corbin (1998) encourage researchers to note down their "gut sense" (p. 150) on their observations or when one should "dance with data" (Hoare et al., 2012, p. 240)? And how "systematically obtained" (Glaser & Strauss, 1967, p. 2) is writing down "gut sense" in relation to data?

If a researcher has the best intentions to be systematic or even merely to 'dance with the data', which approach should be followed, or how should the steps be ordered? The following table illustrates a selection of options and choices to make.

Table 5: Selected options for coding in (A) traditional, (B) evolved, and (C) constructivist grounded theory

Approach to grounded theory	Initial coding	Intermediate coding	Advanced coding
(A) Traditional	Open coding	Selective coding	Theoretical coding
(B) Evolved	Open coding	Axial coding	Selective coding
(C) Constructivist	Initial coding	Focused coding	Theoretical coding

Source: Based on Birks and Mils (2015)

Glaser (1992), for example, published a rebuttal on Strauss and Corbin (1990). Much later, Chun Tie et al. (2019) offered process advice for the novice researcher. Yet it has not been established whether such a novice should embark on Glaser's (1992) earlier, even positivist approach to grounded theory or directly take Strauss and Corbin's (1990) post-positivist approach that Chun Tie et al. (2019) have proposed? As grounded theory is continuously evolving (Ralph et al., 2015), these options are not the only ones.

Secondly, there is the issue of sample sizes and right approach regarding when to stop further empirical investigation, coding, categorisation and theorising. Vasileiou et al. (2018) analyse the field of grounded theory and conclude that deciding on the right sample size remains a field with much debate on conceptual issues and uncertainty in the application phase.

The literature on sample sizes or judgment calls when deciding on theoretical sufficiency or saturation remains vague. There are sources aiming to illustrate what researchers ought to do. For example, regarding saturation Morse (2015) posits that it is 'the most frequently touted guarantee of qualitative rigor offered by authors' (p. 587). For Guest et al. (2006) saturation is the gold standard. Yet, it remains a judgment call. Guidelines for cut-off points for interviews remain generic (Morse, 2015). This is not surprising as there are at least four approaches to saturation according to Saunders et al. (2018).

Each seems firmly established based on the sources they cite. Most importantly, however, why bother about saturation if the goal is to theorise, and following Dey (1999), the more crucial criterion is theoretical sufficiency, i.e. a clear judgment that sufficient depth has been reached to construct the emerging grounded theory?

Hence, conceptual density and conceptual depth might be the more reasonable factors when determining the cut-off point. Arriving at a sufficient conceptual density is separate from pursuing the final limit. In this context O'Reilly and Parker (2012) question whether this final limit is ever realistically achievable as ambiguity enters the fray when a construct is dislocated from its natural context. Such dislocation naturally limits the analysis and underlines the importance of focusing on theoretical sufficiency instead.

Thirdly, there are potential ethical issues to deal with. What researchers can do according to Vasileiou et al. (2018), is to add transparency about the reasoning that underpins their choices on sampling. This has been done in chapter 4. Similarly, quality management in grounded theory suggests embarking on and creating transparency regarding the researcher's reflection on potential biases, as was done in section 3.3. Yet, abstracting from and moving beyond the first round of bias analysis, warrants an extension.

Largely in line with Finlay's (2009) insistence on critical self-awareness, Berger (2013) argues for an ongoing alertness to the effect of the researcher's own lenses. Watanabe (2017) uses the term 'positionality' and prescribes that researchers hone awareness of their own position as such, but also of the interviewees impact on the progress in research. The following figure aims to capture the first and second tier positionality effects as part of my observation of a reflection process.

Figure 12: Positionality effects

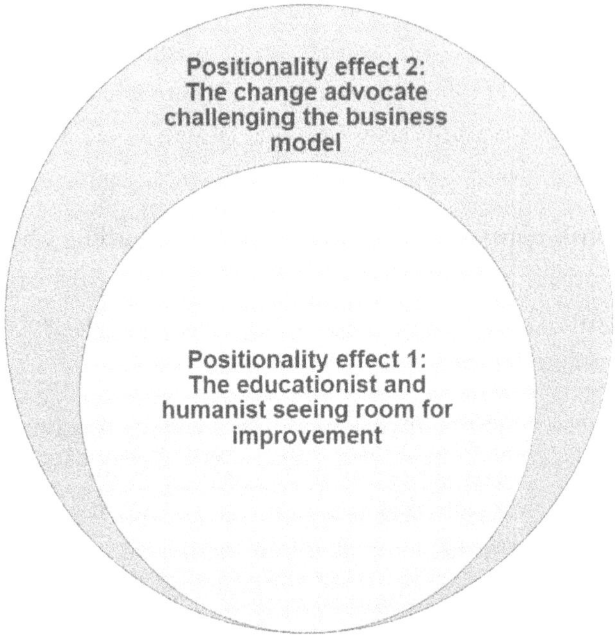

Positionality effect 2:
The change advocate challenging the business model

Positionality effect 1:
The educationist and humanist seeing room for improvement

The first positionality effect has a very positive impact. Understanding in line with the Principles of Responsible Management Education that business schools ought to be role models in terms of ethics and organisational excellence, as the researcher I can detect clear gaps. As an (aspiring) educationist, enhancing, optimising, even maximising the quality and uniqueness of the learning experience and the value created in the classroom, it seems natural to focus on specific obstacles, thus a hygiene factor orientation is not surprising. As a humanist focusing on the dignity of faculty members and students, certain gaps emerge more naturally than others. A demotivated faculty overwhelmed by high teaching loads with practically no training or incentives to innovate cannot create unique learning experiences. In turn, on the student side, this means they receive less value. This reduced value can come in the form of less learning, less employability, less return on their investment, or less respect and acknowledgement of their human dignity and individuality if their learning styles and respective versatility hardly matters or remains unknown.

In agreement with Berger (2013) who posits that any researcher must routinely review their position in light of the ongoing research and process of discovery, there is a second positionality effect. Once this lens has identified faculty as showing a weakness and the next study on students has been presented, it will be crucial to note that a second interpretation is possible and potential repercussions must be made transparent.

If there are hygiene factors to be prioritised before LSV can unfold its full potential, e.g. in having greater visible impact in improved grades as we can deduce from study 1, the researcher not only plays the role of analyst, discoverer or theorist, but to some extent also the role of an (aspiring) change agent for the organisation being studied. The same logic applies for other organisations with a similar setting once more attempts towards generalisations are in place. Figure 1 presents a generic business school model and implies that the more aligned its variables are, the smoother the operations and the better the outcomes.

Based on the interviews conducted on site, the study partner organisation seems to have an aligned setup. Limiting innovation, giving faculty incentives or development might well keep costs low in a context where the school leadership is concerned about funding. Adopting the role of a change agent or supporting change could create a conflict of interest with the owners of the private institutions. The institution needs to optimise the use of faculty resources in a means-end relationship. Actually improving their motivation, their skills to ensure meshing takes place, the time they allocate to innovation, to name but a few examples, can affect the business model in place – and this effect can be negative.

The project I report on here relies on a study without mandatory or coerced participation. It was done with informed consent (Christians, 2000) and the opportunity for any participant to withdraw, of course, without facing any questions, pressure or other adverse consequences. The ensuing data analysis was guided by a 'no harm' value, which is why data was anonymised as suggested by best practices guidelines ideally suited to learning-style-related projects and research, even if applicable in other kinds of projects as well (Pashler et al., 2008). The same abstract logic would apply on the student side. More learning, better learning can become possible, initially to the detriment of the business model and counter to the interest of the institution's owners, at least until a shift to an entirely new system has been accomplished.

To conclude these interim reflections, I would mention that building and applying grounded theory remains somewhat more challenging than the quantitative analyses presented in study 1 in chapter 2. This is especially the case considering a nascent construct like LSV being studied in a complex business school environment. In my experience and when comparing study 1 and 2, administering a survey, organising data on grades, running the regression analysis appear to be manageable. For example, the help function in SPSS as a software package explains statistics. There are axioms regarding acceptable levels of statistical significance, etc. In contrast, coding, categorising, and applying constructive, abductive grounded theory entails more ambiguities.

Chapter 6: Exploring the student view on LSV

– insights from the third empirical study

6.1 Introduction

This third empirical study investigates the second crucial stakeholder group in the learning process – the students. This time, and in contrast to study 1 presented in chapter 2, the research does not aim to substantiate the importance of LSV in general with a quantitative approach. The main research question for the final part of this research project on the nascent concept of LSV is:

"How do students perceive the phenomenon of LSV?"

In light of it being a how-based research question, as detailed below in section 6.3 and following Creswell's (2014) insights, a qualitative approach is the appropriate way to address the question. Similar to study 2 in chapter 4, the research objective is to gain richer insight into the contextual factors, the dynamics at work, and the preconditions and barriers to the students in a particular setting perceiving and responding to the LSV concept. The structure of the analysis is straightforward. Section 6.2 adds additional relevant insights from the literature review. A number of key concepts have been covered in the preceding literature reviews in sections 2.3 and 4.3, i.e. we have explicated the larger higher education context, the challenges of business schools, learning styles and the overall maturity of their field, but also other learning-related constructs, such as grit, growth mind set or absorptive capacity. The purpose of the literature review given here, is not to repeat, but to complement the previously given LSV definitions and to further reflect on the purpose of education within the debate of fostering the big D for dignity versus the big P for performance as fundamental learning targets.

Section 6.3 then continues with outlining the research methodology for this sub-study, once again adopting a qualitative research design based on grounded theory. The empirical foundations for this grounded theory are given in section 6.4, after which section 6.5 presents theorising results. As before in the context of the faculty view, section 6.6 discusses limitations along with implications for theory and practice. In order to inform efforts to generalise in future studies that go beyond the scope of this research project, I include hypotheses for future research before drawing conclusions.

6.2 Elements of an initial literature review

In previous chapters I critically reviewed learning styles and defined LSV. Also, in the earlier chapters I discussed the reasons for and benefits of researching LSV for the contribution it can make to an enhanced orientation towards humanism in business and business schools. Also, LSV research could help in working towards constructively implementing the principles of responsible management. The foregoing chapters further indicated that the main way to cope with a VUCA world might well be learning while relying on LSV.

In this section, following a similar logic to that outlined in section 4.3, the literature review is not a traditional one aiming at exhaustively reviewing all relevant literature to develop a conceptual framework and related hypotheses for subsequent empirical testing. Instead, the idea is to give an overview of material that sensitised the researcher and assisted in shaping an effective interviewing and coding process as prescribed by modern constructivist grounded theory, as suggested by Charmaz (2014). With such a purpose, the scope of this preliminary literature review is therefore extremely concentrated. Nonetheless, it applied the same backward and forward snowballing approach suggested for systematic literature reviews detailed by Wohlin (2014). The guiding principle was to spot sensitising topics similar to the idea of sufficiency – learning sufficiently about what the literature identifies as relevant, not reaching saturation in having covered the field completely. This logic leads to three literature review sections which focus on the following elements:

1. Content and development of learning taxonomies.
2. Constance versus changeability of learning styles, meta-cognition or self-regulation.
3. Insights from leadership development on boosting versatility.

1) Content and development of learning taxonomies

Over the past 65 years, ever since Bloom's (1956) seminal work, a number of learning taxonomies have been suggested. Some authors have revised their own ideas, other authors have adjusted the taxonomies of earlier scholars. Table 6 provides an initial overview of learning taxonomies, giving a variety of classifications of which field to develop in the learning process.

To illustrate the taxonomy development, early on, Bloom (1956) distinguished between learning on cognitive, affective and psychomotor levels. Cognitively, he suggests learners ought to embrace knowledge, a deeper comprehension, abilities to apply, analyse, synthesise, and evaluate new knowledge. Regarding affective learning, the taxonomy is once again ordered, structuring these aspects of learning from simple to complex feelings, including attitudes associated with receiving, responding to, valuing, organising, and characterising new knowledge.

Finally, regarding the psychomotor dimensions of learning, Bloom (1956) identifies reflex movements, fundamental movements, perceptual abilities, physical abilities, skilled movements, and non-discursive communication. Bloom's (1956) framework has for long been considered seminal, with a major impact on educational philosophies and curricula around the world (Rahman & Manaf, 2017). It has also been criticised, e.g. by Case (2013) who sees downsides due to how easily people apply Bloom's framework badly, which then withholds learners from thinking beyond a given sequence of steps. As Viji and Benedict (2017a) show in their review (see the table below), a number of additional taxonomies emerged over the years, each with either more incremental or radical, far-reaching changes.

Table 6: Timeline of selected educational taxonomies

Year	Title	Features
1956	Bloom's taxonomy	Cognitive, affective and psychomotor
1979	Experiential taxonomy	Exposure, participation, identification, internalisation, dissemination
1982	SOLO (Structure of Observed Learning Outcomes) taxonomy	Pre-structural, uni-structural, multi-structural, relational, extended abstract
1989	Mc Cormack and Yager's taxonomy	Knowledge, process, creativity, application, attitude
1990	Revised Bloom's taxonomy	Remembering, understanding, applying, analysing, evaluating, creating
2000	Marzano's new taxonomy	Knowledge, cognitive system, metacognitive system, self-system
2001	Anderson et al.'s taxonomy	Factual, conceptual, procedural, and metacognitive knowledge
2003	Fink's taxonomy	Foundational knowledge, application, integration, human dimension, caring, learning how to learn
2007	Bloom's digital taxonomy	Remembering, understanding, applying, analysing, evaluating, creating
2017	Viji and Benedict's taxonomy	Emphasizing 21st century learning skills, ingenuity, connectedness and a local context

Source: Extending Viji and Benedict (2017a, p. 193)

One of the shifts that took place over time is towards a focus on learning to learn. Fink (2003) presents a less hierarchical taxonomy, positing learning to learn as an explicit sixth category alongside foundational knowledge, application, integration, human dimensions, and caring. Anderson et al. (2001) especially emphasize the addition of the metacognitive level in their revision. Figure 8 in section 4.3 above already provided an overview of the multiple links and relationships between LSV and metacognition. Marzano (2000) reaches beyond classic learning style taxonomy dimensions by suggesting a drastically different model for thinking and learning and moving beyond elements established in past models. In a critical review of the model, Intel (2012) outlines that there is a foundational knowledge domain which includes information, as well as mental and physical procedures when it comes to learning. The model then distinguishes three systems with a clear hierarchy of importance. The most vital system, identified as the self-system, focuses on (1) beliefs about how important knowledge or learning is, (2) beliefs regarding efficacy, and (3) knowledge-related emotions. On the level below, the second metacognition system is the "mission control" (p. 3) which specifies learning goals and monitors the execution of knowledge, clarity and accuracy. The third 'cognitive system' considers knowledge retrieval, comprehension, analysis, and knowledge utilisation.

More recently, Viji and Benedict (2017b) have proposed a new learning taxonomy, their so-called taxonomy of ingenuity and connectedness (TIC), with 21st century learners in mind. These learners have easy access to information, and the new taxonomy should catalyse a drastic innovation of the educational context in India. The authors indicate as well, that India shows strong connectedness. The more other countries and learners increase their level of connectedness, the more this taxonomy of the future will also apply to them. In sum, a more modern approach to learning taxonomies reflects a number of features: technological advancement, learners' (online) behaviour, learning needs that emphasize information search capabilities, the ability to create new insight, enhance creativity, and hone investigative imagination. Such approaches are more just-in-time and more virtual, and less confined to any teacher-driven, physical classroom activities. Wider connectedness in a modern context will be an important element when reviewing the learning experience of the students in this study.

2) Constancy versus changeability of learning styles, metacognition and self-regulation

If a VUCA world would require LSV as a coping mechanism within a requisite variety (Ashby, 2011), then it is important to know whether LSV is a changeable or rather a constant entity. As LSV is still in its nascent state as a concept, it is crucial to review the literature on growth potential and changes in learning preferences.

Before commencing this review, an additional remark is due on how Wohlin's (2014) core task of data extraction as part of the larger scrutiny of the literature review was done. To render the individual contributions and often rather poorly labelled arguments more tangible, I decided to assign clear labels as part of the interpretation process and of distilling the relevant insight that can be drawn from the extant literature. This is an attempt to add more originality and value to this research project. The procedure resulted in a series of labelled arguments explained in the following paragraphs and summarised in table 7.

Regarding the quiddity of learning styles, Claxton and Ralston (1978) emphasize that a person's learning style should be defined as something constant. This could be explained considering the year of publication of their research, because, as outlined below, more insight on the constancy or changeability of learning styles emerged only later. But even the later publication of Willingham et al. (2015) reiterates this idea of learning style constancy which is often understood as (1) "a consistent attribute of an individual" (p. 266), and (2) an attribute which is "constant across situations" (p. 266). Recognizing, roughly, that different people could learn the same content or skills in different ways, was accompanied by an interpretation that I label the **structuring argument** in favour of constancy of learning styles. The analysis of learning styles has to start somewhere, and viewing learning styles as fixed and exogenous allows for a better understanding of impact and context. The question that emerges, asks which factors amplify complexity in this discussion on changeability of learning styles.

Firstly, the poor delineation of constructs is one factor. Willingham et al. (2015) further explain constancy by distinguishing between styles and abilities. For these authors, learning styles address the question of how a person carries out a task, while abilities focus on how well the task is done. They rely on a sport analogy. "Two basketball players may have equivalent ability but different styles on the court. One may take risks, whereas the other plays a conservative game" (Willingham et al., 2015, p. 267). I regard this as a good illustration of the structuring argument. Keeping styles and abilities separate as two fixed entities for the analysis allows for juxtapositions and analysis of relationships between constructs.

The second factor to show the complexity of changeability is linked to definitions and the multidimensionality of the construct. Here we ask whether learning styles mirror preferences or abilities. Are they linked to absorption or processing or both as postulated in the Honey and Mumford (2009) framework? We know little about the impact of varying strength of the preference and/or ability. Seiler (2011) differentiates three levels of preferences strong, moderate and mild, while Honey and Mumford (2009) rate LSV on a scale from very low, through low, moderate, and strong, to very strong, as figure 9 shows. The impact of intensity remains largely unknown, i.e. is not discussed in the learning style literature. This research gap in the literature could possibly reinforce the **structuring argument**. Until research can disclose more about different learning style attributes, the facets that are known to us, are likely to be treated as constant.

Thirdly, there is a pragmatic review of the perception and processing continuum framework of Kolb's (2006) learning cycle, as well as of the linked learning style framework Honey and Mumford (2009) proposed. Convergers differ from assimilators, which in turn vary from being accommodative to being divergent. If these learning styles are linked to another construct in the field of learning, namely wisdom, the following argument can be made relying on Clayton and Birren (1980) who understand wisdom as an outcome of maturation and an adult learning process, resulting in the capacity to understand open or covert truths. Wisdom could at times require divergent thinking styles, possibly also accommodation to dispose of theories that do not fit the intuition of a diverger, or the purely analytical skill of a converger. Nonaka and Toyama's (2007) definition of practical wisdom includes the ability to make judgments and to grasp the essence of situations.

Learning situations are often difficult (Maguire, 1997), thus they require multiple learning styles for students to adequately cope with them. Hawes (2004) outlines how wisdom can be fostered with the help of the right teaching methods, e.g. case studies. Ergo, with wisdom training, at least the skill side of learning style shows it is not just given, but can be shaped. Adler et al. (2004) in one of the rare examples of learning style related studies in business schools, precisely show that teacher-led and student-led cases impact on and balance out learning styles, or put differently, they alter LSV. Beyond this higher level analysis and argument on the quiddity of learning styles, one could narrow down attention to each of the learning styles to an argument against constancy. For example, regarding the ability to create theoretical models and reason inductively, assimilators excel at generating theoretical frameworks, as well as reasoning in an inductive way. Nagel et al. (2015) encourage researchers to seek mentoring and training to hone their research skills. Researchers are in a situation where abilities are not fatalistically constant. Researchers can learn to be more assimilative. Table 7 summarises this logic, and labels this interpretation as the **wisdom-as-trigger-for-change argument.**

Table 7: Opposing schools of thoughts in the learning style literature and their implications for LSV

Feature	School of thought no. 1 on constancy	School of thought no. 2 on changeability
Key positions	▪ **The structuring argument**: Learning is constant (Claxton & Ralston, 1978), learning styles are a consistent attribute, and are constant regardless of the situation (Willingham et al., 2015). ▪ **The born-into-not-made argument**: Both the genetic and social setting into which people are born, impacts their learning styles (Dunn, 1996).	▪ **The non-immunity-to-change argument**: Both the broader adult learning field (e.g. Kegan, 1994) and the narrower learning style field (Dunn & Griggs, 1995) posit non-constancy and change dynamics at work. ▪ **The stimulus-response argument**: Practical learning to complement scholastic studies, is organised (Van den Berg, 2015), as is mere awareness training (Bhagat et al., 2015), and case-based training (Adler et al., 2004), all of which can foster a growth mind-set, and technological innovations impact learning styles. ▪ **The past-cum-future argument**: Not only past learning interventions, but also future career aspirations impact learning styles, and their perpetuation (Van den Berg, 2015). ▪ **The naturally fading argument**: Previous experiences do not necessarily have a lasting impact (Van den Berg, 2015). ▪ **The wisdom-as-trigger-for-change argument**: Wisdom can be fostered, thereby

		implying growth of different learning styles (Hawes, 2004).
Implications for LSV	There is no discretion, nor room to grow, in a rather fatalistic view of learning styles as a stable factor.	There are several means to change through diverse methods (e.g. case writing or practical work). Change can even occur after a short-term experience.
Implication for LSV as an emerging field	The literature remains divided on conceptual foundations and how learning styles persist or evolve. "Developing the flexibility to respond productively to all sorts of instructional situations would be a laudable goal… How best to encourage this flexibility is yet to be determined" (Bhagat et al., 2015, p. 59).	

Fourthly, the field of learning styles overall seems still to be in an early stage. There have been only a very few attempts to turn learning styles from an exogenous to an endogenous variable. Seeing a variable as simultaneously both of these, inarguably renders it more complex to characterise in detail. In this context, Dunn (1996) sees learning styles largely as biologically imposed. Parents could have contrasting learning styles, siblings can learn differently, and children generally can vary in their learning styles as well. This could be labelled the **born-into-not-made argument.** While the classic debate in leadership development on innate versus cultivated leaders focuses on genetic dispositions, Dunn's (1996) study considers the interpretation that it is not only DNA, but also the social setting, which is largely fixed. Therefore, the innate versus cultivated argument relates mostly to a situation of being born into a bio-social setting, and it represents a rather fatalistic view of constancy.

A fifth factor the literature mentions that impacts LSV, is age or time. Abilities theory has long established that cognitive abilities are not constant, although development of ability is not one-directional as Salthouse (2010) indicated. Key abilities such as reasoning, processing speed, or memory grow from childhood to adulthood, while they decrease again as people age. Research now even embraces the idea that learning disabilities are remediable (Robinson, 2012). This is in line with other modern adult learning theories, such as Kegan and Lahey's (2009) theory which assumes the human adult brain to be able to reach higher levels over time, albeit not without effort and by no means in all cases. The authors outline both a certain 'immunity for change' and a non-fatalistic view of how to overcome Kegan's (1994) conceptually and empirically advanced Constructive Developmental Theory (CDT) as they foresee precisely this opportunity for learners to mature and elevate their thought processes, which are dynamic over time.

Dunn and Griggs (1995) believe that an individual's learning styles can change over time. Seiler (2011), however, could not substantiate that learning styles change with age. More empirical evidence is needed. Hence, constancy within the narrower field of learning styles or the broader fields of adult learning, and even theory of the mind, is not necessarily assumed to hold universally and fatalistically. In this regard conceptual efforts need to be perpetuated, because many constructs are not clearly delineated. If learning style research selectively emphasizes ways of processing new input and then differentiates more effective ways to process, especially when the meshing hypothesis is in place, then there is an overlap with the speed factor. This would put 'time' on the abilities side.

While not explicitly underlined, and in contrast to learning style definitions which presume constancy, there is an element of the variable than can entail change. This line of thought that connects adult learning to more or less naturally occurring changes in thought processes, could be labelled the **non-immunity-to-change argument,** which positions it within the semantic world opened up by Kegan and Lahey (2009).

Related to the speed factor is Van den Berg's (2015) research. The table below summarises the development of his ideas as the **stimulus-response argument, a naturally fading argument,** as well as the **past-cum-future argument.** He found that even short periods of a certain activity can change learning styles. For example, medical students, when shifting from their academic work to their internships, thus from theoretical to practical training, showed three effects: (1) practical training alters learning styles even after shorter periods, producing more reflective and theoretically aware learners, applying the Honey and Mumford (2009) learning style framework; (2) past experiences impact learning styles by generating more action-oriented ways of thinking at the beginning of the clerkships (although this effect was not a long-lasting one); and (3) future career choice (different to past or present experiences) also impact learning styles, and the frequency with which abstract learners became pragmatists.

There are two further elements which can be subsumed under the stimulus-response argument. Darlo Digital (2018) interprets the work of Dweck (2015) on the growth mind-set rather freely while transferring it to the concrete context of learning styles. The logic put forward is that as a psychological concept, a growth mind-set could alter a learner's perception of what they are capable of, and what new ways they should absorb in processing information they aspire to access. Altering learning styles would yield new learning abilities to better cope with an ever-challenging world. Bhagat et al. (2015) further underline the importance of the content that is being taught. These authors indicate that mere awareness of learning styles can impact the learning styles people adopt and display. Six consecutive sessions of at most one hour long showed not only an impact on self-awareness, but also portrayed, measurable (at statistically significant levels) changes in learning styles applied. The authors do not elaborate more extensively on the precise timeframe that elapsed between the sessions, nor on the overall start and end dates of the study; however, based on their overall research report, the changes they report were most probably immediate.

Van den Berg (2015) reports on a time frame of roughly two years of medical training, in which learning style changes occur. In contrast, Siriopoulos and Pomonis (2007) report on changes in learning styles within one year. This has implications for return on investment discussions in business schools, as well as on giving space and weight to learning-to-learn elements in curricula. As Kirby (1988) and Pask (1988) mention, the most effective learning style could be the one that does not depend on just one style or style-based consistency in one's approach, i.e. the authors argue in favour of LSV.

Darlo Digital (2018) similarly interprets the Reid's (n.d.) research that suggests even if learning styles do not change fundamentally, we are likely to see adaptations through technology use in the learning process. Both of these points have implications for curriculum design where decisions are made on the content and delivery mode of learning experiences. Learning goals that include a growth mind-set and technology are thus antecedents of learning styles, and as adaptations are explicitly mentioned, possibly also of LSV.

Table 7 summarises these insights. Interpreted from a curriculum design point of view, providing students with opportunities for practical terms in which they encounter a range of learning stimuli, could help them evolve. I have labelled this the **stimulus-response argument**. Preferences with which learners start out, do not seem to last when other learning opportunities arise. I have labelled this the **naturally fading argument**. Finally, as both the past and the future learning experiences impact learning styles, they seem to get shaped by elements of both time dimensions, therefore the label **past-cum-future argument.**

Table 7 above gives a preliminary summary of the field of learning styles, starting off with the assumption of constancy. Yet, revisiting the different definitions, their scope, and how they link to other learning constructs such as practical wisdom as a learning outcome, raises a question regarding constancy, and thus brings doubt regarding a fatalist perspective on individuals' learning styles in an increasingly VUCA world. Following from this, the literature on learning styles can be divided into two opinion camps, one that advocates a constancy perspective, and one that is open to more discretion, options and choices. Constancy, however, entails an assumption which cannot be sustained if the definitions are scrutinised and links to other constructs are considered.

Still, from this constancy-versus-changeability perspective, sound knowledge about learning styles is scant. The foundations do not allow extensive inferences regarding LSV. There is a research gap in general, as well as in business school related studies. The research cited above largely takes place outside of business schools, while medical schools have done substantially more in researching students' learning styles. Bhagat et al. (2015), therefore, summarise the state of the field quite aptly as follows: "developing the flexibility to respond productively to all sorts of instructional situations would be a laudable goal… How best to encourage this flexibility is yet to be determined" (p.59).

3) Insights from leadership development on boosting versatility

The literature review section in chapter 2 drew a parallel between the overall level of maturity of the fields of leadership and of learning styles. The argument then was that studies on leadership had progressed beyond a first stage that predominantly emphasizes definitions, and even beyond a second stage which focuses on leadership styles. Within the field of leadership, it remains important to understand and have clarity on what leadership is and which styles exist. Yet, as Kaplan and Kaiser (2003a) empirically substantiate, leadership versatility emerges as the most crucial leadership skill, because no matter what the situation demands, a versatile leader could most likely cope with it effectively. Continuing the parallel, figure 13 below illustrates one comparative view on the leadership field versus the field of learning and learning styles.

Figure 13: Comparison of developmental phases in leadership versatility research versus LSV research

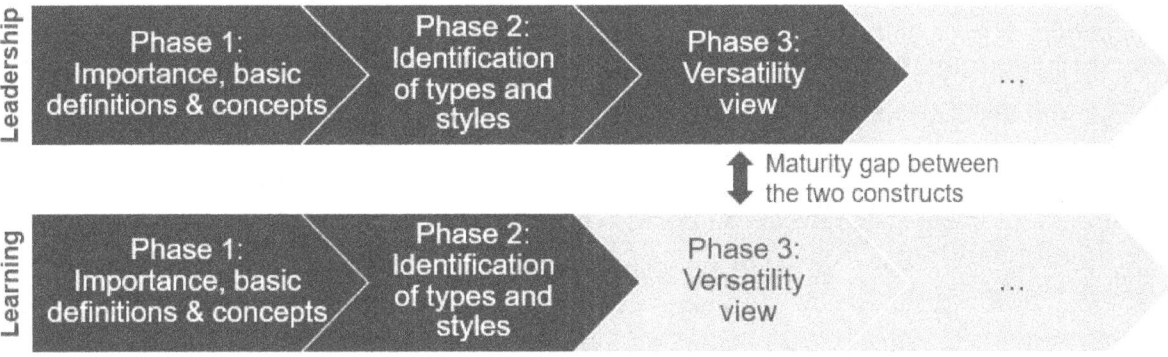

This representation shows that LSV represents a potential next step in maturing the learning style field. The table in figure 9 below summarises this development along with sample publications. Various learning styles have been defined and juxtaposed, and the field is rich in different kinds of approaches as is exemplified in the 71 conceptualisations included in the review by Coffield et al. (2004). However, to the best of my knowledge, none of the articles in the literature moves beyond the dominant questions regarding the best typologies, the soundest theoretical foundation, the best measure, and how to apply the concept of 'learning style' (for example, Romanelli et al., 2009).

Table 8: The development of the leadership and learning style field

Stages in the concept's maturity over time	Leadership field – Sample publications	Learning style field – Sample publications
1st stage: Defining the construct and clarifying its essentiality	Scordato (2015), Connor (2002)	Cassidy (2010), Zajac (2009)
2nd stage: Acknowledging different styles	Weiss et al. (2018), Zhang et al. (2018).	Stander et al. (2019), Keefe (1985), Ahmadaliev et al. (2018).
3rd stage: Emphasizing and fostering versatility	Uhl-Bien and Marion (2008), Robinson (2016), Kaplan and Kaiser (2003a, b).	Gap

85

The contingency theory view (Donaldson, 2001) posits that there are no single best styles. Instead, it is a question of fit. The three empirical studies presented in chapters 2, 4 and 6 delineate a field of tension with the VUCA world which increasingly challenges leaders and managers (Betof et al., 2014; Codreanu 2016; Fassinger et al., 2017.

The response to this growing adversity can be found in re-establishing fit by educating, recruiting, promoting and retaining the right talents in the student body of business schools. Leadership has to be situationally appropriate in order to be effective (Thompson & Vecchio, 2009). For Robinson (2016) leadership and learning have for too long been too far apart. Hodgson and White (2001) propose a learning model of leadership for uncertain environments, reframing leaders as learners. Sticking to one style or to past strengths could possibly have detrimental effects. Kaplan and Kaiser (2003a) argue similarly, and with a huge dataset give evidence on how much more effective versatile leaders are.

The field of research into learning styles has not achieved the same level of maturation as research into leadership has. Learning style research still lacks the insight that neither understanding a style and its theory (Cassidy, 2010; Zajac, 2009), nor differentiating styles as in, for example, Stander et al. (2019), Keefe (1985), or Ahmadaliev et al. (2018) are sufficient. LSV needs to be prioritised in business school research

According to Butler (2008), a Carnegie Foundation report and a Ford Foundation report, both published in 1959, introduced a strong rift, the so-called 'valley of death', between rigorous research and practical relevance. Both reports criticised business school research as insufficiently theoretically rigorous, calling for the integration of natural sciences' approaches and tools.

To the present, the divide that emerged as a consequence continues to be a challenge (De Frutos-Belizón et al., 2018), and the phenomenon has been a theme of discussion in numerous top journals, such as the Academy of Management Journal (2001), the British Journal of Management (2001), Human Resources Management (2004), the Journal of Management Studies (2009), Organization Studies (2010), the Academy of Management Perspectives (2012), and the Journal of Business Economics (2014). Research in business schools should overcome this rift by triggering more research on how to create more versatile learners in the business context.

Thus, we need to reflect on what insights the development of leadership versatility might inspire, or what could spill-over into the field of learning styles. Learning style, similar to leadership style, has a cognitive and a behavioural component, and similarly has to address a foundational question of whether the skills are innate or socially developed. As it is, leadership development represents a core field within executive education and business schools, which also raises questions on a similar place for learning style and strategy development. The following section provides a literature review in the form of a brief overview, which as before, serves merely the purpose of identifying topics that will help sensitise readers for the field work of study 3.

Two more contemporary areas within the literature on leadership development appear to be relevant for this research. The first is the aforementioned area of leadership versatility as outlined by Kaplan and Kaiser (2003a) and Goleman (1998), which refers to superior performance regarding outcomes such as productivity or engagement at organisational, unit or team levels. The second is an area captured by the concept of strategic leadership, identified as "blue ocean leadership" (Kim & Mauborgne, 2014).

The following analysis focuses on these more modern approaches, fully acknowledging though that contingency theories have decades of publications on effectiveness of leadership depending on circumstances, thus being very situational in nature. Early work includes the model on situational leadership by Hersey et al. (1969), or Vroom and Yetton's (1973) tool in the form of decision-making trees to account for situational idiosyncrasies. Beyond leadership, and referring to more general strategies and skills, Donaldson (2001) describes how, considering there is no perfect setup, entire organisations ought to pursue "fit", because organisational achievement relies largely on the fit and alignment of internal and external factors. More recent approaches, however, adopt very modern views as outlined below, introducing such topics as emotional intelligence, the sophisticated measurement tools of a leadership versatility index, or strategic thinking to their reflection on leadership.

Kaplan and Kaiser (2003a) propose a similar contingency framework as Goleman (1998) does when the latter presents six leadership styles of which the results are determined on what is situationally needed. The only important conceptual difference is that Goleman (2000) adds the perspective of emotional intelligence as "the ability to manage ourselves and our relationships effectively" (p.6) when addressing versatility.

Kaplan and Kaiser's (2003a) model spans a 2x2 matrix focusing on forceful versus enabling, as well as strategic versus operational style. In terms of the level of reductionism and as a duality-oriented framework, it is comparable to Honey and Mumford's (2009) framework. Another possible contribution to the field of learning styles and LSV is a new set of semantics, i.e. new terminologies, such as lop-sidedness, hypertrophy (describing an overdevelopment of one side of leadership), or atrophy (pointing to the negligence of another). Kaplan and Kaiser (2003a) also point to mental models becoming skewed by the need to explore basic assumptions, beliefs, values, attitudes and behaviours. The leadership style discussion is one often still reduced to preferences and behaviours.

Kaplan and Kaiser (2003a) suggest ways to gain more leadership versatility. They propose that working on self-awareness as an out-of-balance leadership approach or style emanates from an ill-fitting belief system, similar to the contingency view for LSV presented in figure 5 in chapter 2. Further, according to these authors, the emotional side and awareness of various possibilities represents the start of developing one's leadership versatility.

The measurement tool they provide helps elevate this process of self-awareness to one that is not only idea-based, but also data-driven. Interestingly, Bhagat et al.'s (2015) research mentioned above on learning styles, similarly points to the importance and impact of awareness. Dunn (1996) links these tools to holistic learning style programmes, also illustrating a plethora of tools to measure learning styles. In the same way, Kaplan and Kaiser (2003a) mention the importance of looking ahead to recognise particular jobs' requirements. This is a parallel to Van den Berg's (2015) insistence on linking learning styles and their persistence to career objectives.

Here, the leadership field might already be more developed than the learning style field as there are several clear models of so-called leadership pipelines (e.g. Charan et al., 2011). They clearly outline the expectations associated per leadership level from the early pre-leadership level of merely being a team member to senior corporate and multi-business unit executive levels.

Kaplan and Kaiser (2003a) continue by outlining a third element of honing versatility in the form of addressing and conquering fear in the process of overcoming weaknesses. Nevertheless, they do not share specific steps to take beyond self-awareness. Finally, they encourage individuals, even while remaining somewhat vague, "to do some internal work" (Kaplan & Kaiser, 2003a, p. 25). They apply the analogy of developing muscle growth through training to prevent atrophy, thus being overdeveloped to the stage of hypertrophy, while undertraining other areas. Thus they hint at the need to adjust certain practices and to learn to emphasize differently. Their final suggestion for working towards more versatility, is to avoid binary thinking, as in completely discontinuing one line of action in response to feedback that the action was done too energetically, or in aggressively overdoing an action due to feedback that a bit more was required. Otherwise, Kaplan and Kaiser (2003b), mention no additional step other than working towards a personalised development plan.

Goleman (1998) remains similarly vague when it comes to specifying how to implement the four core emotional intelligence capabilities, which have been broken down to 20 competencies that are held to better implement the six leadership styles situationally. Goleman (1998) recommends starting the journey towards more leadership versatility with self-awareness and recognition of lacking EQ competencies, followed by a commitment to "work assiduously" (p.14) and practice.

An additional coping strategy would be to assemble a team with skill sets complementing one another, rather than trying to develop individuals towards possessing higher leadership versatility. Identical to Kaplan and Kaiser (2003a, 2003b), Goleman (1998) adopts elements of a growth mind-set and changeability by suggesting that in contrast to the largely genetics-based and rather stable IQ, EQ is seemingly learnable "at any age" (p. 15).

A third, recent innovation in the field of leadership development is positioned very differently, yet with parallels to discussions within the learning style field. Kim and Mauborgne (2014) argue, while transferring insights from strategic management, that leadership must be reframed. It should abandon the heavy trait or preference orientation which might either be more difficult or more time consuming in enhancing leadership versatility, and with versatility would not even be necessary. They further argue that being more versatile and effective should not take extra time.

Their blue ocean leadership strategy foresees orienting leadership efforts towards all those not yet fully following the leaders. In some countries, more than 80-90% of staff members are disengaged from leadership. Versatility can overcome this pitfall. The authors recommend four steps going forward: (1) leaders should openly face their leadership reality, starting with more self-awareness and taking stock, ideally with external feedback; (2) they should canvas alternative leadership profiles in comparison to existing behaviours. This once again should entail external feedback to inquire what should be reduced slightly, what should be somewhat increased, what should be added completely to the leadership repertoire, and what should be erased from the leadership behaviours; (3) there should be a negotiation and 'selling' process to stakeholders, before (4) the new leadership behaviour is institutionalised building the corresponding routines.

The biggest insights to be gained from blue ocean leadership are, once again, a focus on the right dosage, the fundamental belief in changeability and thus a non-fatalistic view, and most importantly the encouragement to ignore predispositions or preferences. Leadership, if it is to become more effective and versatile, could feel somewhat uncomfortable. By institutionalising and through routines, thus by practices similar to what Goleman (1998) suggests, progress can be made.

In the context of learning styles, Dunn (1996) points to the insight that learning can take place even via a style normally thought to be unsuitable, very much in line with blue ocean leadership thinking. The possibility that the dual nature of learning style could be understood as both preference and absorption ability would emphasize it as a processing skill. The following figure summarises how the three leadership models discussed above envisage growth journeys towards more versatility.

Figure 14: Insights on how to grow leadership versatility based on selected frameworks

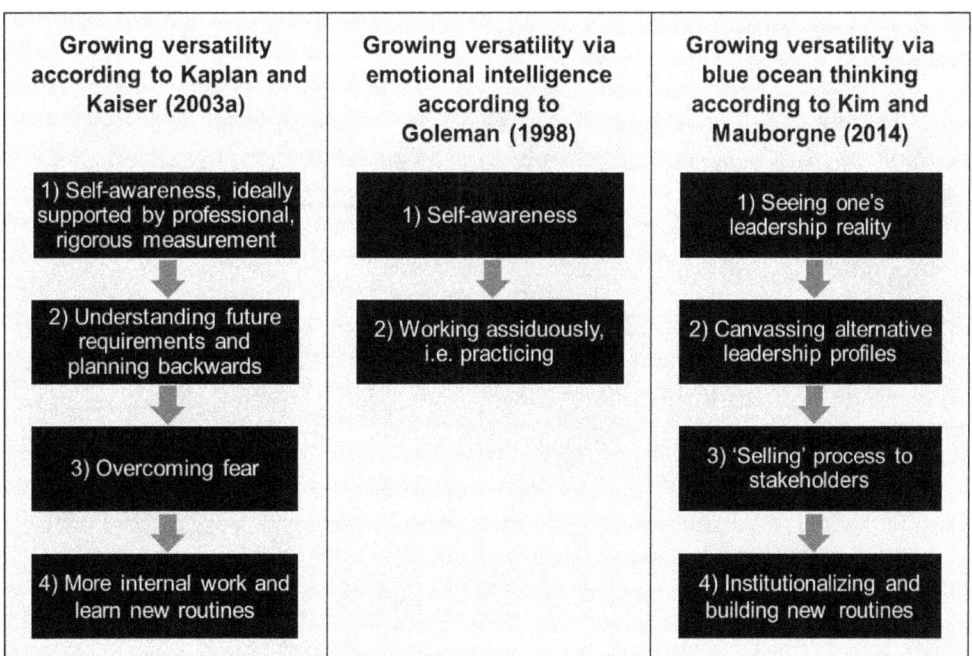

Summary of research gaps and sensitising topics

The preliminary literature review aimed at sensitising readers to emerging topics had three sections. The first section led to the conclusion that modern learning taxonomies embrace different levels of learning. LSV represents a part of this view, thereby exceeding a more classic knowledge orientation for which the Bloom (1956) taxonomy became famous.

The second section of this preliminary literature review dealt with the two opinion camps and arguments abstracted from the literature. As outlined in table 7, the first opinion camp adheres to the **structuring argument** and the **born-into-not-made argument** which both emphasize the view that learning styles are given, and therefore more constant. The second opinion camp adheres to the **non-immunity-to-change argument**, the **stimulus-response argument**, the **past-cum-future argument**, and the **wisdom-as-trigger-for-change** argument, which in turn, all speak in favour of a non-fatalistic view on learning style. There are initial implications for LSV, but overall, the level of the available insights does not reflect substantial maturity. This seems to have advanced more in research in other settings than business schools. The overall body of knowledge can best be described by researchers active in the field itself: "Developing the flexibility to respond productively to all sorts of instructional situations would be a laudable goal… How best to encourage this flexibility is yet to be determined" (Bhagat et al., 2015, p.59).

The third section of this preliminary literature review explained the strong parallels to the field of versatility development in leadership. The leadership field inspired this research project's questions regarding LSV in the first place. Leadership versatility has given some additional insights on developing versatility in the field of learning styles, yet there are also limitations. Rolfe et al. (2001) provide a useful set of questions to solve problems, asking, What? So What? Now what? These questions can also be used in critically reviewing literature, in this case the selected readings on leadership versatility. Models seem to be biased content-wise to the initial, more descriptive content, putting less emphasis on the prescriptive part dealing with how to actually implement versatility development. The ensuing grounded theory study explores this build-up of versatility based on students' perceptions. How exactly the research question is addressed will be outlined in the next section.

6.3 Methodology and method

Grounded theory is one of the most important and influential approaches in qualitative analysis (Lindlof & Taylor, 2011). Study 2 on faculty members' views presented in chapter 4, already relied on this theory, critically discussing its major features. A similar logic applies to this study. Starks and Trinidad (2007) recommend grounded theory as the perfect fit for research questions with the development of an explanatory theory as their goal and with the target of exploring how a chosen social process takes place in a specific environment. This third empirical study investigates how students, as a key stakeholder group in learning, experience the dynamics related to LSV. Addressing this research question with grounded theory represents a match – it is a functional fit.

Arino et al. (2016) re-emphasize the importance of qualitative research in this context, especially when it comes to rich, complex constructs that emerge from data in specific contexts. The grounded theory used in study 2, presented in chapter 4, underlined the crucial role context plays in general, as well as in terms of the LSV related perceptions and practices in a particular research partner institution. This third study is based on the logic and ontological assumption that reality exists in such social settings. From an epistemological point of view, relevant and new knowledge is then produced by interpreting the actors' narrated perceptions. In this sense, this study is true to the non-deductive nature of grounded theory set by post-positivist Glaser and Strauss (1967) from the very beginning.

As Parry (2003) mentions, researchers who are new to grounded theory can easily be overwhelmed by the diversity of approaches to it. The following section provides a brief overview. Glaser and Strauss (1967), who established grounded theory, differentiate two types of theories, one labeled substantive theory that is more context-specific, and the second labeled formal theory that is more generic. Yet, regarding the process and overall position of grounded theory, greater divergence soon followed. Morse and Niehaus (2009) identify the following five major branches:

(1) Corbin and Strauss (2008) described the strongly symbolic interactionist Straussian grounded theory which built on Strauss and Corbin (1990) and Strauss and Corbin (1998). This version of the theory detailed a more prescriptive coding technique. (2) Glaser (1978, 1992), but also Stern (2009), described what became known as Glaserian grounded theory. Glaser (1978, 1992) focused more on the constant comparative method than on axial coding as Strauss and Corbin (1990) did. (3) Key publications by Bowers and Schatzmann (2009) and Schatzmann (1991) articulated what is known as Dimensional analysis. (4) Charmaz's (2006, 2009) constructivist analysis was the basis for Charmaz (2014), that eventually detailed her approach. For her, grounded theory serves the purpose not of uncovering reality, but of discovering it based on a set of collected data. She criticises the founders of grounded theory for remaining rather objectivist by merely suggesting an approach to theorising as a way of discovering reality in collected data. In turn, she aims to offer a constructivist method which she claims constructs reality. This takes place first by a line-by-line coding and subsequently a more focused coding, along with noteworthy, value-adding memo-writing in which theorising takes place too. (5) Finally, there is situational analysis (Clarke, 2005). According to Morse and Niehaus (2009), these further developments that reached beyond Glaser and Strauss (1967), pursued slightly diverging purposes and led to different end outputs. Hence, an additional qualification placing an approach within the field of grounded theory, is needed. The next section sheds light on the chosen positioning of this third and final study on LSV.

The grounded theory approach chosen for data analysis

There are several approaches that can be applied in carrying out grounded theory, therefore, following Suddaby (2006), basic assumptions and choices have to be made explicit. For this study, the choice remained with a highly constructivist approach which differs fundamentally from a more objectivist alternative. The differences are summarised in table 10 below, and are detailed in the following descriptive text.

As explicated in Charmaz (2016), constructivist grounded theory distances itself from a positivist epistemology. As table 10 shows, Charmaz finds that constructivist grounded theory has very different assumptions to an objectivist approach. Especially with rather new and complex topics, such as LSV, I share the assumptions Charmaz (2016) posits. As the researcher, I take part in the sense-making, and drive the development of a new context-specific substantive theory grounded in data and based on the co-created meaning. The grounded theorising process is unlikely to yield the same results if carried out by other researchers. I bring certain assumptions to the analysis about the involved disciplines (education and business schools, research, etc.), as well as theoretical perspectives. If epistemology comprises the truths, beliefs and justifications (Steup & Neta, 2020) regarding key themes, my own epistemology builds on the beliefs that business schools ought to be role models, committed to continuous improvement to contribute earning the right to educate, operate in an economically sound but highly responsible way or that leadership in business schools should be just as efficient and effective as in non-academic corporations. This sets high expectations.

Table 9: Constructivist versus objectivist grounded theory

Constructivist grounded theory	Objectivist grounded theory
<ul><li>Prioritises the phenomena as part of the research focus, viewing both data and analysis as emanating from the researcher and study participants' joint experiences;</li><li>Methods are a mere tool or means to an end, they do not guarantee knowledge;</li><li>Researchers explore the construction of meaning as well as action;</li><li>Researchers pursue proximity to this experience creation;</li><li>Data analysis is a reflection of the ways in which researchers think, and of the situational nature of the data (context, culture, time, location);</li><li>Sense does not reside in the data alone.</li></ul>	<ul><li>Data exists, carries the sense, is objective and factual;</li><li>Sense-making relies primarily on the data and is an objective process;</li><li>The focus is on meaning in the data, which is discoverable in the real world;</li><li>Unbiased researchers observe and record the data;</li><li>Researchers are conduits, not creators of discovery processes;</li><li>Researchers play the role of authority external to the phenomenon, and are distant and separate from the participants;</li><li>Participants readily share core facts, with the focus on explicit themes;</li><li>Care in applying methods leads to a thorough understanding, and researchers ought to follow core steps with great discipline.</li></ul>

Source: Based on Charmaz (2012)

Other researchers would not have read the same literature, carried out the same quantitative or qualitative studies on the topic as I have. Their interests might be different to mine, and they would not have identical access to this unique study context at the research partner institution in India in order to pragmatically create an idiosyncratic study as part of their quest to improve the situation and prepare for their own careers and publication strategies.

To add critical views to the chosen methodology, the following needs to be pointed out: Charmaz (2006) discourages an overly rigid process that attempts to follow in full detail. This entails flexibility on the one hand, and ambiguity on how to proceed, on the other. The literature shows either inconsistencies or dynamics over time. Ralph et al. (2015) summarise Charmaz's (2000, 2006) key steps for grounded theorising with the task list as outlined in the left column of table 11. On the right, I give a juxtaposition of Charmaz' (2012) suggestions with less key phases.

Table 10: Exemplified ambiguity in Charmaz's constructive grounded theory

Core elements of Charmaz' (2000, 2006) constructivist grounded theory according to Ralph et al. (2015, p. 2)	Core elements of constructivist grounded theory according to Charmaz (2012)
<ul><li>Initial coding and data categorisation</li><li>Writing memos</li><li>Concurrent data gathering & analysis</li><li>Constant comparative method</li><li>Theoretical sampling</li><li>Theoretical sensitivity</li><li>Focused & axial coding</li><li>Identifying core categories</li><li>Theoretical coding</li><li>Theorising</li></ul>	<ul><li>Coding data</li><li>Memo writing</li><li>Theoretical sampling</li><li>Integrating the analysis</li></ul>

This can easily be confusing. For Fendt and Sachs (2008), the apparent contradictions represent a more general issue with grounded theory as a field because besides the field's growing fragmentation, they find it suffers from one or more of the following: (1) method-inherent inconsistencies (see tables 9 and 10), (2) inconsistencies regarding the semantics (see, for example, table 5 in section 5.2), (3) misinterpretation of key texts, and subsequently misleading teaching and writing, (4) insufficient researcher training, especially at doctorate level, (5) lack of sufficient coaching and/or attention to process details, and (6) a potentially poor fit between research and research questions.

I realised that I needed clarification and simplification for my own study. I reviewed several approaches and explored which would match my own ontological and epistemological assumptions best. The chosen route was to proceed by keeping closely to Charmaz's (2012) guidelines, and to avoid multi-source confusion by not considering other sources. This was done bearing in mind that she understands grounded theory and process guidelines only as guidelines, not as an overly confined research process. The impact on my study was straightforward. Applying analogies, I gained a map, not a tight corset. I gained confidence that by following an example and mimicking the level of analytical depth as well as reporting practice, my systematic approach is sufficient. Charmaz (2014), and in a more elaborate way Charmaz and Belgrave (2019), encourage substantially more creativity, prioritizing that over any blind process compliance. As an interim summary, the originally rather ambiguous grounded theory process became much more tangible.

The next section shares details on how interviews can help implement this constructivist grounded theory study. Details on interview cut-off considerations follow, with an explanation of risk mitigation strategies for anticipated or encountered ethical concerns. A critical self-assessment of the method closes this section.

Target group selection and interview process

In order to ensure contextual consistency across interviewees, the same private research partner organisation as was identified before, in one of India's major cities served as source of student level interviewees. Interviews represent a major method for data collection in grounded theory (Thompson, 2011).

England (1994) identified research as "a process, not just a product" (p. 82). The following sections aim to create transparency about this process. In line with Bourke (2014), I show and reflect on self-scrutiny and self-conscious awareness regarding the bond between interviewee and interviewer. Additionally, Eisner (1998) clarifies that the credibility of qualitative research increases when a more coherent report, additional insights and transparency on the instrument utility are added. Finally, Hall (1990) adds that positionality is "the space in which objectivism and subjectivism meet" (p. 18). Bourke (2014) complements this line of thought by arguing that trying "to achieve pure objectivism is a naïve question, and we can never truly divorce ourselves of subjectivity" (p. 3). Therefore, in what follows I share subjectivity and comment on impressions in the research process.

To assist, the partner institution's dean tasked the associate dean of research to support the selection of interviewee candidates. Here Blaxter et al.'s (2006) statement that "research is the art of the feasible" (p. 157) can be observed in action. Before I travelled to India, an email was sent to all students, announcing and explaining the study and sharing the information sheet plus the consent forms. A town hall meeting with all students presented the project and allowed for questions, also for distributing the information sheet and the consent form a second time. The researcher reiterated that participation was voluntary and that data would only be analysed on an aggregated level, and anonymously. The positive atmosphere with general questions indicated that as much as this seemed possible, I had managed to minimise fears or any perceived pressure to participate. The associate dean went to all classrooms on consecutive days, selecting a handful of students from undergraduate and graduate courses, so that all classes and business subjects were represented. The only selection criteria were ones that would ensure a gender balance similar to the overall class distribution, which is in line with the group composition of responses in study 1 presented in chapter 2 of this submission. Thus, interviewees were 60% male and 40% female.

In grounded theory studies, the exact number of interviewees is not defined *ex ante*. Sufficiency versus saturation guided the process of adding further interviews. Established sampling techniques were therefore not applied, i.e. an *ex ante* set probability sampling ensuring that participants have an equal chance to be interviewed as outlined by Etikan et al. (2015). These authors distinguish non-probability sampling in the form of convenience or purposive sampling, and encourage researchers to describe how their sample could differ from random ones. According to these authors, convenience sampling relies on easier accessibility and availability. Purposive sampling chooses study participants based on specific, explicit and predefined qualities.

Other than observing a gender quota reflecting the overall student body, there was no further predefined quality or selection criteria, such as grades, region of origin, age or caste. Therefore, the chosen approach does not fully depict purposive sampling in the narrow sense. There was no technical system in place to randomise the selection principle, and the selection might be considered as a convenience sample. Any potential biases on the side of the associate dean of research were not investigated further. When asked how he selected them, he described his approach as random. This is a rather subjective interpretation, yet one could argue in favour of each student receiving an equal chance to participate. The students I encountered showed diverse backgrounds, personalities, majors, etc.

Interviews took place in person on site during November 2019. I spent five days at the research partner organisation to carry out one-on-one meetings. Two rooms were made available. The associate dean of research made sure that in the first 50 m^2 waiting room, there would always be five to ten students lined up waiting for their turn. There was a long table with enough chairs, a water cooler and a ceiling fan to ensure that the wait was not too uncomfortable, as temperatures were rather high. The 12 m^2 interview room was next-door, only accessible through the waiting room, with a glass door and wall separating it. This set-up was not chosen before the trip to India, but offered by the school. Carrying out these interviews required a certain degree of 'going with the flow', as when interviews started with some delays in the morning. Spontaneously, after the interviews, the board members, the president or other deans invited me for a cup of tea to learn more about the project or to give a short presentation.

The glass wall separating the two rooms ensured two crucial aspects. On the one hand, students waiting for their interview could not overhear anything discussed in confidentiality in the actual interview room. On the other hand, they could follow with interest and calm their initial nervousness. They could see that the discussion in the meeting room took place in a casual way, in a less hierarchical but overall friendly atmosphere over a cup of tea if an interviewee wanted one.

The guidelines for the interviews were repeated at the beginning of the interview to ensure that everything was perfectly understood. Students were reminded that participation was voluntary, that they could stop at any time without giving an explanation and without any consequences for them. When asked, interviewees did not like the idea of being recorded, but they readily agreed to notes being taken. I immediately noted key statements verbatim and repeated the text back to the students, regularly asking if, for example, a more daring statement could be used as a quote. None of the study participants objected.

Following what Morse and Niehaus (2009) identify as an underlying trait of all grounded theories, I carried out unstructured interviews. Charmaz (2012) lists a number of reasons motivating the use of such interviews for constructivist grounded theory studies. For example, they ensure more control in collecting and analysing data than other approaches, most notably enabling ethnography as well as text analysis. Interviews for exploring the phenomenon of interest with open-ended questions assure much needed flexibility in the research process to probe and pursue emerging themes when eliciting experiences.

While video-recording systems have a number of advantages, they have downsides, too, as set out by Nehls et al. (2015). Initially, students participating in this study were asked whether videotaping or sound recording the interviews would be acceptable. Yet, as none initially agreed, the attempt to capture the interviews digitally was abandoned. The participants did not share reasons for their refusal explicitly, which was also not required. Their hesitation might have been overcome at a later stage after having built a trusting relationship with the researcher. They might have feared that recordings could be used in a way that would embarrass them, although the research ethics guidelines ensured this would not happen.

Meetings in person overcame the problem of technology like video-recording possibly failing due to the still limited technological endowment of the institution, even for a reliable WhatsApp or Zoom connection. Face-to-face meetings would enable bonding and better rapport between researcher and participant, as well as building trust and the required assurance of confidentiality. McCoyd and Kerson (2006) refer to face-to-face interviews as the gold standard in avoiding risks of trust, sincerity, etc. In contrast, they find that technology-based setups for qualitative research interviews produce inferior data. Even as recent as in 2019, Archibald et al. (2019) mention the lack of data to confirm the advantages of, e.g. Zoom as a method for data collection, and thus advise that methods associated with data standards need to be revisited.

During interviews, it was easy to establish rapport and maintain it, as a positive interview atmosphere was a priority. I took notes while trying to keep eye contact as much as possible, only intermittently glancing at my notes. I continued my notes and observations during the lunch break, at the end of the day and on my return after the visit, to provide a sound foundation for memos. Overall, the many risks outlined by Daymon and Holloway (2010) that could theoretically materialise during note taking, such as a negative impact on the bond, disruption of the flow of the conversation, fear of what might actually get noted, were not observed. I had my notes on the table in front of me, sitting opposite the interviewees and reading back key statements to ensure their correctness. I also noted contextual information for further analysis at a later stage.

A number of factors came together to create a positive impact. Offering tea, asking for permission, explaining rights and process, checking on statements, to name but a few actions, impacted the rapport building and bonding processes positively. Merriam et al. (2001) explain that "positionality is thus determined by where one stands in relation to 'the other'" (p. 411). Showing respect, working towards agreement, and preventing strong hierarchical behaviour in the interview process allowed me to take on several positions in parallel. I was an outsider to the institution, as I was neither a student, nor staff or faculty, let alone part of the school leadership. Yet, I feel I managed to build stronger rapport with the students than the faculty or school leadership could, thus becoming more of an insider when it comes to the students' learning interest. The students clearly saw faculty or staff as "them", with at times starkly diverging interests (learning and career chances versus mere teaching and minimising cost). I did not perceive race, that Harley et al. (2011) identified as a factor contributing to positionality, to be a problem. This could be linked to my having travelled to India repeatedly before, an effect also described in the literature (Dwyer, 2004).

Having done a number of interviews for other projects, including the simultaneous note taking, integrating lessons learnt from the first grounded theory study presented in chapter 4, relying on circular questioning, I am confident that I have captured the content of the interviews as accurately as possible.

Saturation as interview cut-off criterion

Regarding the number of interviews to be recorded, there are two main criteria for the decision on cut-off, namely sufficiency and saturation (Charmaz, 2014). The chosen constructivist grounded theory foresaw these interviews being carried out until saturation. Similar to what was outlined for study 2 in chapter 4, saturation is a judgment call the researcher has to take. I had a virtually inexhaustible pool of interviewees, limited only by the overall number of enrolled and present students, as I had the full support of the school leadership and the curiosity of the students. Students became interested in the study during the town hall meeting and after hearing about it from peers who had been selected. In this study, the notes taken during interviews 54, 55 and 56 were very short as basically no new information that could have enhanced the fieldwork in a noteworthy way, was forthcoming. Grounded theory, as explained before, proceeds differently from a mailed survey, which works with response rates achieved. This approach does not pre-define a sample size and cut-off point before starting the data collection. In this case, having interviewed 56 students, the perception was substantiated that no new knowledge was to be gained by continuing the interviews. Morse (2004) defines this point as "the phase of qualitative data analysis in which the researcher has continued sampling and analysing data until no new data appear and all concepts of the theory are well developed… and their linkages to other concepts are clearly described" (p. 1123).

For Charmaz (2006), there is still no agreement on the precise way of determining saturation. Aldiabat and Le Navenec (2018), but also Francis et al. (2010), disagree as, based on their review of the literature, they see the source of problems and ambiguity in the challenge of articulating the saturation point clearly and substantively. In order to do that aptly, semantics can help. Here, Hennink et al.'s (2016) typology of saturation is helpful. They distinguish type 1 as code saturation that occurs when researchers have a heard-it-all moment, type 2 as meaning saturation that occurs when researchers reach an understand-it-all point in their research. For these authors, one of the two types of saturation is sufficient. In contrast, Morse (2015) requires reaching both.

This study on LSV related perceptions reached both of these saturation points. Regarding code saturation, Hennink et al. (2016) suggested that the point of no new, diverging cases for each code, is often achieved substantially earlier than meaning saturation in terms of what the codes according to each of the interviewees, stand for. Based on this insight, this study continued until 56 interviews had been completed and both code and meaning saturation had subjectively been achieved. This allowed for opportunities to probe whether any more codes could be added and whether the insights gained and condensed could be enriched or reinterpreted further. After 56 interviews, this was no longer deemed possible.

The first grounded theory-based study presented in chapter 4 relied on sufficiency based on the researcher's judgment as described by Charmaz (2006). Interviewees from the faculty body shared views that were largely consistent. Theoretical sufficiency was achievable quite soon. Students might not have had the eloquence in sharing thoughts that their professors had had after years of experience in communicating in classrooms and research-oriented publications. Also, students seemed to show larger diversity, as will be outlined in the next section. A choice was made to orient the interview cut-off point at saturation – the perception by the researchers that additional interviews would not yield any further valuable additional insights.

The duration of the interviews varied between 15 and 45 minutes. In twelve cases a second round of interviews was organised, albeit shorter, just to double-check on some answers. Interviews took place in a closed meeting room with only the interviewer and one student present to ensure a confidential atmosphere.

Critical self-evaluation of the method
This section describes a self-critical review of the chosen methodology, focusing on key elements of the research design. Table 11 summarises these discussion points.

Firstly, the study is clearly positioned, and its method within grounded theory, which relies on number of interviews is established. This "unassailable" (Charmaz, 2012, p. 676) interview method is based on several insights and guidelines in the grounded theory literature. Thompson (2011) gives the average number of interviews in his review of more than 100 grounded theory-based studies as 25. Larger numbers were linked to research questions with a broad reach (e.g. Troiano, 2003), which is not the case with this study's focused question. Therefore, this study's new insights are based on a larger than average number of interviews. Yet, Hennink et al. (2016) require study designs to be tailored to the nature of interviewees as study participants. While the faculty members for study 2 in chapter 4 were assumed to – and turned out to be – communicatively well-resourced to articulate their ideas clearly and concisely, students, in contrast, often shared more information than was required, e.g. on their background or career aspirations (sometimes asking the researcher's advice). Interviews were less straightforward and thus a larger number of study participants contributed to a better understanding of the dynamics at work. This was not surprising as several sources in the literature, such as Sobal (2001) and Morse (2000), assert that the nature of the phenomenon being studied, if more complex or abstract, can easily overwhelm.

Table 11: Critical self-assessment of the chosen method

Strengths of the method	Weaknesses of the method
• A clearly positioned grounded theory approach;	• Grounded theory remains a challenging approach due to multiple kinds of approaches and method-inherent subjectivity;
• Above-average number of interviews were carried out;	
• More interviews helped cope with limited straightforwardness of some student participants compared to faculty members as interviewees;	• There is an interviewer/positionality effect with some interviewees;
• Explicit elaboration of approach to interview cut-off points;	• Interviews were the primary way of collecting data, thus limited triangulation with other data sources;
• Approach to saturation seeks a combined code and meaning saturation point.	• Issue of recording the data – triangulation could have been employed at the end of the interview by going back to the notes, confirming participants' representations.

Secondly, this study's method embraced Aldiabat and Le Navenec's (2018) criteria for better grounded theory which clarify how the "often anxiety-provoking" (p. 246), "mysterious, subjective, non-linear, gradual and unfixed process" (p. 258) of stopping interviews in general, and of saturation more specifically, should be addressed. As Bowen (2008) indicates, numerous qualitative studies lack an explanation of what their stance towards saturation is or how it might have been achieved. The study relied on Hennink et al. (2016) in detailing options and illustrating what lower (i.e. code saturation) and higher quality standards (i.e. meaning saturation, which is more difficult to achieve) are. The study at hand further complies with Morse's (2015) high standards for grounded theory studies emphasizing both code and meaning saturation.

There are downsides as well. The first disadvantage of using grounded theory is linked to the advantages. There is substantial subjectivity in the field. For example, Morse et al. (2009, p. 244) state that "good grounded theory… surprises and delights". However, 'surprising' and 'delighting' are vague concepts of which the meaning remains unclear. Charmaz (2006) reiterates that grounded theory-related guidelines can only "give you a handle on the material, not a machine that does the work for you" (p. 115). Fendt and Sachs (2007) argue similarly, that a too orthodox application of a rigorous process undermines the sought-after strengths of grounded theory.

In addition, Aldiabat and Le Navanec (2018) see potential limitations for grounded theory-based studies in three factors, namely that conducting grounded theory in shorter time frames is difficult, budget constraints can be limiting, and general resource limitations, which could include elements of training and monitoring, can be barriers. They apply conceptual insights to handling these kinds of circumstances, suggesting that focus days be spent on nothing but interviewing, writing memo's, constantly comparing notes, coding, and probing and checking with interviewees, i.e. not multitasking with other activities. The authors warn, though, the information power can be limited in shorter timeframes of exposure. Onwuegbuzie and Leech (2007), as well as Maltrued et al. (2016), mirror this need of ensuring sufficient intensity in interviewer-interviewee contact and strengthened dialogue. As LSV represents an emerging, complex phenomenon, interviewees could find it challenging to articulate their perceptions explicitly. Charmaz (2006) also confirms that the complexity and novelty of the research question can require more time for interaction and for completing the study. In this study, this disadvantage was mitigated by two choices. One was to continue with every interview and proceed to more interviews until both moments a heard-it-all and understand-it-all were reached. There was no time limit on either the side of the interviewer or interviewee to stop the meeting, thus we continued until all questions had been answered.

Monitoring, mentoring and training represented a bottleneck in this process. Having read a number of articles and attended research seminars could only advance the research skills to a certain level. Recognizing potential own blind spots as part of a Johari window analysis (cf. Luft & Ingham, 1955) on one's skills is not easy. Even articles, such as Aldiabat and Le Navenec (2018) encourage novices in grounded theory to use their "subjectivity, wisdom and intuition" (p. 246). This seems to be an oxymoron, as linking a novice to wisdom in research seems contradictory. If a younger researcher were to exhibit and apply wisdom in a concrete research project, the label 'novice' would not be justified, and it is not clear how an expert would then be described.

Aldiabat and Le Navenec (2018), which intended to create transparency on how to professionally determine the cut-off point with interviews, ends up recommending mentoring. This study is the second grounded theory study I have carried out as a researcher. Fortunately the two studies were conducted within one year, so that everything I learnt in the first study and from additional readings, had remained fresh for the second. The strong dogmatism in the field regarding which grounded theory approach is the right one, inhibits cumulative learning across sources, and obliges one to follow Nagel et al. (2015) by finding a suitable mentor, which is what I did, after reading widely on grounded theory from a conceptual point of view and going through sample studies in a variety of fields.

From a process point of view, I could perceive the benefits of relying on an auto-didactic approach to learn about grounded theory. At first, I formed my own opinion, then increasingly relied on my epistemological, ontological and axiological assumptions to develop a firm stance about the best fit. Mentoring or monitoring in the process of assigning codes, inducting and theorising could challenge the way in which the researcher can subjectively drive the theorising process. One mitigation strategy I deployed was sought not in mentoring or monitoring *per se*, but in reading widely to see how individual grounded theory experts tackled various core areas of the research process within a grounded theory frame. One such insight was gained from Wright and Leahey (2013) who promote the procedure of asking a variety of types of circular questions aimed at identifying differences, effects, or developments over time. Charmaz (2012) add their suggestions on effective questions as well.

Further, and having carried out an earlier study using this method of data collection with faculty members of the same institution, using grounded theory has its strengths and weaknesses. The question again was whether 'guilty knowledge' (Williams, 2009) in the form of any preconceived understanding of the research partner institution could impede a fresh unprejudiced approach. Self-awareness can help mitigate this risk. Charmaz (2017) adds methodological self-consciousness as a key element to self-awareness, and suggests turning a deeply reflective gaze back at ourselves and the research process, as well as at the empirical world (p. 350) in order to produce higher quality research.

There are researchers within grounded theory that do not see disadvantages in being well-informed about a target group. For example, Le Navenec (1993) encourages a triangulation approach not only in data collection, but also in sample selection. Dillon (2012) sees positive aspects and even essential support for theorising when exploring the context not only from the learners' side, but also from the teachers' side – together the different perspectives could give a more comprehensive view (similar to the faculty interviews in study 2 in chapter 4).

If grounded theory is based on symbolic interactionism as described by Denzin (1992), having covered the faculty perspective of the interacting parties can help with understanding the context. As defined early on, symbolic interactionism explores the social settings and individuals' understanding of their experience (Blumer, 1969). In addition, Chenitz (1986) mentions the possibility of commencing the research by investigating an unrelated theoretical framework, which the researcher can then reshape to fit the data. Thus, the grounded theory literature is aware of researchers' possibility to enter a study with preconceived notions. Having prior knowledge of the interaction partner, i.e. via the faculty who are teachers and supervisors of the interviewees of this study, could help accelerate the process of gaining a thorough understanding of the study context.

Continuing the critical evaluation, I anticipated and observed an interviewer and positionality effect. It relates to the high power distance between faculty and students in India, in which, following Hofstede (2011), students are on the low end of the power scale (see section 4.5). Further, this is accompanied by a natural distribution of more or less shy individuals in any given group. An older foreigner as interviewer introduced as a person whose requests they ought to comply with and answer to, instructed by the institution's leadership, resulted in 15% of the cases showing reticence in relative shyness initially, introversion and an inclination to take on the role of a good ambassador for the school instead of primarily giving information honestly and as an equal partner. As interviewing an individual progressed, this effect mostly disappeared. In one case, however, I had the impression the interviewee was growing increasingly anxious as the interview continued, therefore I ended it and removed all this participant's data from the study, thereby also complying with a clear no-harm policy.

To mitigate effects of participant's awareness of the interviewer, various strategies were employed. A literature review considering, e.g. West and Blom's (2016) overview and synthesis of interviewer effects in more general terms and Scott's (2004) critical review of aspects of shyness and coping mechanisms, proved to be helpful. This way, following Thompson's (2011) advice to the interviewer, I made a conscious effort to proactively address the researcher's interference as a potential factor that might impede high quality studies. Unsurprisingly, Jette et al. (2003) link such specially honed researcher acumen to the possibility of getting greater benefit and better results from a given sample.

Finally, although interviews were the main data collection instrument, Morse and Niehaus (2009), list a number of data sources that could complement the primary instrument, such as observations or different kinds of documents. Saturation in terms of a perceived understand-it-all clearly refers to insights to be gained from the interviews.

To conclude, besides symbolic interactionism on the research philosophy side of grounded theory, pragmatism comes in to make clear choices in favour of and against some aspects given in the data (Aldiabat and Le Navanec, 2011). The research question was not to explore how LSV would be formed over a longer time span. Also, the focus was not primarily on dynamics within the classroom for which an ethnographic study combined with grounded theory would be necessary.

The aim in this study was to gather data from students as the second core stakeholder group, to complement study 2 while also bearing the study 1 results in mind. This would support the goal of providing a thorough, holistic, even if still preliminary and highly context-specific, three-partite study on the emerging phenomenon of LSV. Tashakkori and Teddlie (1998) explain that pragmatism encourages researchers to rely on approaches that work well, if not best, when it comes to a chosen research problem, such as LSV in this study. Kaushik et al. (2019) add that pragmatism as a philosophy firmly links individuals' actions to their experiences and beliefs. The authors continue by pointing to the importance of an action's situation and context. Creswell and Clark (2011) show clearly how pragmatism assumes the possibility of multiple realities. In this sense, pragmatism, with its emphasis on experience, is very compatible with this study. Grounded theory represents this fit with the research problem that pragmatism solicits. Interviewing instructors and learners represents an effective and productive, pragmatic approach. Grounded theory primarily emphasizes experience (Starks & Trinidad, 2007), as does pragmatism. What remains at the core of both grounded theory studies given in this research project, is an abductive, constructivist research process, which defines the quiddity of these studies.

6.4 Empirical results producing the grounded theory of 'emergence' for a student-oriented view on LSV

This section reports on the empirical results according to the key stages Charmaz (2012) suggests for future researchers to follow her published framework and the empirical results of their particular study. This allows us to cumulatively build up knowledge on grounded theory as more illustrative studies become available. The following sections, therefore, include stage 1 on coding, stage 2 on memo writing, stage 3 on theoretical sampling, and stage 4 on integrating the analysis. These stages are not purely chronologically sequential. As mentioned, to capture perceptions and observations thoroughly, memo writing took place during the coding process, as well as before and after the theoretical sampling, and even after stage 4. Ongoing memo writing was also aimed at fostering reflexivity and a more robust grounded theory.

Stage 1: Coding data

As recommended by Charmaz (2012), coding represents the first step in the analysis to move from mere description to conceptualisation. Coding was done line-by-line paying close attention to the data. As suggested by the framework for the analysis, I was attentive to sensitising concepts I came across in frequent reflective moments. A guiding question in this process was Glaser's (1978) general one which enquires about what becomes obvious by looking at the data. Initially, I did open coding that entails first analytical decisions, and subsequently focused coding which processes the most frequently used codes. This helped with sorting, synthesising, and conceptualising the data. As in study 2, this was done by using active language, specifically using gerunds. A search for more data on these processes was then pursued.

Charmaz (2012) alerts the researchers to the possibility that new directions can emerge during the coding and subsequent interviews, thus taking the analysis beyond the initial scope and themes. This happened in study 3 when a second group, a second cluster of students, seemed to be emerging. Further interviews revealed that particular features did not belong only to an initially small group of outliers that did not fit the first apparently homogeneous interviews and emerging insights. Selective or focused codes were, as suggested by Charmaz (2012), more incisive, general and abstract, while also serving a categorising role. They reached beyond a single interview as well, and enabled comparisons and fit assessment beyond a rudimentary framework for theorising and the actual situation in the data. Table 9 exemplifies this process. Iteratively comparing recurring themes in interviews, doing the open coding on a very granular level, coding and categorising labels on a more abstract focused level across dozens of interviews, took a considerable amount of time. The emerging categories provided the foundation for emerging frameworks.

Tables 12 and 13 below provide an overview of the coding process and emerging categories. Table 12 shares interviewee quotes which are coded and categorised according to elements of the student's ecosystem. What becomes apparent, is a distinction between students who view their environment primarily as positive and full of opportunities and those who view it as something deterministic and thus fatalistically negative.

Table 12: Sample coding and emerging categories in student-external factors

Interviewee	Comment	Code	Category
I1	"Technology is cool. I am on websites like YouTube a lot to learn more about the topics."	Going beyond a professor's offer	Perceiving environment as enabling
I2	"I browse, go beyond books."	Realising opportunities	
I3	"School is irrelevant… learning to learn is not discussed… they think learning is memorising."	Understanding limitations of institution	
I5	"Now we have maximum freedom. Some professors really give their best effort, whatever they can do. We take it forward."	Seeing the positive value	
I6	"I read, go on YouTube, try to experience, see what is working."	Experimenting	
I4	"In school, it is a last minute rush, we learn for exams, it is not practical at all. I would rather do something practical."	Resigning to the status quo	Perceiving environment as limiting and negative
I7	"The class is useless."	Getting frustrated about the institution	
I8	"Classes don't work… I learn alone… Need to adapt as I love the job I have in mind."	Accommodating	
I9	"Here it is 70% dictation, 30% watching videos. If you are interested in learning, then what?"	Seeing limitations surrounding the student	
I10	"There is no speaking about learning to learn in school, 80% of the class is lecturing. The professor does not tell us how to have a new idea."	Being stuck	
I11	"Here is competition, it is not good."	Seeing the non-enabling environment	
I17	"I watch YouTube, I cannot understand what the professor is saying. They sometimes just send the PowerPoint files without explanations."	Feeling let down by teachers	

Table 13 provides a selective overview of the open and focused coding process, considering another type of insight, which addresses the learner as such. Besides the nature of the environment as core to the phenomenon of LSV, in terms of being conducive to fostering self-awareness, reflexivity or experimentation, the role of the student can be categorised as being either more active or more passive.

One has to bear in mind that placing the term "category" or the categorisation process in a binary-style, in an in-versus-out list, does not necessarily do justice to the more fine-grained continuum on which students' responses could be placed. There are varying degrees to which they fulfil each category. The next section, following the description of data coding, explores memo writing as a crucial phase of analysing the data, codes and categories.

Table 13: Codes and categories of the learners

Interviewee	Comment	Code	Category
I1	"For learning, I do what I feel. It is my instinct… books do not give me anything."	Being self-aware, noticing what is working and what not	Being active
I2	"Learning is finding out new things, not just the textbook stuff. I browse, go beyond books. I look for practical applications and want to do things."	Taking initiative in light of one's learning preference	
I3	"I search, help myself, explore, look for projects…"	Being active	
I5	"I go for true understanding, which is not memorising. I need to do more for true understanding which is learning. I always try to reflect and ask myself what it means for me."	Going beyond the status quo in the classroom	
I6	"I learn by self-study. I learn by doing … on the job … I am curious and adapt what I do … I am self-driven … I pursue field work."	Realising the current offer from professor is insufficient	
I16	"I am self-driven, I search myself. Up to 100% of classes are lecturing at times. I need to overcome the work-study gap."	Being eager to succeed in studies and the job market	
I13	"I listen, I was brought up like that."	Accepting a passive role	Being passive
I14	"The class is more about content, not skills, no feedback on learning. We listen, that is it."	Complying	

Stage 2: Memo writing

Continuing to follow Charmaz's (2012) guidelines, memo writing is viewed as an interim step serving the purpose of linking codes to initial drafts within a more coherent analysis. I wrote such memos in lunch or coffee breaks, at the end of each interview day, as well as in the morning before commencing the next round of interviews and after reflecting on the data. I continued memo writing in the days after returning from the research partner location. Notes were written in a quick, shorthand way, at times even using dictation software before editing in word processing software in order to capture all pivotal thoughts. A total of 15 pages were accumulated as a consequence of this form of memo writing.

Following Chandrasegaran et al.'s (2017) recommendation, visualisations drawn on paper and in PowerPoint frames complemented the dictations and compiled texts. They were essential to ensure insights and emerging theory-related observations that originated from working solely with the data, and not with literature in the first place. Notably, memos changed over time as situations were better understood after more interviews had been carried out. Texts and figures matured over time. Memos lead to probing questions for further analysis and comparison. I tried to avoid the perfectionist trap, i.e. trying (as a non-native speaker) to write each memo in the most perfect way, let alone embarking on language editing with a language editor such as the online website grammarly.com. Similar to what Charmaz (1999, 2012) indicated, as the writing progressed there was a growing sense of competence as well as confidence.

At the same time, memo writing contributed to understanding better how the learning environment can be very restrictive to the students. To name but one example, some professors were perceived as being exceptionally helpful. Others, and this was mentioned repeatedly, merely distributed PowerPoint slides without even giving verbal or written lecturing notes on them. Tables 14 and 15 give an impression of how the notes written as *aide de memoire* of interviews, were written. These memos rely on verbatim quotes from the interviewees.

Table 14: Excerpt 1 from memo writing

On diverging student views regarding the learning environment
… It is interesting to note just how diverse perceptions are when it comes to learning environment. I24 shares "I learn more if the professors use our lingo. They do not need to rap but make it understandable. Younger teachers understand us better. I usually get 10% from the professor in average, the rest from other sources. Some professors, very few, make it lively. They have games and simulations, which can help us learn, but also experiment. I am a shy person as being a good listener is expected from me as a girl in our culture. We do not speak up at home. Our parents would deem it rude. Parents expect us to be book worms, just like the professors, the normal ones, the older ones. We then copy and paste for the exam. I learn best though, as I found out, through practical things, by applying things, or in internships. I am actually not a book worm. I have been conditioned to be one by the parents and teachers."

Fostering Learning Style Versatility in Business Schools

> Equally, I26 communicates "learning depends on the topic. But the professor often merely rushes through the .ppt. They sometimes just send the file even without talking about it in class. I need to practice it though." I27 mentions "in order to become a more versatile learner, we need to personalise what is happening. Some professors make an effort which I appreciate. I like reading, my family encourages me. I tried doing activities but it was not well done. I know it may take years to become a more versatile learner. I want to build confidence, we need small steps. If I do more, I will change". I31 continued by sharing "they do not even have a proper calendar, which is very demotivating, e.g. exam dates change all the time, some start earlier, others later. The results of exams are not posted in months, why? The bathroom hygiene is not good. The dust bins are always full". I34, in turn, says "they just have lectures, don't ask about my ideas. There is only one textbook for a class of 35 students. We take a picture with our phone". In contrast, I41 states "It is not what I expected, but I am grateful. I understood the classes are just theoretical, so I help myself, I review, practice, discuss. Special classes where we practice could help, but I organise all myself. Google and YouTube are super"…

Further, the written memos helped clarify the initially counterintuitive observation and interpretation that there were two completely different groups in the student body at the research partner situation. Some differences were so stark, I almost questioned whether these students were at the same school at all. One group of students were extremely passive, complying, subordinate, trusting and modest. Another cluster, in a diametrically opposed way, arranged themselves and showed proactivity beyond what the teacher offered or expected. Major elements of the learning culture seemed to be rather heterogeneous.

Table 15: Excerpt 2 from memo writing

On students taking charge or not
… Students seem to have a different stance to what is happening to them. Some perceive the environment is an absolute given, as something imposed, and the situation reflects a very fatalistic nature. I32, for example, illustrates this the following way "I cannot focus in class. The professor sends .ppt. Some are typed, some notes are even handwritten only. They are hard to read. I try so hard to listen. We need 75% of attendance otherwise we cannot take the exam. We then have to write down what mam says. That is it. Professor does not know that I do not like lectures or that I would like examples, or experience something. When we will work, we will do things, not theorise, we need to improve and prepare. We are not given any chance to explore."
In turn, I38 shares "I am working on becoming an extrovert. I try to interact, learn from speaking to others. I organise activities and projects. Overall, I learn at least 40% from projects, discussions, presentations. I organise them. If I waited for the professor, it would not happen". Students seem to recreate the hierarchies they know from home. I39 shares "our parents expect us to learn by listening, for a long time". I found out, however, I am better at interacting. I want to be a

> professor, but one that is modern. Yes, students will adapt to the challenges, but need more help. I do it so far without the help. That is why I want to become a professor, to improve things, there is much more we call can do."
>
> Students seem to be divided in those that accept their fate and those that understand that for things to improve, they have discretion, they have to change and take charge. There seems to be no gender difference as both male and female students provide similar answers. National culture seems to matter such as coming from households organised with strong hierarchies and roles for the youngers. The question arises when individuals should experiment with LSV if not for the very latest in business schools before starting their careers? Starting a job will represent a drastic shift of learning mode from reducing 'theorist' and lecture-oriented learning to much more activist-style based learning interventions….

Finally, Charmaz's (2012) recommendation to include interview quotes and excerpts from the interviews in the memos to ground them in the data and 'keep them real', proved beneficial. The memos became a unique way of capturing thoughts as otherwise, over time, one is inclined to forget a substantial amount of detail. During memo writing a number of categories already crystallised, yet grounded theory foresees a further substantiation as the next section explains.

Stage 3: Theoretical sampling

This stage was aimed at exploring additional cases for the development of the categories. The purpose was to check for completeness of the categories, explore variations within them, and possible features shared between them. Regular, ongoing comparison can then lift concepts to the theoretical level. For this to happen, saturation is required (Charmaz, 2012).

In the context of this study, further interviews substantiated previous codes. Here are further illustrative excerpts of students' comments that colour the environment positively. The ecosystem referred to here, goes beyond the classroom and includes technology.

- I40: "I like experiments, the few that we do, very much. I learn a lot. I leant that I learnt a lot from them. And now with Google, it is so easy. Technology really makes all the difference. If I don't get it from the class, I watch videos until I understand it."

- I50: "Practical work helps us best. Business law class had a few cases and a trip. Google helps with assignments. There are mentoring sessions and advisory. If there is a problem in class or family, they help. During orientation day, they gave us a value orientation as well, about being disciplined…"

- I52: "We recently had micro-economics. Teacher explained properly… she encouraged me, motivated me by saying 'you can do it'."

- I53: "We google a lot. Becoming a more versatile learner depends on the topic. At times videos help, other topics have theories or not, for others you need real life experience and practice. We can do it. Students experiment ... can lead to short-term change... tests give good feedback."

At the same time, students' comments on the ecosystem being less enabling increased as more interviews were conducted. The following examples illustrate such relatively negative comment on the environment.

- I45: "The syllabus comes from the government. There is nothing we can do within the school context... there is nothing the school can or should do... too much learning versatility is not encouraged as this raises expectations. The profs cannot do it."

- I43: "Teachers should focus more on EQ. When you think about it – who are we? We have not seen the world. Most of the teachers have not seen a business. They just teach it... Teachers do not recommend us to google stuff... why take the programme? Parents pressure us to get a BBA. Parent pressure is a sign of love. An MBA gets you something, which is what they say, is what everyone says, it opens doors, farming doesn't. But professors only lecture, we take notes."

- I46: "Teachers start to lecture, students listen."

- I47: "School needs more projectors, some do not work. Reading and writing is the dominant way of learning."

- I48: "You need to be friendly with teachers, otherwise... they think 'keep it mean to keep them learning'."

- I51: "There is no team building, many sub-groups in class. There should be more bonding, to learn from each other, to help, to practice with each other. Study is for work and make money, but we should learn also. This is not possible now really."

On being active and taking their own initiative, rather than merely being stuck in a deterministic situation, students shared:

- I40: "Learning is my responsibility."

- I41: "Students need to adapt."

- I45: "How I learn best is up to me, I need to figure it out. I am doing it. It is totally dependent on our efforts. We have to work hard. We adapt."

In contrast, the quotes and codes of the students who took a more fatalistic and thus more passive stance, were as follows:

- I42: "We do not have the power to change the schools. The programme is for the sake of certification, to get a job. Many of us still need to figure out what we want to do. At least with the certification we can get a job and figure it out then. We study to please the parents. A degree gives us safety, then they leave us alone. We might have wasted years then, but we go with the flow."

Making a preliminary summary of the theoretical sampling stage, it became obvious that in the evoked set and within the relevant set of topics frequently mentioned, there were recurring core themes. The last three interviews brought no new information, which induced an obvious heard-it-all and understood-it-all moment allowing me to realise that I had reached saturation. Probing questions produced answers very much in accordance with known codes and categories. The final step, as outlined in the following section, was to be undertaken next, namely integrating the quotes, codes, categories, memos, insights and interpretations into one substantial theory and framework. The next section sheds light on this.

Stage 4: Integrating the analysis

This integration process relies on both these categories (classroom environment and actors) emerging as concepts, as well as on their rich analysis during memo writing. The memos brought clarity and a minimum degree of generalising in the emerging grounded theory, which can be understood as a story that unfolds (Charmaz, 2012).

As shown in figure 15 below, this narrative is about an observed process. 'Emergence' is about the way a student embraces both adversity and opportunity in a classroom environment, and about the potential additional complementary factors offered, such as technology and rich pools of information available for self-study helping to hone LSV. Some students do so more quickly, some lag behind. This resulting grounded theory of emergence starts by two perceptions of what the classroom environment is in a narrower or broader sense. One group of students view the classroom environment as rather rigid. They do as they are told. They comply with expectations and imposed learning style boundaries.

Their counterparts, however, have broadened their horizons. They turned their learning environment into a multi-site "classroom". Learning can take place within the actual, physical classroom, online on their mobiles, as well as online or offline at home. For them location boundaries are more fluid.

Two drivers catalyse the efforts of the second group, namely adversity and additional opportunities. What emerges is insight in the tremendous flexibility of how, where and when to learn. Technology constitutes the main pillar that brings complementary tools into their ecosystem. In addition, a few, often younger, teachers inspire and encourage in an otherwise rather dull, mono-teaching style environment, which allows no LSV potential to prosper, let alone being discovered as part of honing higher order learning, e.g. on the metacognition level.

Figure 15: Emergence framework as grounded theory for student-oriented LSV dynamics

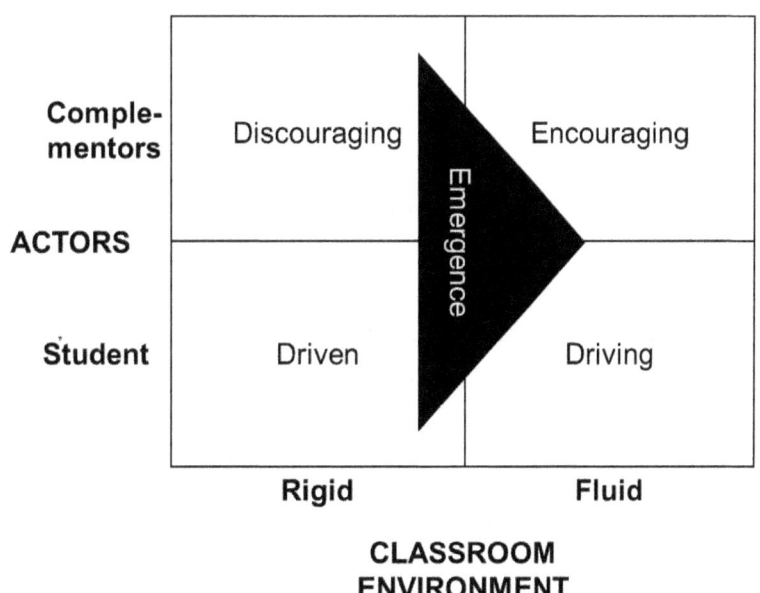

A central question eventually refers to how students perceive LSV. The data shows that it strongly depends on their perception of the classroom environment. We need to know whether it is as rigid as portrayed, and whether such perceptions are driven by the faculty. If students adopt the view of a rigid classroom set up as the only possibility, they usually also embrace passivity. They neither show interest in diversifying their repertoire of learning styles, nor do they see the need to enhance their LSV.

In contrast to passive participants, a larger group of students showed that they embrace a world view in which classroom boundaries and guardrails for learning are fluid. They are proactive and drive their own learning journeys. They steer their own development, taking own responsibility for it. They experiment with different modes of learning. If they find the faculty not up to their standards, they move beyond and find out what works elsewhere. They embark on peer learning and take note of what others are doing. Strong competition for jobs, careers and social mobility, as well as unrealistically high family expectations of many in the Indian culture accelerate them, driving their learning as well as their learning skills. It is the adversity that energises learning, propels experimentation, and avoids that individuals get too comfort and convenience oriented.

Besides adversity, there are other complementors to count on if the students embrace resulting opportunities as outlined below. Technological innovation to some extent assures that students can be less reliant on faculty members in their learning. If faculty do not share information on learning skills or explicitly on LSV, individuals can grow, even on an unconscious level, with the help of online learning offers. Online offers can include specialised learning apps, websites and platforms that are either free or proprietary, or mere google searches and YouTube videos. They would not per se exclude the possibility for theorists to learn more traditionally from books, articles or notes, but they do encourage experimentation.

The notion of emergence fits in this kind of study for two reasons. On the one hand it refers to something that moves from being concealed to being visible. What has been difficult to explore, experiment with, and hone, such as one's LSV, according to study participants, is now emerging as an actual new form of behaviour. Emergence further refers not only to something that was concealed before becoming visible, it also reflects something coming into existence and even gaining prominence. Still at a largely unconscious level, learning to learn and becoming a more versatile learner emerges as a key to survival in the future job market, in the degree programmes and courses, as well as in participants' private social lives, e.g. with parents and other close relatives who impose performance pressure.

In addition, the notion of emergence clearly refers to an ongoing process which is not completed, and has not reached all students. Finally, in light of the very limited focus on the learning-to-learn concept among faculty or on the larger institutional side, further stages in the emergence process are likely to be seen. The more technology grows and related behaviours spread, the likelier we will see an acceleration in the adoption of a learning skills and LSV view.

6.5 Discussion of results and second literature review on the student-oriented grounded theory and emerging hypotheses

This section will further detail and discuss the emergence framework while relying on links to the literature. Five main sets of hypotheses will be detailed. Immediately, hypotheses are included to possibly take the theorising efforts forward. Hypotheses need to be directly testable. This requires not only a variable conceptualisation, but also an operationalisation before the hypothesis testing becomes fully feasible. While these two processes have not yet taken place, and could be suggested for original work in subsequent research, there are several hypotheses that emerge for testing in quantitative research designs. It needs to be re-emphasized that the purpose of a substantive context-specific grounded theory is not to readily generalise across settings, yet merely to explore and understand a particular setting better.

Firstly, complementors can accelerate LSV. Their nature and presence help to explain performance. The label "complementor" alludes to an extension of Porter's (2008) five forces to analyse environment in general and industries in particular. Brandenburger and Nalebuff (1996) add a sixth force as complementor. In this grounded theory, there are complementors that help students by providing general technology, such as Google and YouTube, as well as more specialised learning apps. Complementors can also be linked to actor-network theory (David, 2007), assuming that even non-human elements within a system or network can play an active agency role

There are two more stakeholder categories. One such category is the teachers (some better trained and more enabling than others), who give support beyond their frequently encountered lecturer role. This agrees with Pintrich's (1995) view that good faculty members can accelerate learning efforts related to their subject. If they are present in the role model version, students benefit more. They are frequently absent in this additive and more advantageous educator role, and thus can impede as well as accelerate. Second, parents are complementors whose impact can be twofold as well. If they overemphasize passive reading and listening, or impose career expectations, they could eventually exert an influence different to what they intended to. This leads to the study's hypothesis 1:

H1: The more enabling complementors are present in the environment of a learner, the higher the learner's LSV.

Secondly, still considering the complementors, parents often comply with traditional Indian values which represent a high power distance culture, leaving less room for their children to exercise discretion, experimentation and self-actualisation. Dunn (1996) pointed to the major role of national culture in educational learning journeys - an insight substantiated in this study. Mantiri (2013), for example, establishes this link of culture-specific idiosyncratic ways to teaching, while Gay (2002) encourages teachers' awareness of the unique influence national culture can have, so that they will create suitable culturally responsive learning experiences. Myers (1990) posits that there surely are some predispositions that are innate, yet beyond this nature view, the nurture view emphasizes just how important the right social environment is. Ramirez (1989) links learning behaviour to very early experiences in the family setting. Dunn (1997), in turn warns against oversimplifying. There is not necessarily a single dominating learning style within a nation, race or culture. Yet, future research can at least test an influence of culture on LSV. Awareness of cultural difference in terms of power distance, leads to the following hypothesis:

H2: High power distance cultures are correlated with less opportunities to develop LSV.

Thirdly, a key observation gained from the 50+ interviews relates specifically to the term "emergence framework". Besides external factors that develop LSV, internal factors of personal self-development were brought to the interviewer's attention. While the initial literature review given in section 6.2 above identifies research which largely emphasizes externally regulated factors that change learning styles and thus also LSV with an added time dimension, interviewees shared their contrasting perceptions. They seemingly self-regulate their study behaviour, practically representing Gardner's (1991) view that individuals are not solely shaped by a given culture, but that they create their own ways of thinking too. Cox and Ramirez (1981) add that this line of thought has ethical and educational policy implications as it counters oversimplification, misunderstanding, stereotyping and affords less opportunities which a culturally determinist position would find just and justified. Gardner (1991) continues by outlining that compliance with one culture could lead to conflict with another, divergent culture. If markets, technology and the flow of people, capital and information become increasingly international, even if not fully global as pointed out by Ghemawat (2011), business schools in one context might not adequately prepare students for international careers. Bennis and O'Toole (2005) point generally to a frequently encountered complaint that business schools in general lack relevance. The interviewees of this study, relatedly, seem to confirm a special form of being less culturally versatile.

Filling the void in preparing for the international business scene in classrooms, there is an emerging behaviour of adaptation that does not accept this limitation as fatalistic. One section of students start to use discretion for more self-regulated learning, thus in agreement with Pintrich (1995) who indicates such a possibility. Zimmermann (2000) reviews several areas that matter, including the relationship between the self and a person's behaviour on the one hand, and the appropriate behaviour in a chosen environment on the other. As the model posits, this study shows considerable self-reflection on what works and what does not among a substantial part of the interviewees. A number of them express intrinsic motivation to understand, self-instruct, focus attention, self-experiment, self-evaluate, and find self-satisfaction in terms of learning and learning cut-off points.

A second model on self-regulated learning put forward by Boekaerts (1991) emphasizes three purposes for self-regulation, which include thirst for knowledge and skills expansion, avoiding threats and harm to oneself, and protecting commitments, even if it means reliance on coping mechanisms that do not immediately ensure well-being (for a full review of key self-regulation models, cf. Panadero, 2017). These purposes become obvious among participants of this study as well. Although Pintrich (1995) underlines the possibility of faculty helping students to achieve self-regulation, a substantial group of students drive learning themselves, even in the absence of good faculty support. This leads to hypotheses 3a, 3b and 3c on self-regulated learning in the LSV context:

H3a: The poorer the externally regulated learning stimuli, the more the individual learner self-regulates.

H3b: The more rigid the classroom setting is perceived to be, the lower the LSV.

H3c: There is a positive correlation between the degree of self-regulation and more LSV.

Fourthly, technology seems to play a particularly important role. While the literature review in section 6.2 already pointed to the impact an enabling, externally regulated learning environment can have on learning style changes, this insight is also broadly received in the literature on learning in general. Todorov et al. (1997) showed empirically how technology can accelerate the learning of more complex topics. Raja and Nagasubramani (2018) are probably using hyperbole when, in their review of technology's impact in education, they say that next to life, technology is the "greatest of God's gifts" (p.33).

Still, there is a point in valuing technology as supporting learning. Interviewees in this study on LSV share that they can pick-and-choose among available technologies, be it more passive video watching or relying on self-chosen learning exercises not available in their classrooms. They indicate that they can experiment and drive their own learning which can have a motivating effect. This is in line with Milgram et al. (1993) who argue that having opportunities to diversify the learning experience helps. Also, active involvement alters learning styles, as Siriopoulos and Pomonis (2007) have explained. The earlier literature review highlighted relatively modern learning taxonomies, among them Viji and Benedict (2017b) who argue in favour of innovative learning for the interconnected learner. Among the interviewees of this study, there certainly are such interconnected learners who nowadays have access to numerous and often openly available technologies via Google or YouTube, where no paid subscription is required.

These considerations must be linked to the frequently recurring statements made about the learning style differences based on gender (e.g. Siriopoulos & Pomonis, 2007), which are, however, not confirmed; see for example, Van den Berg's (2015) work that did not observe and thus could not confirm such differences. Male and female interviewees did not answer differently. Still, further research could give clarity on the emerging field of LSV's stance in this regard. In line with the previously outlined stimulus-response argument, the fourth set of hypotheses states:

H4a: The better the access to affordable learning technologies, the higher the LSV.

H4b: There is no significant gender difference when it comes to accessing technologies.

H4c: Gender does not moderate the link between accessing technologies and building LSV.

Fifthly, the preliminary literature review in section 6.2 explored several arguments in favour of changeability, and it explored how a related field (leadership) suggests honing learning styles and possibly building more LSV. This section leading up to the next set of hypotheses does not explore new literature, but links this study's results to the previously identified literature to assess the extent to which they contain sensitising concepts for the empirical study actually were confirmed. We need to ascertain whether interviewees' responses touch upon the mentioned ideas.

Students clearly express the wish to survive and be competitive in the job market. They orient themselves towards what might be needed in the future, and intend to learn accordingly, which speaks in favour of both the past-cum-future argument as well as the naturally fading argument. This future mapping and calculating backwards might not materialise in as conscious a way as the blue ocean leadership approach with its canvassing does. Further, the interviews justify the conclusion that students do not reflect on styles, related capabilities and numerous competencies, nor consciously use emotional intelligence to leverage change. They have not been given formal sessions on LSV awareness, nor do they operate in an environment that otherwise fosters learning style awareness. Thus, a key ingredient of becoming more versatile as outlined in the field of leadership, is clearly missing in the research context at the partner organisation for this project. The process of developing awareness is substantially less conscious, yet to a noteworthy extent, is still future driven. By force of adversity, the aforementioned strategic learning and coping mechanism can lead to learning adaptations, from which LSV emerges. This leads to the following final set of proposed hypotheses:

H5a: Groups with awareness training for LSV show a higher level of LSV than groups without training.

H5b: The clearer the job aspirations, the more efforts are invested in honing LSV.

Testing these hypotheses would help generalise the grounded theory in similar settings and eventually bring research to a more generally applicable and richer body of knowledge, also developing theories on LSV. The following section outlines limitations that each study has, also the study presented here as study 3. Implications of the findings for theory, practice and for grounded theory researchers, follow.

6.6 Limitations and implications for research and practice

This section will first outline the study's limitations. To start with, one possible way of taking the research forward would be to explore beyond interviews and the single-organisation view. Interviews, as noted when describing and critically reviewing this method, are frequently used to collect data in grounded theory (Thompson, 2011). Yet, the essence of grounded theory is to explore interesting psycho-social processes and generate theory in the aftermath, as explicated by Aldiabat and Le Navenec (2018). These authors, along with others such as Morse and Niehaus (2009), emphasize the importance of triangulation and mixed method study designs. This has the potential to generate even thicker datasets than single methods can do (Le Navenec, 1993). Thickness could refer to information elements not covered, nor easily coverable, by interviews. Dillon (2012), for example, went into the classroom for further observations. As Charmaz (2012) states, for a researcher who pursues proximity that will create an experience, interviews remain, in her own words, unassailable. Even so, this kind of data could be complemented. Sense is not only captured in the data, but develops also in the theorising process, thus proximity to participants and their shared experiences could be beneficial. Future research is encouraged to investigate this avenue of multi-method data collection designs, most notably by considering classroom interactions.

Secondly, in agreement with this line of thought and also addressing a choice made in this study's design, a longer timeframe for interviews could be a productive avenue for further exploration. We would like to know whether LSV grows over time, e.g. we would assess LSV capacity at the beginning and at the end of the programme. That would give answers to questions regarding among which students LSV develops well, why this happens and how. Also, how would perceptions change? Who drives the change – and how is it done effectively? Who can accelerate or add more value? Future studies can embrace a range of research questions which lead to finer detail than the current study's research questions. Also, an analysis on a more granular level, by adding not only direct observation but, also a time dimension to the analysis, would take our insight further. A whole set of timing dimensions could be explored, involving pace and rhythm dynamics, which encourages investigating multiple points in time, or *ex ante* and *ex post* interviewing. Aldiabat and Le Navenec (2011) rightly point out that the boundaries between grounded theory on the one hand and ethnography on the other, could then become blurred. Yet, any related decision on the research design would be contingent on the future research question and ensuring a fit method-wise.

The third limitation is linked to a point raised in the critical self-evaluation of the method, and was observed in the implementation and execution phase. Nagel et al. (2015) advise researchers to explore mentoring or noteworthy training to hone grounded research related skills. In the execution phase of both study 2 in chapter 4 and this empirical study, the learning curve on grounded theory continued to be extremely steep. There is substantial learning by doing. Parry (2003) notes that grounded theory can easily overwhelm. This study relies on constructivist grounded theory where the researcher, regardless of the skill level he or she might have, is an essential part of the grounded theorising process. It is likely that a person who previously carried out more grounded theory studies than the one presented in chapter 4, would have more confidence and process clarity. Considering various ways to report results of grounded theory studies, this study relied on Charmaz (2012) as a blueprint, yet any constraints or limitations this source of inspiration might have had, would have been transferred too. This leads to the conclusion that a seasoned grounded theorist would have approached the studies undertaken here, differently. Any shortcomings of younger researchers carrying out studies like this one, do have an inherent limitation. After outlining the study's limitations here, the following sections outline implications for researchers and practitioners.

Finally, the alignment of research objective, question, and method represents a choice to produce a grounded theory. Generalisations and further empirical testing of the suggested hypotheses had to fall outside the scope of this study. More progress with advancing the field of LSV would have been desirable, but was out of scope.

Implications for practice

There are a number of implications to draw from this study. To start with, we consider what practitioners can learn. Two types of practitioners ought to be differentiated though. In this case there were the students as well as business school staff members in their leadership and on the academic side.

Regarding students as practitioners, the core insight is to encourage pragmatism. Learners should drive their own learning by assuming full responsibility for it. Once they become aware of inhibitors, which can come in the form of national culture, family pressure and roles, understanding what is presented in the classroom as given rather than fluid, they should explore the potentials that inarguably exist.

This applies to the technological opportunities outside of business schools, but also to the ready and basically free access to ideas on learning how to learn. At no time before in human history has there been such knowledge available on how to become more self-aware, to learn and to grow. A technologically savvy, pervasively connected online learner depends significantly less on the teacher. In the study, a major part of the student participants seem to operate according to a starkly different logic. Students in general are encouraged to become more reflective and explore how to benefit more by extending learning beyond the classroom. The following figure helps to take this discussion to a more abstract and conceptual level, as well as to integrate the literature on education.

Bolat and Bas (2018) detail four main schools of thought in educational philosophy as shown in figure 16 below. The faculty members in the study, as expressed by the student-level interviewees, seem still to operate based on an essentialist philosophy. They view their role as one replicating a society's culture by following existing role models, which construct students as passive recipients of their wisdom. Non-compliance leads to punishment, while compliance brings rewards. Students, some sooner and more extensively than others, have started to realise that the world is changing, that they can use discretion, and that input from faculty members, as well as they may be teaching, could be insufficient. This reflectivity, paired with subsequent adaptations in learning behaviour, represents core implications for students. They can drive their own development as they assume more responsibility for it. The following section turns attention to the study's implications for business schools and to the practitioners on the administrative and academic staff.

Firstly, LSV does not necessarily depend on major new budgets that school leadership has to grant, and which might go against profit seeking motives of a private business school in an ever growing process of commercialising higher education in general (Bok, 2003). Schools might be able to extend LSV without major investments in technology. There seems to be sufficient, enabling technology available and freely accessible, or at least at very affordable levels. The research partner institution, to name just one example, in one instance made only one textbook available to the entire class, seemingly to minimise cost. Yet, this might be overcome in an environment with accessible technology to support learning efforts. Such technological support can enable effective learning, also in the form of learning to learn and growing one's LSV.

Figure 16: Divergent educational philosophies of students versus faculty members encountered in this study

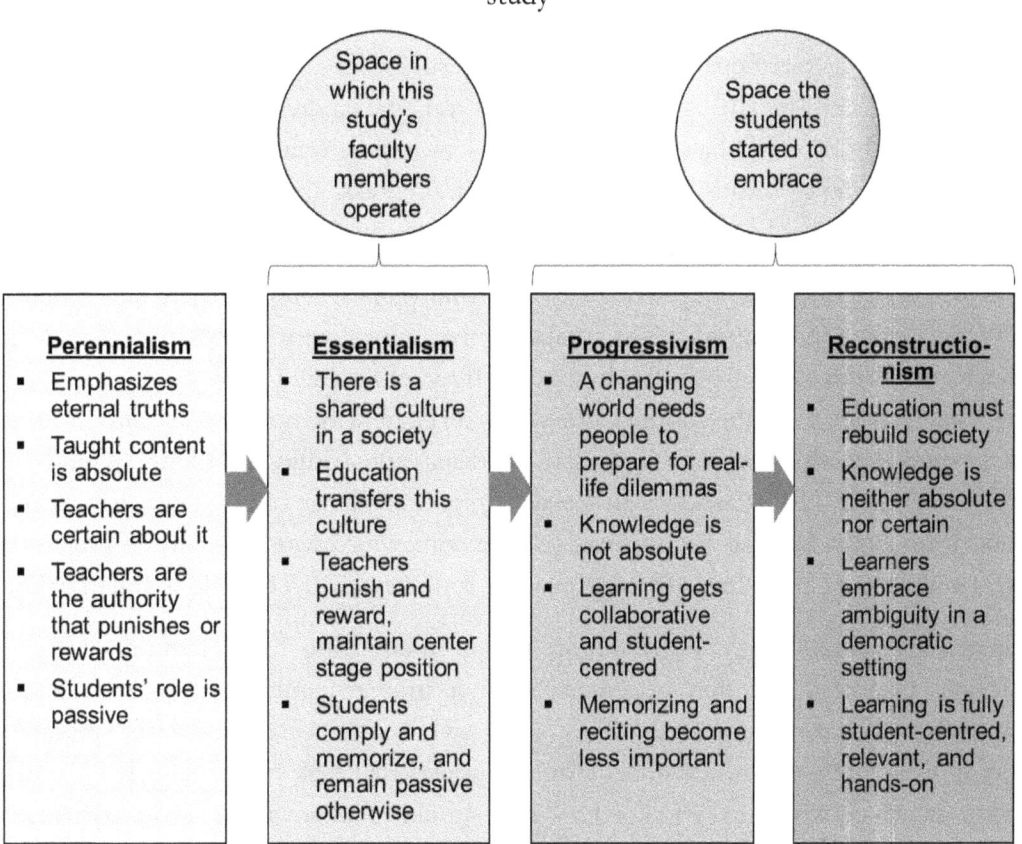

Source: Author, based on Bolat and Bas (2018)

For this to happen, more awareness training ought to take place. The field of leadership versatility development seems once more to be a step ahead in conceptualising ways to hone versatility. However, the learning style literature also alerts practitioners to how they can create an environment where students can externally regulate the development of learning styles and LSV. So far, the students at the research partner organisation seem to be left to themselves. This adversity triggers very positive dynamics as was shown by the students. If they perceived what was given to them not as fatalistically determined, but rather as situated in a fluid environment, and if they tapped into what complementors offer, they could grow their LSV. But if they were helped further with excellent instructors as an additional complementor rather than inhibitor in learning, more rapid progress could be possible. Emergence of and increasing students' LSV could be more actively facilitated. Awareness sessions can have an impact in timeframes reported and empirically proven to produce statistically significant differences in learning styles, i.e. in less than one (Siriopoulos & Pomonis, 2007) or two years (Van den Berg, 2015).

The frameworks put forward by Kaplan and Kaiser (2003a, 2003b), Goleman (1998), and Kim and Mauborgne (2014) on leadership versatility all start with awareness and eventually could move forward to intense practicing or institutionalising new ways through building routines. All three groups of these authors on leadership suggested quantitative ways to measure the status quo, which can also be done at cost effective levels and initiate change processes on the individual learner level as well as organisationally, based on clear, objective data. Besides awareness training, workshops can help in the process, e.g. on managing emotions such as fear, anxiety or stress, and career management sessions to create clarity on what future jobs would mean. These sessions could help the process of LSV emergence.

The active involvement of stakeholders who take opportunities to self-regulate and experiment, continue to be key. As Siriopoulos and Pomonis (2007) stated, active involvement alters learning styles and should be maintained as an effective process component. If practitioners follow through on this study's suggestions, they can leverage the insights the study brought with both of its parts, the emergence framework grounded in the 50+ interviews and its discussion within a preliminary and subsequent literature review. Overall, LSV represents an interesting new challenge not only for the research partner organisation of this study, but also for business schools somewhat more generally, as the literature does not indicate a wide-spread body of knowledge on how to foster LSV. The field is still in its infancy.

Finally, Mintzberg et al. (2009) provide one more insight in clarifying that practitioners often make the mistake of over planning, and that in general such a strategy could limit the development of a phenomenon that should be emergent. This study, while still focusing on the research partner organisation and the interviewees it made available, suggests that LSV might have been approached in an emergent way, which would truly foster LSV that should metamorphose into a partially emergent, but also partially planned, externally regulated process.

As mentioned earlier, this can be done in a cost-effective way with one resource person leading the way for all classes across the undergraduate or graduate courses, starting to offer learning style awareness sessions. It could be a part of the regular course directors' responsibilities.

This is in agreement with blue ocean thinking outlined in the literature review according to which transformational change should not merely be added, but should be integrated in the core of activities, roles and responsibilities. Once again, keeping a strong focus on the research partner organisation without global generalisation, figure 17 below could be described in a potential change model. As Glaser ad Strauss (1967) originally mentioned, grounded theory aims at generating and discovering a theory.

Charmaz (2012) added a constructivist perspective to it. Yet, deeply inherent in exploring the phenomenon of LSV is the question of being holistic and addressing all three core questions of a theory that Rolfe et al. (2001) put forward. This study explored the "What?" question and its implication for building an exploratory framework with the help of the grounded theory.

Section 6.2 critically reviewed what we learnt from the leadership versatility view, and one weakness emerged, namely that the learning style field often ignored the "Now what?" question. The following figure provides an initial attempt to visually specify the "Now what?" for practitioners and for the specific context of the research partner organisation.

The school leadership, according to this framework for a possible change process, starts with an awareness session for members of the school leadership, key faculty members and course directors. Keeping project governance and organisational efforts lean, one person can lead the designing and implementing of a pilot project. Subsequent awareness sessions with students should be backed up by individual test scores. Throughout the process they should maintain the crucial role of self-regulated learning. They should increase cultural awareness with regards to high power distance cultures and the technological potential readily available to complement what the school offers. Career workshops and emotional intelligence sessions can help sustain the momentum of this initiative and ensure the pilot is holistic enough, as Dunn (1996) suggested for learning style related programmes. Finally, success needs to be tracked and a version 2.0 integrating key organisational learnings from this pilot ought to follow within a reasonable timeframe.

Figure 17: Change model towards more LSV as value added in a competitive world

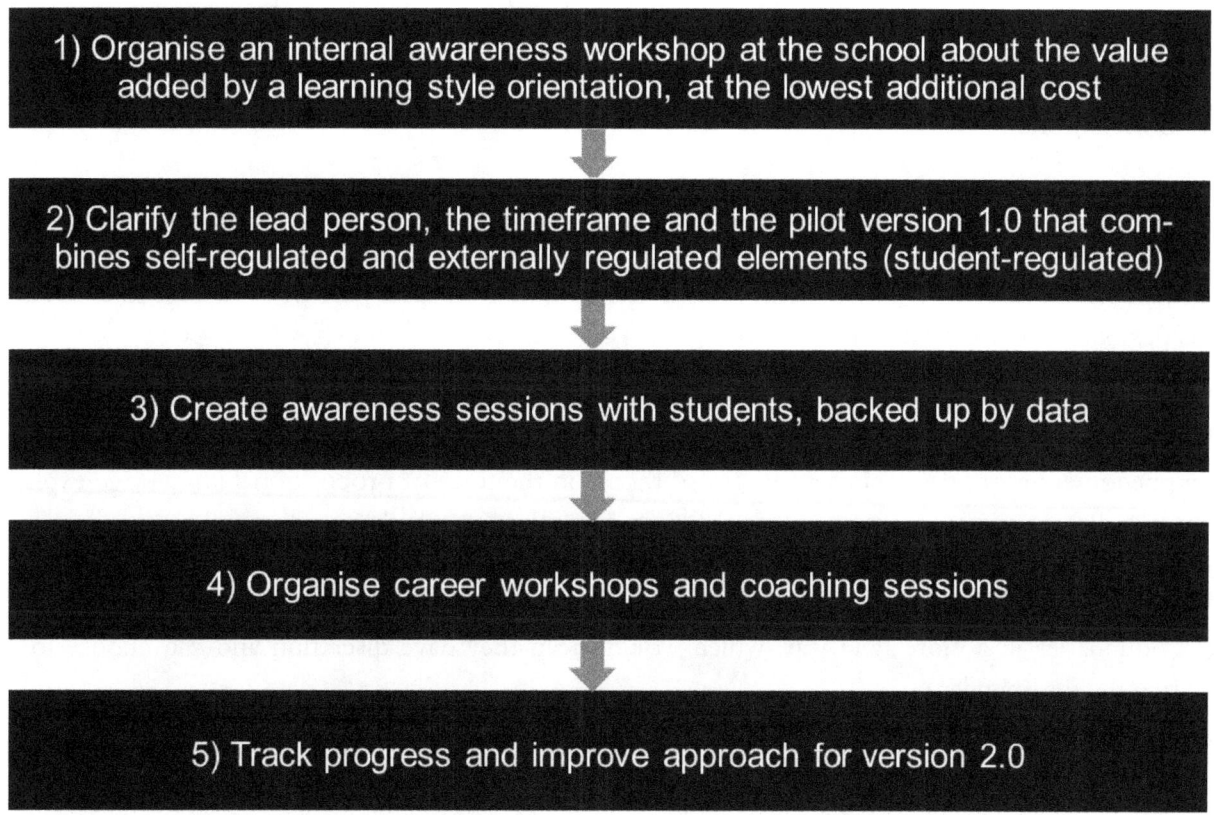

Implications for researchers

This third study on LSV produced an exploratory framework giving researchers insight into the student view on LSV in a specific setting at the research partner organisation in which a profit orientation and a culture of 'keep it mean to keep them learning' prevails. Section 6.5 produced a comprehensive set of hypotheses for future empirical testing so that findings can be verified and generalised. These efforts, although important for developing the LSV area of research, clearly lie outside the scope of this study. Further research ought to test whether similar, or for that matter different, settings show convergent or divergent dynamics. Since national cultures, organisational culture and faculty level factors, very much parallel to study 2 in chapter 4, were such dominant elements in creating adversity, studies in homogeneous and heterogeneous settings ought to follow.

From a theoretical point of view, a number of factors proposed in the literature as antecedents to learning styles, could be extended to LSV as well. The analysis above and the resulting hypotheses illustrate this. The field of LSV remains in an early stage of development, and the field of leadership versatility continues to be a strong source of inspiration for its sister field of LSV. Opportunities to advance and mature the field of LSV continue to emerge. This study's findings speak in favour of the learning experience on the one hand, but actual learning is also heavily affected by initiatives oriented to LSV, or the lack thereof.

6.7 Conclusions

The study presented in this chapter addresses the gap in the literature regarding LSV. This section responds to what Bhagat et al. (2015) eloquently described as: "Developing the flexibility to respond productively to all sorts of instructional situations would be a laudable goal … How best to encourage this flexibility is yet to be determined" (p. 59).

With this third study on LSV that focuses on the student view, I constructed a framework grounded in data based on a number of interviews with students in order to better understand how they experience the phenomenon of LSV. This new grounded theory in the form of propositional knowledge explains that two dimensions matter tremendously. Firstly, we reflect on whether students take a fatalistic view on what the school offers, which would mean learners simply comply with what is required. Alternatively, we investigate whether a learner understands the classroom with all of its opportunities and boundaries in a more fluid way, which would mean they have discretion and can choose to go beyond the set boundaries.

Secondly, we relate to what the individual learner does in light of the ecosystem in more general terms. We investigate whether learners spot, embrace, and utilise accessible complementors by relying on the few teachers who use modern and helpful methods, as well as on the seemingly vast potential technology offers. Additionally, we determine whether individual learners understand that they have discretion in either choosing to comply, or at least partly to move beyond the limitations a high power distance culture imposes. Such limitations show in strong pressure and boundaries set by the national culture and family expectations.

Based on the 'emergence' grounded theory that views LSV as driven by self-regulating learners in a situation of partial adversity and partial potential in their ecosystem, this study has outlined implications for practitioners while retaining its focus on the single organisational setting of the research partner organisation. It provides a foundation for future studies by producing hypotheses for future research. Overall, the study could serve as a crucial step in a larger theorising process on LSV, from a student view but also from a broader perspective, as the results can be linked to the previously presented studies 1 and 2.

Moving beyond the concept of LSV, the research outcomes can be interpreted as arguing in favour of Viji and Benedict's (2017b) proposed taxonomy of ingenuity and connectedness (TIC) for an ever more connected learner. Technology has been liberating to the individual learner, complementing the learning journeys offered by the business school in focus, and compensating for some weaknesses. Future studies can contribute to generalising this insight to be applicable beyond the research partner organisation. This study makes no claim of universal validity, as it was not in the scope of the research objectives and linked methodology.

Chapter 7: Implications for theory and practice

7.1 Overview of the findings in light of the research projects

A number of researchers in the educational field apply grounded theory as a method with which to investigate practical issues that aim to trigger change and improve situations as well as lives (Dillon et al., 2000). The studies in this research project on LSV follow this logic, yet first posit the necessity to work towards better understanding the phenomenon of LSV and its importance. This section revisits the research objectives of this study originally presented in chapter 1.3. Table 16 below summarises the outcomes.

Firstly, the research aimed to explore whether learning versatility is in fact, to date, an under-researched construct. The literature reviews of the three studies included in this project lay out several related concepts, yet none of them cover the LSV concept with a comparable focus or scope and in a comparably explicit way. Therefore, this research objective has been achieved.

Secondly, the research aimed to trigger a process of not only conceptualising, but also operationalising LSV so that researchers could start to learn more about the LSV proxies and would be able to improve them over time. To my best knowledge, based on three literature reviews applying backward and forward snowballing techniques along with feedback after presenting initial results at learning related conferences, this study provides the first scale to operationalise LSV, as is described in chapter 2.

Thirdly, the research intended to show that LSV can be an important construct within the field of learning. This was done by means of a regression analysis in a quantitative research design. LSV has been found to impact students' grades in a statistically significant way. Therefore, this research objective has been achieved as well. There were several other learning related outcomes, such as satisfaction. Yet, it seems that even with less evidence of LSV, students can be satisfied with what is offered to them.

Fourthly, the study pursued exploratory research that would give more insight on how faculty members perceive the LSV construct. Chapter 4 presented a grounded theory model illustrating hygiene factors that institutional leaders in the study's partner organisation should attend to if they aspire to make progress with introducing and gaining advantage from the construct. Hypotheses for further testing and generalisation completed the analysis.

The research project also intended to gather more insights and construct a grounded theory on students' perspectives on LSV. The third empirical study presented in chapter 6 sheds more light on this aspect. Similar to the preceding qualitative study, the aim was not to generalise, but first to secure rich insights and theorise. Overall, the research objectives have been achieved. There are limitations, however, which are set out in the next section.

Table 16: Overview of outcomes based on research objectives

	Research objectives	Outcomes
1)	To establish whether learning versatility is in fact a hitherto under-researched construct and how LSV relates to other key learning related constructs.	LSV can be distinguished from other constructs. It represents one way to further evolve the learning style field.
2)	If so, to trigger the process of operationalising LSV in order to commence the crucial process of measuring and building proxies for it.	Chapter 2 proposes and applies a first proxy of an LSV scale.
3)	To show the construct's importance, i.e. to investigate whether LSV impacts study performance, for example in the form of grades as being representative of study outcomes.	Chapter 2 provides an initial empirical substantiation of the construct, within the constraints of the study. Chapters 4 and 6 allude to the potential to improve learning
4)	Gather additional qualitative insight, by means of interviews, on how faculty members and students perceive LSV.	Chapters 4 and 6 provide a context-rich, in-depth analysis of both the instructor as well as the student view on the phenomenon and propose new grounded theories.

7.2 Limitations

The individual studies presented in chapters 2, 4 and 6 all have limitations that are discussed in dedicated sections in each case. As mentioned before, "research is the art of the feasible" (Blaxter et al., 2006, p. 157). Therefore, for this study it was necessary to take decisions on the position of the research as well as the research design (cf. the more detailed discussion on pragmatism in chapter 6.3). This section intends to make the study's limitations more transparent so that future research can overcome them. Table 17 summarises these limitations.

Table 17: Summary of limitations across the three empirical studies on LSV

Limitations of study 1 and the quantitative research on the importance of LSV for learning outcomes	Limitations of study 2 and the qualitative research on the faculty view on LSV	Limitations of study 3 and the qualitative research on the student view on LSV
• The study was purely descriptive, not prescriptive. More research is needed to investigate how grades can be improved with attention to LSV. • The results for non-grade related learning outcomes were inconsistent and weak. More research needs to explore the link between LSV and outcomes other than grades. • The quantitative research design was not able to shed light on the main scenarios of eco-effectiveness, eco-sufficiency, eco-inefficiency, and eco-ineffectiveness. Qualitative studies on these scenarios can provide rich insight for completing the analysis. • The operationalisation of the first LSV proxy was pragmatic. Future studies should work on better conceptualisations and operationalisations.	• The qualitative study was situated in a mono-culture setting, which limits how much one can generalise. Future studies would benefit from repeating the study in the same and in different cultural contexts. • The study investigated a single organisation and a specific ownership setting. Future studies ought to revisit the impact of ownership and the business model in place. • There is disagreement on what the right process is for grounded theory. Future studies could elaborate on the impact of both the chosen grounded theory approach, as well as the impact of the researcher in the subjective, abductive process. • The study could not differentiate between the actual behaviour of faculty members and their potential to hone LSV. Future studies could take a prescriptive approach and test its outcomes.	• A single-organisation study offers depth but does not capture the diversity possible across settings. • The study carried out interviews at one point in time. Accompanying students over time could capture more of the dynamics, e.g. by carrying out *ex ante* and *ex post* interviews. • The study relied on interviews which the grounded theorist Charmaz (2012) described as indispensable for this type of study. Still, in-class observations could have led to even more proximity to those perceiving the phenomenon. • The learning curve on carrying out even the second study was quite steep. Efforts were made to carry out blind spots, but more experience would have been helpful. • Generalisations were out of the study's scope.

The studies' limitations originate from the very nascent state in which the research field of LSV currently is. The study entails a first-time conceptualisation and operationalisation, first-time exploration of faculty and student views, first-time scrutiny of the concept at this level of integration, all of which had to start somewhere. The single-organisation setup should be overcome in future studies by collecting similar empirical data from multiple organisations.

7.3 Implications for theory – towards a future research agenda for learning styles versatility

The first implication is the following. While the field of leadership has transitioned to a point where versatility is acknowledged (see the in-depth discussion in chapter 6.2, figure 13), the field of learning styles lags behind. Until now and more specifically, business schools have not proactively reoriented themselves towards this kind of versatility. Study 1 suggests work towards something similar to, or even a replication of Kaplan and Kaiser's (2003a) efforts in changing the focus from leadership styles towards leadership versatility with an equal large-scale empirical testing effort. Based on the results of this research initiative on LSV, I have presented an initial step in this direction. For the first time, quantitative evidence has been collected which substantiates the call for more attention to LSV. Statistically significant results have been produced. The main task is to view the gap outlined in the table above, and to address it with new data. To date, there is no other study that quantitatively gives evidence of the importance of LSV.

Business schools are complex adaptive systems (Tuncer & Ali, 2017). For actual change to take place, the quantitative analysis has to be complemented by qualitative, in-depth insights as I have done in studies 2 and 3. The first study acknowledges that especially the initial operationalisation of LSV has to be pragmatic in order to trigger a learning process that will inform us on suitable instruments.

The following figure summarises a provisional path for current and future research efforts based on a mapping framework suggested by Peng (2006). By adding the versatility view to learning styles in this study, as was done earlier in the field of leadership, I was able to add a new twist to a known domain. Quantitatively, study 1 substantiated and elaborated the importance of LSV. Study 2 provided a new theory – a hygiene factor-based framework and a specific stakeholder orientation in which faculty members make up the stakeholder group that I interviewed and whose views I then analysed. A grounded theory reflection on students in terms of LSV complemented this view.

In the literature, to date, no LSV measure has been conceptualised or operationalised. Peng (2006) suggests a framework for describing possible research projects and their intended outcomes as part of mapping trajectories in research agendas. After confirming that a switch from a style orientation towards a versatility orientation has taken place in a related field, the research I present here indicates that the next stage in the learning style field is opening up.

Figure 18: Categorising research efforts and showing a path for research related to LSV

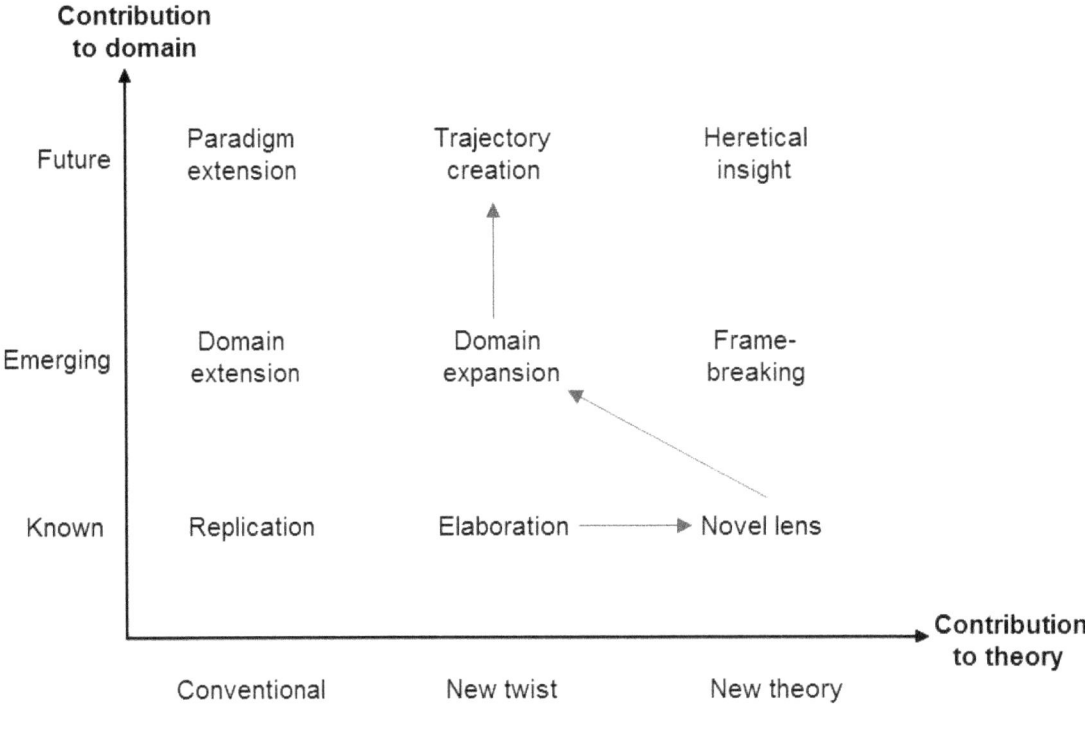

Source: Based on Peng (2006, p. 5)

Thus, the research links Ashby's (2011) law of requisite variety to the concept of LSV, and drafts two matrices which eventually identify four conceptual cases of an integrated versatility-oriented ergo-ecology. In line with the research trajectory outlined in figure 19 above, this should bring a domain expansion and build a trajectory for the learning style versatility field.

Throughout the three studies, potential emerged for expanding the domain of learning styles and LSV further. Study 1, for example, indicated that women have a higher average LSV than men. Adding the gender perspective could have two effects. Firstly, gender is an under-researched topic in the field of learning styles and LSV. Therefore we can recognize potential for developing a gender-oriented versatility view. Secondly, the gender view alluded to in study 1 can enrich the field of gender studies in general. Figure 20 places this potentially new view in the context of gender studies, thus extending the review of periods suggested by Joshi et al. (2015).

Figure 19: Periods in gender studies

| Period 1 in the 70s: acknowledging the plight of women | Period 2 in the 80s: Identifying the barriers | Period 3 in the 90s: Rendering the barriers view more sophisticated | Period 4 in the 2000s: From gender differences to dissimilarity and diversity | Period 5 from 2019 on: Focus on learning superiority? |

Source: Extending Joshi et al. (2015)

Besides the potential of expanding the domain of learning styles and LSV, the domain of gender studies could equally be enriched by adding considerations not only of equality or general diversity, but also of abilities to learn in a VUCA world.

Finally, and in line with Peng (2006), the task of overall trajectory construction remains. Considering the aforementioned limitations, the trajectory for LSV could be described as given in the following paragraph. A new study should replicate this one in similar and dissimilar settings so that results can be confirmed or disproven. This applies for the quantitative as well as the qualitative studies. This would be a key step towards the kind of generalisation this study could not claim. Researchers should then continue the quest to generalise by testing the hypotheses derived here among stakeholders.

Methodologically, other researchers have called for more grounded theories to gain a better understanding of the individual researcher's role and how this changes in diverging contexts. Finally, research needs to move from a descriptive towards a prescriptive approach, largely similar to developments in the leadership field, where considerations on how to become increasingly versatile have been discussed more extensively although not as holistically as this could have been done.

7.4 Implications for practice – students, faculty and business school leadership

This research project aimed to produce a better understanding of the phenomenon, a 'proof of concept' in terms of substantiating the importance of the concept, and initial actionable knowledge for business schools and its key actors, such as deans, programme directors, admission team members, faculty and students. As part of a lifelong learning initiative, this study was also intended to equip me as a researcher and business school faculty member with such knowledge. The three audience categories (managers, lecturers, students) and the beneficiaries on the practice side of this research are dealt with separately in the following sections.

Implications for the practitioners

When it comes to deans, programme directors and faculty members, this research project and its constituting three studies have produced several important insights. Firstly, there is an emerging insight on how to deal with the situation in which business schools are attacked for fostering unethical behaviour and becoming irrelevant (e.g. Mintzberg, 2004). Three key messages emerge:

Firstly, a greater focus on LSV complies with the principles of responsible management education because teaching unfolds with more attention to the individuality, and therefore to the human dignity, of a key stakeholder group – the learners.

Secondly, for too long, too little value has been offered to students. Moving beyond teaching and honing hard skills in organisational functions, such as procurement and supply chain management, operations, marketing and the support functions of human resources, finance, IT, etc., helps differentiate institutions. Thus, those institutions that adopt the logic of attending to learning, learning styles, and LSV sooner, and offer clear added value in an ever-more complex or VUCA world (detailed in chapter 2.2) are bound to be better equipped and thus better rated. Learning to become a more versatile learner represents a clear competitive advantage to the careers of business school graduates.

Thirdly, embracing the concept of LSV can challenge the business model of a school, such as one that is highly profit-oriented but that has less human dignity awareness, as is illustrated in the example given in this research project. Choosing to change the fundamental logic of what they will teach, learn and focus on, even if their outlook is profit-oriented, constitutes a litmus test for business school deans, programme directors and faculty members. It offers a clear and constructive way of addressing and implementing the addendum principle of the United Nations Global Compact Principles of Responsible Management Education on attention to human dignity and sustainability in education. The literature reviews allow for the conclusion that, so far, instilling such ideals of integrity in students has not been afforded adequate attention. Embracing the concept of LSV can help a school to advance.

Tempelaar (2006) explains that honing metacognitive skills generally turns out to be more challenging than sharpening students' cognitive skills, such as is done in teaching finance, operations or strategy in the business school context. This has implications for the faculty side of a business school. The school needs to be reoriented towards a holistic, integrated selection, promotion, development, retention and incentivisation of faculty. In appointing faculty members, business schools should prioritise candidates who are interested in and show the potential to observe human dignity, so that the respective skills will be built up and learning journeys redesigned.

Kabele (2010) refers to the debate on structure versus agency in this context of faculty and learning journey development. The question is whether the business school as the institution or structure, should primarily drive students' learning journey, or whether individual faculty members should act as agents and take the initiative even when the structures in which they work are less conducive to their learning. There is no general answer to this question, because each school has its own situational characteristics. All deans and programme directors are called upon to foster these human dignity and LSV concerns, as such a choice is morally better and represents more value. At the same time, all faculty members are called upon to launch experiments that will enable a positive learning curve even if their institutions do not promote learning innovations in terms of LSV as part of considering human dignity. The individuals turning out to be more effective at it can then serve as role models for others.

Besides the ethical considerations, the idea underlying LSV as a concept and as a research agenda, is one that steers away from the publish-or-perish culture which is currently rampant in the business school world, as was discussed in chapter 2.2.

Rather, the intention is to overcome the relevance gaps in both business school research and teaching which were highlighted in the criticism articulated in the literature reviews. LSV has the potential to become a new dominant logic (Hill, 2000) for business school learning. Institutional theory identifies such kinds of dominant logic in industries, and shows that the current dominant logic focuses too limitedly on ethics, while presenting fragmented coursework across corporate functions, with insufficient relevance as the literature review sections revealed.

Considering myself as a practitioner as well, I include implications the work has for my work more generally. Working both as academic program director and as faculty member on several masters programs, I have for a number of years been using learning style surveys at the beginning of programs, introducing them on the launch day. I discuss learning styles at the beginning of the program to alert participants to the various learning modes and their preferences. The main shift this research project triggers for such introductory surveys, is that in future I would emphasize individual style or preferences less. Rather, I will discuss participants' learning style versatility and reflect on how to possibly improve it further. Working in an institution that puts extremely high emphasis on quality, I would use the one-on-one coaching session I usually schedule with course participants to discuss individual learning style versatility along with development ideas. Thereby, I would clarify who shoulders which responsibility for an individual learner's development.

Summary of the implications for practice

As the introductory chapter clarified, the field of learning styles shows controversies. Proposed options to overcome dilemmas include either abandoning the field, or innovating it. I chose the latter, especially in light of the tremendous needs within business schools to add more value. Attacking institutions without presenting constructive alternatives is the easy route; this research project preferred a more constructive procedure. It informs school leaders, course directors and faculty members that learning style versatility can matter and demonstrates how (within the constraints and limitations of the three-partite study) the phenomenon can be better understood. Such insight is crucial to trigger action. The The research project encourages and equips managers and faculty to reflect on whether applicants' learning style versatility could be added to the selection criteria as it impacts students' ability to perform. Also, contextual factors matter. Practitioners should reflect on whether they operate in an equally disenabling environment as the sample organization. Then, hygiene factors ought to be taken care of first. As for students, schools can encourage them to pragmatically move beyond what is offered, to drive their learning. Since the establishment and growth of business schools, we have probably not had 'complementors' as enabling as they are today!

7.5 Implications for grounded theory researchers

Research involving grounded theory ought to be reflective. Active experimentation can help advance the learning curve. There are limitations to what can be acquired by reading or attending research seminars focused on sharing conceptual knowledge. The key to learning in business school contexts is that researchers can embark on practice grounded theory studies before embracing the main studies on LSV so as to advance their learning by doing. Peer discussions and further reading can and should accompany the process of training but might not necessarily suffice; success in training could eventually be contingent on the learning style.

Further, the literature demonstrates just how divergent and fragmented grounded theory as a field has become. Researchers should be alert not to focus on the differences only, but also help others to learn more about similarities. After a phase of divergence, what grounded theory possibly needs is to converge within and across the respective opinion camps.

7.6 Summary

I have carried out three studies that complement one another. Each study had a specific focus with an aligned approach regarding the literature review, a research methodology and method, corresponding field work with primary data collection, and subsequent analysis. The module structure of this doctorate study's programme, relates to these studies that represent the three submissions for three modules of a structured doctorate programme. There are limitations as outlined above, yet there are also clearly demarcated knowledge gains. LSV matters, and so does the context in which faculty function; also, students show unique behaviour when they are challenged to cope with a complex situation regarding the aims, courses, teaching modes and materials in business schools considering the principles of management education in a fast-changing world, today.

Chapter 8: Conclusions

8.1 Complying with the Principles of Responsible Management Education

This study has frequently mentioned the crucial role of the UN's PRME as directing a moral course of action. It is important that business schools, researchers and practitioners more than merely acknowledge the existence of such principles; importantly, they should also implement them, e.g. by acknowledging the individuality of learners which shows in personal LSV. Application of the PRME further shows in business schools offering relevant value to the students, as well as a learning environment where faculty can reach good performance levels. The addendum principle prescribes that schools themselves must become role models.

The research presented in this submission consciously complies with this call for more research initiatives to improve organisations and practice in general. Two grounded theory studies helped with a true, in-depth 'verstehen'. LSV has great potential in light of the call to build more ethical business schools, research agendas and learning journeys. National culture and profit optimisation that shows, for example, in poor faculty development and a weak learning philosophy, can impede progress. Students, in turn, seem to adapt swiftly by embarking on coping behaviour and leveraging technology potential now available outside of what is offered by the school. This reflects a pragmatic, self-regulated process which could benefit from being further facilitated by the school.

8.2 The strong case for Ashby's law of requisite variety

Besides the moral anchor with which the PRME has provided this study, I have relied on Ashby's (2011) law of requisite variety for theoretical underpinning. It encourages organisations to internally mirror the complexity encountered in the external environment. LSV represents a promising construct. In a VUCA world, LSV can be a suitable coping mechanism to establish and ensure fit. In line with Marzano and Kendall's (2007) role of the self-system, LSV could be one of the decisive factors that would allow learners to feel self-efficacy to an extent that spurs their interest in a topic, encourages their motivation, and assists in maintaining it; it could support them in learning more, and in feeling sufficiently able to cope with VUCA world subjects. Still, fostering LSV requires the skills to build up precisely this complexity in the right place. While this study's single-setting-based grounded theories did not aim to deliver generalisable results, it supports the idea that hygiene factors, as well as the type of students and their particular interests can play a role.

8.3 The case for a self-structured leadership pipeline for business schools

An important question that remains is whether aspiring future leaders in business schools should wait for their institutions to provide the right training for a multi-year development, or should take an active agency role and innovate in the courses they teach or direct. It could save a great deal of time if such aspiring future leaders were to take full responsibility of their own developmental journey. They are encouraged to develop the next generation of organisational solutions so that when their time to lead comes, they have prepared initiatives and are more prepared for their new responsibilities than they would otherwise have been. This study offers them insight on an emerging field in which they could proactively learn more. Put more abstractly, this study should also be understood as an example. These three studies could assist in developing new insights that prepare students in advance to become future leaders in business schools within a reasonable time frame. Therefore, this study encourages future leaders in business schools to proactively prepare for and drive their own learning.

8.4 Effectively addressing a research gap

Reviewing the literature, it soon became obvious that "developing the flexibility to respond productively to all sorts of instructional situations would be a laudable goal ... How best to encourage this flexibility is yet to be determined" (Bhagat et al., 2015, p. 59). This tripartite research project gathered initial empirical insights to confirm the statement that LSV is important (cf. study 1). Being a more versatile learner is linked to better grades in a statistically significant way – based on an initial quantitative study. The literature on learning styles can and should be extended to include more LSV considerations. Statements and insights, such as Irvine and York's (1995) "all students are capable of learning, provided the learning environment attends to a variety of learning styles" (p. 494), could evolve to now assert the following: all students are capable of learning and gaining more success, the better their learning versatility is developed. A strong LSV would enable them more readily to cope with different environments.

How best to encourage additional flexibility or versatility then depends on the stakeholder view (cf. study 2 and 3). Without generalising, yet actively exploring and understanding LSV in a very specific business school context, this study has produced two grounded theories. A number of hygiene factors emerged as prerequisites for faculty to build a high performance system towards more LSV. Students represented in this study showed great pragmatism and, as the emergence framework outlined, started to leverage potential for their own learning success. Finally, the study also produced a roadmap and research agenda for future research in this still nascent field of LSV. Therefore, next steps, e.g. on confirming derived hypotheses, are clear. I trust that the pointers given here will inspire and catalyse further research to build momentum in this field now that it is – within the constraints of the implemented studies – understood better.

Reference list

- Aalto, A., Heponiemi, T., Väänänen, A., Bergbom, B., Sinervo, T., & Elovainio, M. (2014). Is working in culturally diverse working environment associated with physicians' work-related well-being? A cross-sectional survey study among Finnish physicians. *Health Policy*, *117*(2), 187–194.

- Adler, R., Whiting, R., & Wynn-Williams, K. (2004). Student-led and teacher-led case presentations: Empirical evidence about learning styles in an accounting course. *Accounting Education*, *13*(2), 213–229.

- Ahmadaliev, D., Chen, X., & Abduvohidov, M. (2018). A web-based instrument to initialize learning style: An interactive questionnaire instrument. *International Journal of Emerging Technologies in Learning*, *13*(12), 238–246.

- Aldiabat, K., & Le Navenec, C. (2011). Philosophical roots of classic grounded theory: Its foundations in symbolic interactionism. *The Qualitative Report*, *16*(4), 1063–1080.

- Aldiabat, K., & Le Navenec, C. (2018). Data saturation: The mysterious step in grounded theory methodology. *The Qualitative Report*, *23*(1), 245–261.

- Al-Saadi, H. (2014). *Demystifying ontology and epistemology in research methods*. https://www.researchgate.net/publication/260244813_Demystifying_Ontology_and_Epistemology_in_Research_Methods?enrichId=rgreq-3329e770cfe503f5ad798fefd5c9ee15-XXX&enrichSource=Y292ZXJQYWdlOzI2MDI0NDgxMztBUzoxMDMzMTY4NzI3NjEzN DRAMTQwMTY0NDA3MDE1Mg%3D%3D&el=1_x_2&_esc=publicationCoverPdf

- Alzain, A., Clark, S., Ireson, G., & Jwaid, A. (2018). Learning personalization based on learning style instruments. *Advances in Science, Technology and Engineering Systems*, *3*(3), 108–15.

- Amann, W., & Goh, J. (Eds.). (2017). *Phronesis in business schools: reflections on teaching and learning*. IAP.

- Amann, W., & Stachowicz, A. (Eds.). (2013). *Integrity in organizations – Building the foundations for humanistic management*. Palgrave.

- Amann, W., & Khan, S. (2011). The business schools' role in developing leaders: silent partners in crime or the cradle of a new generation? *Human Resource Management Journal*, *6*, 11–17.

- Amann, W., & Khan, S. (2012). Complexity capabilities as a prerequisite for organizational innovations and successful responses for universal equilibrium. *International Journal of Organization Theory and Behavior*, *15*(4), 502–519.

- Amann, W., & Khan, S. (2013). A complexity view on integrity dilemmas in leadership – How conceptual clarity impacts practices. *Journal of Organization and Management*, *5*, 43–56.

- Amann, W., & Khan, S. (2017). *Internationalization journeys: The impact of internationalization on organizational culture*. Winterwork.

- Amann, W., & Stachowicz, A. (Eds.). (2012). *Business integrity in practice – worldwide case studies*. UN PRME.

- Amann, W., & Tripathi, S. (2017). *Corporate yoga: A primer for sustainable and humanistic leadership*. IAP.

- Amann, W., Fenton, P., Zackariasson, P., & Kerrets, M. (Eds.). (2012). *New perspectives in management education*. Excel Publishing.

- Amann, W., Kleinhempel, M., Nieffer, R., Lewis, A., Tripathi, S., & Stachowicz, A. (2015). *Implementing the anti-corruption toolkit*. Greenleaf.

- Amann, W., Khan, S., Tripathi, S., & Stachowicz, A. (Eds.). (2014). *Innovations in executive education*. Winterwork.

- Amann, W., Khan, S., Tripathi, S., & Stachowicz, A. (Eds.). (2018). *Responsible executive education*. Winterwork.

- Amann, W., Nedopil, C., & Steger, U. (2011). The meta-challenge of complexity for global companies. *Journal of Database Marketing and Customer Strategy Management*, *18*(3), 200–204.

- Amann, W., Nedopil, C., & Steger, U. (2012). Understanding and managing complexity. *European Business Review*, March/April, 52–57.

- Amann, W., Pirson, M., Spitzeck, H., Dierksmeier, C., & Von Kimakowitz, E. (Eds.). (2011). *Business schools under fire – humanistic management education as the way forward*. Palgrave.

- Amann, W., Puempin, C., & Sornette, D. (2008). How power laws may shape the future of strategy. *Critical Eye*, *17*, 21–26.

- Amann, W., Spitzeck, H., Pirson, M., & Von Kimakowitz, E. (Eds.). (2011). *Humanistic management in practice*. Palgrave.

- Amann, W., Tripathi, S., Khan, S., & Janardhanam, K. (2017). *Making management studies matter – towards phronesis 2.0 in business schools and companies*. Himalaya Publishing.

- Anderson, L., Krathwohl, D., Airasian, P., Cruikshank, K., Mayer, R., Pintrich, P., Raths, J., & Wittrock, M. (Eds.). (2001). *A taxonomy for learning, teaching, and assessing: A revision of Bloom's taxonomy of educational objectives*. Allyn & Bacon.

- Andreff, W. (2017). Complexity triggered by economic globalization – the issue of online betting-related match fixing. *Systems*, *5*(12), 1–18.

- Aramburu, N., Sáenz, J., & Rivera, O. (2006). Organizational learning, change process, and evolution of management systems. *The Learning Organization*, *13*(5), 434–454.

- Archibald, M, Ambagtsheer, R., Casey, M., & Lawless, M. (2019). Using Zoom videoconferencing for qualitative data collection: Perceptions and experiences of researchers and participants. *International Journal of Qualitative Methods*, *18*, 1–18.

- Argyris, C. (1977). Organizational learning and management information systems. *Accounting, Organizations and Society*, *2*(2), 113–123.

- Arino, A., LeBaron, C., & Milliken, F. J. (2016). Publishing qualitative research in academy of management discoveries. *Academy of Management Discoveries*, *2*(2), 109–113.

- Arumugam, P., & Christy, V. (2018). Analysis of clustering and classification methods for actionable knowledge. *Materials Today: Proceedings*, *5*(1), 1839–1845.

- Ashby, W. (2011). Variety, constraint, and the law of requisite variety. *Emergence: Complexity and Organization*, *13*(1/2), 190–207.

- Averbook, J. (2014). HR's ultimate survival guide: The only thing constant is change, but this Time it's now or never. *Workforce Solutions Review*, *5*(1), 5–6.

- Baeten, M., Kyndt, E., Struyven, K., & Dochy, F. (2010). Using student-centered learning environments to stimulate deep approaches to learning: Factors encouraging or discouraging their effectiveness. *Educational Research Review*, *5*(3), 243–260.

- Bennett, C. (1995). *Comprehensive multicultural education*. Simon & Schuster.

- Bennis, W., & O'Toole, J. (2005). How business schools lost their way. *Harvard Business Review*, *83*(5), 96–104.

- Berger, R. (2013). Now I see it, now I don't: researcher's position and reflexivity in qualitative research. *Qualitative Research*, *15*(2), 1–16.

- Betof, E., Owens, L., & Todd, S. (2014). The key to success in a VUCA world: leaders as teachers is the winning strategy that great companies have used to manage volatility, uncertainty, complexity, and ambiguity (VUCA) confronting their leaders. *T+D*, *68*(7), 38–44.

- Bhagat, A., Vyas, R., & Singh, T. (2015). Students' awareness of learning styles and their perceptions to a mixed method approach for learning. *International Journal of Applied & Basic Medical Research*, *5*(1), 58–65.

- Bhattacharya, A. (2010). Management of Indian management education. *Economic and Political Weekly*, *45*(24), 14–17.

- Billett, S. (2001). Learning through work: workplace affordances and individual engagement. *Journal of Workplace Learning, 13*(5), 209–214.

- Birks, M., & Mills, J. (2015). *Grounded theory: a practical guide*. Sage.

- Blaxter, L., Hughes, C., & Tight, M. (2006). *How to research*. Open University Press.

- Bloom, B. (1956). *Taxonomy of educational objectives: the classification of educational goals*. Longmans.

- Blumer, H. (1969). *Symbolic interactionism: Perspective and method*. Prentice Hall.

- Boekaerts, M. (1991). Subjective competence, appraisals and self-assessment. *Learning and Instruction, 1*, 1–17.

- Bok, D. (2003). *Universities in the marketplace: The commercialization of higher education*. Princeton University Press.

- Bolat, Y., & Bas, M. (2018). The perception of the educational philosophy in the industrial age 4.0 and the educational philosophy productivity of teacher candidates. *World Journal of Education, 8*(3), 149–161.

- Bourke, B. (2014). Positionality: Reflecting on the research process. *The Qualitative Report, 19*, 1–9.

- Bowen, G. (2008). Naturalistic inquiry and the saturation concept: a research note. *Qualitative Research, 8*(1), 137–152.

- Bowers, B., & Schatzman, L. (2009). Dimensional analysis. In J. Morse, P. Stern, J. Corbin, B. Bowers, K. Charmaz, & A. Clarke (Eds.), *Developing grounded theory: The second generation* (pp. 186–126). Left Coast Press.

- Brandenburger, A., & Nalebuff, B. (1996). Inside Intel. *Harvard Business Review. 74*(96), 168–175.

- Brennenstuhl D., & Catalenello (1979). Using learning styles to improve academic effectiveness. *Journal of Experiential Learning and Simulation, 1*, 29–37.

- Bryman, A. (2008). *Social Research Methods*. Oxford University Press.

- Burd, E., Smith, S., & Reisman, S. (2015). Exploring business models for MOOCs in higher education. *Innovative Higher Education, 40*, 37–49.

- Butler, D. (2008). Translational research: Crossing the valley of death. *Nature, 453*, 840–842

- Cameron, R., Clark, P., De Zwaan, L., English, D., Lamminmaki, D., O'Leary, C., Rae, K., & Sands, J. (2015). The importance of understanding student learning styles in accounting degree programs. *Australian Accounting Review, 25*(3), 218–231.

- Canfield, J., Hansen, M. V., Hewitt, L., & Kasuma, H. (2015). *The power of focus*. Sendirian Berhad.

- Case, R. (2013). The unfortunate consequences of Bloom's taxonomy. *Social Education*, *77*(4), 196–200.

- Cassidy, S. (2010). Learning Styles: An overview of theories, models, and measures. *Educational Psychology*, *24*(4), 419–444.

- Chandrasegaran, S., Badam, S., Kisselburgh, L., Ramani, K., & Elmqvist, N. (2017). Integrating visual analytics support for grounded theory. Practice in qualitative text analysis. *Computer Graphics Forum*, *36*(3), 201–212.

- Charan, R., Noel, J., & Drotter, S. (2011). *The leadership pipeline: how to build the leadership powered company*. Jossey-Bass.

- Charmaz, K. (2000). Constructivist and objectivist grounded theory. In N. Denzin & Y. Lincoln (Eds.), *Handbook of qualitative research* (2nd ed., pp. 509–535). Sage.

- Charmaz, K. (2006). *Constructing grounded theory: A practical guide through qualitative analysis* (1st ed.). Sage.

- Charmaz, K. (2012). Qualitative interviewing and grounded theory analysis. In F. Gubrium, A. Holstein, A. Marvasti & K. McKinney (Eds.), *The SAGE Handbook of Interview Research: The complexity of the craft* (pp. 675–694). Sage.

- Charmaz, K. (2014). *Constructing grounded theory* (2nd ed.). Sage.

- Charmaz, K. (2016). The power of stories, the potential of theorizing for social justice studies. In N. Denzin & M. Giardina (Eds.), *Qualitative inquiry through a critical lens* (pp. 41–56). Routledge.

- Charmaz, K. (2017). The power of constructivist grounded theory for critical inquiry. *Qualitative Inquiry*, *23*(1), 34–45.

- Charmaz, K., & Belgrave, L. (2019). Thinking about data with grounded theory. *Qualitative Inquiry*, *25*(8) 743–753.

- Chenitz, W. (1986). Getting started: The research proposal for a grounded theory study. In W. Chenitz & J. Swanson (Eds.), *From practice to grounded theory: Qualitative research in nursing* (pp. 39–47). Addison-Wesley.

- Christians, C. (2000). Ethics and politics in qualitative research. In N. Denzin, & Y. Lincoln (Eds.), *Handbook of qualitative research* (pp.133–154). Sage.

- Christensen, H., Horn, M., & Johnson, C. (2010). *Disrupting class: how disruptive innovation will change the way the world learns*. McGraw-Hill

- Chun Tie, Y., Birks, M., & Francis, K. (2019). Grounded theory research: A design framework for novice researchers. *SAGE open Medicine*, 7, https://www.ncbi.nlm.nih.gov/pmc/articles/PMC6318722/#bibr12-2050312118822927

- Clark, A., & Sousa, B. (2018). Definitively unfinished: Why the growth mindset is vital for educators and academic workplaces. *Nurse Education Today*, 69, 26–29.

- Clarke, A. (2005). *Situational analysis: Grounded theory after the postmodern turn*. Sage.

- Claxton, C., & Ralston, I. (1978). *Learning styles: Their impact on teaching and administration*. National Institute of Education.

- Clayton, V., & Birren, J. (1980). The development of wisdom across the life-span: A reexamination of an ancient topic. In P. Baltes & O. Brim (Eds.), *Life-span development and behavior* (pp. 103–135). Academic Press.

- Codreanu, A. (2016). A VUCA action framework for a VUCA environment. Leadership challenges and solutions. *Journal of Defense Resources Management*, 7(2), 31–38.

- Coffield, F., Moseley, D., Hall, E., & Ecclestone, K. (2004). *Learning styles and pedagogy in post-16 learning. A systematic and critical review*. Learning and Skills Research Center.

- Cohen, L., Manion, L., & Morrison, K. (2007). *Research methods in education. Professional development in education*. Routledge.

- Cohen, L., Manion, L., & Morrison, K. (2011). The ethics of educational and social research. In L. Manion & K. Morrison (Eds.), *Research methods in education* (pp. 75–104). Routledge.

- Collins, J. (2001). *Good to great why some companies make the leap... and others don't*. Random House Business.

- Compton, D., & Compton, C. (2017). Progression of cohort learning style during an intensive education program. *Adult Learning*, 28(1), 27–34.

- Connor, A. (2002). Broadening the definition of leadership: Active citizens as leaders of change. *Mental Health Review Journal*, 7(4), 15–17.

- Cook, D. (2005). Learning and cognitive styles in web-based learning: theory, evidence, and application. *Academic Medicine*, 80(3), 266–278.

- Corbin, J., & Strauss, A. (2008). *Basics of qualitative research: Techniques and procedures for developing grounded theory* (3rd ed.). Sage.

- Corbin, J., & Strauss, A. (1996). Analytic ordering for theoretical purposes. *Qualitative Inquiry*, 2(2), 139–150.

- Cox, B., & Ramirez, M. (1981). Cognitive styles: Implications for multiethnic education. In J. Banks (Ed.), *Education in the 80's* (pp. 94–103). National Education Association.

- Creswell, J. (2014). *Research design: qualitative, quantitative, and mixed methods approaches*. Sage.

- Creswell, J., & Clark, V. (2011). *Designing and conducting mixed methods research*. Sage.

- Crotty, M. (1998). *The foundations of social research: Meaning and perspective in the research process*. Sage.

- Cumming, T., Shackleton, R., Förster, J., Dini, J., Khan, A., Gumula, M., & Kubiszewski, I. (2017). Achieving the national development agenda and the Sustainable Development Goals (SDGs) through investment in ecological infrastructure: A case study of South Africa. *Ecosystem Services, 27*, 253–260.

- Curry, L. (1981). Learning preferences in continuing medical education. *Canadian Medical Association Journal, 124*, 535–536.

- Darlo Digital (2018). *Can learning styles change?* https://darlodigital.com/can-learning-styles-change/

- Datar, S., Garvin, D., & Cullen, P.(2010). *Rethinking the MBA: business education at a crossroads*. Harvard Business School Press.

- Davies, J. (2016). Are business school deans doomed? The global financial crisis, Brexit and all that. *Journal of Management Development, 35*(7), 901–915.

- David, L. (2007). Actor-network theory (ANT) in tearning theories. https://www.learning-theories.com/actor-network-theory-ant.html.

- Daymon, C., & Holloway, I. (2010). *Qualitative research methods in public relations and marketing communications*. Routledge.

- De Frutos-Belizón, J., Martín-Alcázar, F., & Sánchez-Gardey, G. (2018). Managing the "valley of death" between the management research and the management practice: An empirical academic evidence. *Cuadernos de Gestión*. https://www.researchgate.net/publication/327865117_Managing_the_valley_of_death_between_the_management_research_and_the_management_practice_An_empirical_academic_evidence

- De Vita, G. (2001). Learning styles, culture and inclusive instruction in the multicultural classroom: a business and management perspective. *Innovations in Education and Teaching International, 38*(2), 165–74.

- Denison, D. (1984). Bringing corporate culture to the bottom line. *Organizational Dynamics, 13*(2), 4–22.

- Denzin, N. (1992). *Symbolic interactionism and cultural studies: The politics of interpretation*. Blackwell.

- Dey, N. (1999). Globalization of business education in India. *The Indian Journal of Commerce*, *49*(189), 151–163.

- Dierksmeier, C., Amann, W., Pirson, M., Spitzeck, H., & Von Kimakowitz, E. (Eds.). (2011). *Humanistic ethics in the age of globality*. Palgrave.

- Dillon, D. (2012). *Grounded theory and qualitative research*. Blackwell Publishing.

- Dillon, D., O'Brien, D., & Heilman, E. (2000). Literacy research in the next millennium: From paradigms to pragmatism and practicality. *Reading Research Quarterly*, *35*, 10–26.

- Donaldson, L. (2001). *The contingency theory of organizations*. Sage.

- Druckman, D., & Porter, L. (1991). Developing careers. In D. Druckman & R. Bjork (Eds.), *In the mind's eye: Enhancing human performance* (pp. 80–103). National Academy Press.

- Duff, A., & Duffy, T. (2002). Psychometric properties of Honey & Mumford's Learning Styles Questionnaire (LSQ). *Personality and Individual Differences*, *33*(1), 147–163.

- Dunn, R. (1996). *How to implement and supervise a learning style program*. http://www.ascd.org/publications/books/196010/chapters/All-About-Learning-Styles.aspx

- Dunn, R. (1997). The goals and track record of multicultural education. *Educational leadership*, *54*(7), 74–77.

- Dunn, R., Beaudry, J., & Klavas, A. (1989). Survey of research on learning Styles. *Educational Leadership*, *46*, 50–58.

- Dunn, R., & Griggs, S. (1995). Practical approaches to using learning styles in higher education: The how-to steps. In S. Griggs (Ed.), *Practical approaches to using learning styles in higher education* (pp. 54–66). Greenwood.

- Durand, T., & Dameron, S. (2017). Trends and challenges in management education around the world. In T. Durand & S. Dameron (Eds.), *The future of management education* (pp. 1–22). Palgrave Macmillan.

- Dweck, C. (2015). Carol Dweck revisits the 'Growth Mindset'. *Education Week*. https://www.edweek.org/ew/articles/2015/09/23/carol-dweck-revisits-the-growth-mindset.html

- Dwyer, M. (2004). More is better: The impact of study abroad program duration. Frontiers: The Interdisciplinary Journal of Study Abroad, IX, 151–164.

- Dyllick, T., & Hockerts. K. (2002). Beyond the business case for corporate sustainability. *Business Strategy & The Environment*, *11*(2), 130–14.

- Ebernacer, J., Lombo, J., & Murillo, J. (2015). Editorial: Habits: Plasticity, learning and freedom. *Frontiers in Human Neuroscience*, 9. https://www.frontiersin.org/studys/10.3389/fnhum.2015.00468/full

- Eisner, E. (1998). *The enlightened eye: Qualitative inquiry and the enlightenment of educational practice*. Prentice Hall.

- England, K. (1994). Getting personal: Reflexivity, positionality, and feminist research. *The Professional Geographer*, *46*(1), 80–89.

- Engels, P., & De Gara, C. (2010). Learning styles of medical students, general surgery residents, and general surgeons: Implications for surgical education. *BMC Medical Education*, 10. https://www.ncbi.nlm.nih.gov/pubmed/20591159

- Etikan, I., Musa, S., & Alkassim, R. (2015). Comparison of convenience sampling and purposive sampling. American Journal of Theoretical and Applied Statistics, 5(1), 1–4.

- Eudy, R. (2018, July 18). What is a learning ecosystem? And how does it support corporate strategy? ej4.com. https://www.ej4.com/blog/what-is-a-learning-ecosystem

- Eyisi, D. (2016). The usefulness of qualitative and quantitative approaches and methods in researching problem-solving ability in science education curriculum. *Journal of Education and Practice*, *7*(15), 91–100.

- Fassinger, R. E., Shullman, S. L., & Buki, L. P. (2017). Future shock: Counseling psychology in a VUCA world. *The Counseling Psychologist*, *45*(7), 1048–1058.

- Fendt, J., & Sachs, W. (2007. Grounded theory method in management research: User's perspectives. *Organizational Research Methods*, *11*(3), 430–455.

- Fink, L. (2003). *Creating significant learning experiences: An integrated approach to designing college courses*. Jossey-Bass.

- Finlay, L. (2002). Negotiating the swamp: The opportunity and challenge of reflexivity in research practice. *Qualitative Research*, *2*(2), 209–230.

- Finlay, L. (2009). Debating phenomenological research methods. *Phenomenology & Practice*, *3*(1), 6–25.

- Fragueiro, F., & Thomas, H. (2011). *Strategic leadership in the business school keeping one step ahead*. Cambridge University Press.

- Francis, J., Johnston, M., Robertson, C., Glidewell, L., Entwistle, V., Eccles, M., & Grimshaw, J. (2010). What is an adequate sample size? Operationalizing data saturation for theory-based interview studies. *Psychology and Health*, *25*, 1229–1245.

- García-Acosta, G., Pinilla, M., Larrahondo, P., & Lange Morales, M. (2014). Ergoecology: fundamentals of a new multidisciplinary field. *Theoretical Issues in Ergonomics Science*, *15*(2), 111–133

- Gardner, H. (1983). *Frames of mind: The theory of multiple intelligences*. Basic Books.

- Gardner, H. (1991). *The unschooled mind: How children think and how schools should teach*. Basic Books.

- Gardner, H., & Davis, K. (2013). *The app generation. How today's youth navigate identity, intimacy, and imagination in the digital world*. Yale University Press.

- Gay, G. (2002). Preparing for culturally responsive teaching. *Journal of Teacher Education*, *53*(2), 106–116.

- Ghemawat, P. (2011). Bridging the globalization gap at top business schools: curricular challenges and a response. In Canals, J. (Ed.) (2011). *The future of leadership development*. Palgrave, 178–217.

- Glaser, B. (1978). *Theoretical sensitivity*. Sociology Press.

- Glaser, B. (1992). *Basics of grounded theory analysis: Emergence vs. forcing*. Sociology Press.

- Glaser, B. (2001). *The grounded theory perspective: Conceptualization contrasted with description*. The Sociology Press.

- Glaser, B., & Strauss, A. (1967). *The discovery of grounded theory: Strategies for qualitative research*. Aldine.

- Glaum, M., & Oesterle, M. (2007). 40 years of research on internationalization and firm performance: more questions than answers? *Management International Review*, *47*(3): 307–317.

- Godemann, J., Haertle, J., Herzig, C., & Moon, J. (2014). United Nations supported Principles for Responsible Management Education: Purpose, progress and prospects. *Journal of Cleaner Production*, *62*(16), 16–23.

- Goleman, D. (2002). Leadership that gets results. *Harvard Business Review*, March-April. http://www.powerelectronics.ac.uk/documents/leadership-that-gets-results.pdf

- Goleman, D. (1998). *Working with emotional intelligence*. Random House.

- Gravett, L., & Caldwell, S. (2016). *Learning agility*. Palgrave.

- Griggs, S. (1992). *Learning style counseling*. Educational Resource Center for Counseling and Student Services.

- Gröschl, S., & Gabaldon, P. (2018). Business schools and the development of responsible leaders: A proposition of Edgar Morin's transdisciplinarity. *Journal of Business Ethics*, *153*(1), 185–195.

- Guest, G., Bunce, A., & Johnson, L. (2006). How many interviews are enough? An experiment with data saturation and variability field methods. *Field Methods*, *18*(1), 59–82.

- Gunder, M. (2011). Fake it until you make it, and then…. *Planning Theory*, *10*(3), 201–212.

- Haar, J., Hall, G., Schoepp, P., & Smith, D. (2002). How teachers teach to students with different learning styles. *Clearing House*, *75*(3), 142–145.

- Hall, S. (1990). Cultural identity and diaspora. In J. Rutherford (Ed.), *Identity: community, culture, difference* (pp. 2–27). Lawrence & Wishart.

- Hamzah, M., Othman, A., Hassan, F., Razak, N., & Yunus, N. (2016). Conceptualizing a schematic grid view of customer knowledge from the Johari window's perspective. *Procedia Economics and Finance*, *37*, 471–479.

- Harley, D., Jolibette, K., McCormick, K., & Tice, K. (2011). Race, class, and gender: A constellation of positionalities with implications for counseling. *Journal of Multicultural Counselling and Development*, *30*(4), 216–223.

- Hawes, J. (2004). Teaching is not telling: The case method as a form of interactive learning. *Journal for Advancement of Marketing Education*, *5*(Winter), 47–54.

- Hayes, J., & Allinson, C. W. (1993). Matching learning style and instructional strategy: An application of the person-environment interaction paradigm. *Perceptual and Motor Skills*, *76*, 63–79.

- Hennink, M., Kaiser, B., & Marconi, V. (2016). Code saturation versus meaning saturation: How many interviews are enough? *Qualitative Health Research*, *27*(4), 1–18.

- Hersey, P., Blanchard, K., & Johnson, D. (1969). *Management of organizational behaviour*. Prentice Hall.

- Herzberg, F., Mausner, B. & Snyderman, B. (1959). *The motivation to work* (2nd ed.). Wiley.

- Hill, C. (2000). Dominant logic and the iron cage. In J. Baum & F. Dobbin (Eds.), *Economics meets sociology in strategic management* (pp. 187–191). Emerald Group Publishing.

- Hoare, K., Mills, J., & Francis, K. (2012). Dancing with data: an example of acquiring theoretical sensitivity in a grounded theory study. *International Journal of Nursing Practice*, *18*(3), 240–245.

- Hodgson, P., & White, R. (2001). *Relax – It's only uncertainty*. Pearson FT Press.

- Hofstede, G. (2011). *Dimensionalizing cultures: The Hofstede model in context*. https://scholarworks.gvsu.edu/orpc/vol2/iss1/8/

- Hofstede, G., & Minkov, M. (2010). *Cultures and organizations: Software of the mind: International cooperation and its importance for survival*. McGraw-Hill.

- Honey, P., & Mumford, A. (2009). *The learning style helper's guide*. Peter Honey Publications.

- House, R., Javidan, M., Hanges, P., & Dorfman, P. (2002). Understanding cultures and implicit leadership theories across the globe: An introduction to project GLOBE. *Journal of World Business*, *37*(1), 3–10.

- Howard-Jones P. (2014). Neuroscience and education: myths and messages. *Nature Reviews Neuroscience*, *15*, 817–824.

- Thomas, H., & Peters, K. (2012). A sustainable model for business schools. *Journal of Management Development*, *31*, 377–385.

- Hung, L., Phinney, A., Chaudhury, H., Rodney, P., Tabamo, J., & Bohl, D. (2018). Appreciative inquiry: Bridging research and practice in a hospital setting. *International Journal of Qualitative Methods*, *17*. https://journals.sagepub.com/doi/full/10.1177/1609406918769444

- Hwang, G., Sung, H., Hung, C., & Huang, I. (2014). A learning style perspective to investigate the necessity of developing adaptive learning systems. *Educational Technology & Society*, *16*(2), 188–197.

- Iñiguez de Onzoño, S., & Carmona, S. (2012). Red Queen approach to the fading margins of business education. *Journal of Management Development*, *31*(4), 386–397.

- Intel (2012). *Marzano's new taxonomy*. https://www.intel.com/content/dam/www/program/education/us/en/documents/project-design/skills/marzano-taxonomy.pdf

- Irvine, J., & York, D. (1995). Learning styles and culturally diverse students: A literature review. In J. A. Banks & C. A. Banks (Eds.), *Handbook of research on multicultural education* (pp. 199–213). Macmillan.

- Ivory, Chr., Misekll, P., Shipton, H., White A., & Moeslein, K. (2006). *The future of UK business schools*. AIM research. http://wi1.uni-erlangen.de/files/busschool.pdf

- Jagadeesh, R. (2000). Assuring quality in management education: the Indian context. *Quality Assurance in Education*, *8*(3), 110–119.

- Jans, V., & Leclerq, D. (1997) Metacognitive realism: a cognitive style or a learning strategy? *Educational Psychology*, *17*(1-2), 101–110.

- Jette, D., Grover, L., & Keck, C. (2003). A qualitative study of clinical decision making in recommending discharge placement from the acute care setting. *Physical Therapy*, *83*, 224–236.

- Johanson, J., & Vahlne, J.-E. (1977). The internationalization process of the firm-a model of knowledge development and increasing foreign market commitments. *Journal of International Business Studies*, *8*, 23–32.

- Joshi, A., Neely, B., Emrich, C., Griffiths, D., & George, G. (2015). Gender research in AMJ: An overview of five decades of empirical research and calls to action. *Academy of Management Journal*, *58*(5), 1459–1475.

- Juhasz, I. (2014). The workforce in Indian organizations: an analysis based upon the dimensions of Hofstede's model. In J. Karlovitz (Ed.). *Economics Questions, Issues and Problems* (pp. 38–45). International Research Institute.

- Kabele, J. (2010). The agency/structure dilemma: A coordination solution. *Journal for the Theory of Social Behaviour*, *40*(3), 314–338.

- Kaplan, R., & Kaiser, R. (2003a). Developing versatile leadership. *MIT Sloan Management Review*, *44*(4), 19–26.

- Kaplan, R., & Kaiser, R. (2003b). The turbulence within: How sensitivities throw off performance in executives. In R. J. Burke and C. L. Cooper (Eds.), *Leading in turbulent times* (pp. 31–53). Blackwell.

- Kaushik, V., Walsh, C., & Lai, D. (2019). Pragmatism as a research paradigm and its implications for social work research. Social Sciences, 8 (225), https://www.researchgate.net/publication/335662764_Pragmatism_as_a_Research_Paradigm_and_Its_Implications_for_Social_Work_Research

- Keefe, J. (1985). Assessment of learning style variables: The NASSP Task Force Model. *Theory into Practice*, *24*(2), 138–44.

- Kegan, R. (1994). *In over our Heads: The mental demands of modern life*. Harvard University Press.

- Kegan, R., & Lahey, L. (2009). *Immunity to change: How to overcome it and unlock potential in yourself and your organization*. Harvard Business School Press.

- Keller, G. (2013). *The ONE thing the surprisingly simple truth behind extraordinary results*. Bard Press.

- Kellerman, B. (2012). Becoming leadership literate. In S. Snook, N. Nohria & R. Khurana (Eds.), *The handbook for teaching leadership: Knowing, doing, and being* (pp. 35-45). Sage.

- Khatun, A., & Dar, S. (2019). Management education in India: the challenges of changing scenario. *Entrepreneurship Education, 2*(1), 19–38.

- Kim, W., & Mauborgne, R. (2014, May). Blue ocean leadership. *Harvard Business Review.* https://hbr.org/2014/05/blue-ocean-leadership

- Kinnunen, R., & Vauras, M. (1995). Comprehension monitoring and the level of comprehension in high-and low-achieving primary school children's reading. *Learning and Instruction, 5*, 143–165.

- Kirby, J. (1988). Style, strategy and skill in reading. In R. Schmeck (Ed.), *Learning strategies and learning styles* (pp. 229–274). Plenum Press.

- Kirkpatrick, D. (1976). Evaluation of training. In R. Craig (Ed.), *Training and development handbook: A guide to human resource development* (pp. 317–319). McGraw Hill.

- Knefelkamp, L. (2003). *Effective teaching for the multicultural classroom.* http://www.diversityweb.org/Digest/F97/curriculum.html

- Knoll, A., Otani, H., Skeel, R., & Van Horn, K. (2016). Learning style, judgements of learning, and learning of verbal and visual information. *British Journal of Psychology, 108(3),* 544-563.

- Knowles, M. S., Holton, E., & Swanson, R. (2011). *The adult learner: the definitive classic in adult education and human resource development.* Elsevier.

- Köksalan, M., Büyükbaşaran, T., Özpeynirci, Ö., & Wallenius, J. (2010). A flexible approach to ranking with an application to MBA Programs. *European Journal of Operational Research, 201*(2), 470–476.

- Kolb, A., & Kolb, D. (2006) Learning styles and learning spaces: A review of the multidisciplinary application of experiential learning theory in higher education. In R. R. Sims & S. J. Sims (Eds.), *Learning styles and learning: A key to meeting the accountability demands in education* (pp. 45–91). Nova Science.

- Korn Ferry (2015). *FYI – For learning agility.* http://static.kornferry.com/media/sidebar_downloads/82199-FYI_Learning_Agility_2nd_BLAD.pdf

- Kosower, E., & Berman, N. (1996). Comparison of pediatric resident and faculty learning styles: Implications for medical education. *American Journal of Medical Science, 312*(5), 214–18.

- Kumar, S., & Dash, K. (2011). Management education in India: Trends, issues and implications. *Research Journal of International Studies, 18*, 16–26.

- Kutay, H. (2006). *A comparative study about learning styles preference of two cultures*. [Unpublished doctoral dissertation]. Ohio State University. http://citeseerx.ist.psu.edu/viewdoc/download?doi=10.1.1.860.7071&rep=rep1&type=pdf

- Labib, A., Canós, J., & Penadés, C. (2017). On the way to learning style models integration: A learner's characteristics ontology. *Computers in Human Behavior, 73*, 433–445.

- Lanz, K. (2013). The art of self-awareness. *Training Journal, 11*, 65–69.

- Le Navenec, C. (1993). *The illness career of family subsystems experiencing dementia: Predominant phases and styles of managing* [Doctoral dissertation]. University of Calgary, Calgary.

- Lee, S., & Hoffman, K. (2015). Learning the ShamWow: Creating infomercials to teach the AIDA model. *Marketing Education Review, 25*(1), 9–14.

- LePage, A. (1991). Anthony Robbins: He finds success by selling success. *San Diego Business Journal, 12*(34), 1–3.

- Lindlof, T., & Taylor, B. (2011). *Qualitative communication research methods* (3rd edition). Thousand Oaks, Sage.

- Lombardo, M., & Eichinger, R. (2000). High potentials as high learners. *Human Resource Management, 39*(4), 321–329.

- Lorange, P. (2008). *Thought leadership meets business*. Cambridge University Press.

- Lorange, P. (2012). The business school of the future: The network-based business model. *Journal of Management Development, 31*(4), 424–430.

- Luft, J., & Ingham, H. (1955). *The Johari window, a graphic model of interpersonal awareness. Proceedings of the Western Training Laboratory in Group Development*. University of California Press.

- Luhmann N. (1991). *Soziale Systeme: Grundriss einer allgemeinen Theorie*. Suhrkamp.

- Maguire, S. (1997). Business ethics: A compromise between politics and virtue. *Journal of Business Ethics, 16*(12/13), 1411–1418.

- Malterud K., Siersma V., & Guassora, A. (2016). Sample size in qualitative interview studies: Guided by information power. *Qualitative Health Research, 26*(13):1753–1760.

- Mantiri, O. (2013). The influence of culture on learning styles. http://dx.doi.org/10.2139/ssrn.2566117

- Markman, A. (2017, September 12). Gender differences among adults in business school – Why do women perform worse than men in many classes in business school? *Psychology Today*.

https://www.psychologytoday.com/ca/blog/ulterior-motives/201709/gender-differences-among-adults-in-business-school

- Markovsky, B. (2004). Theory construction. In G. Ritzer (Ed.), *Encyclopedia of social theory* (Vol. II, pp. 830–834). Sage.

- Marzano, R. (2000). *Designing a new taxonomy of educational objectives*. Corwin Press.

- Marzano, R., & Kendall, J. (2007). *The new taxonomy of educational objectives* (2nd ed.). Corwin Press.

- Matten, D. & Moon, J. (2004). Corporate social responsibility. *Journal of Business Ethics, 54,* 323–337.

- McCoyd, J., & Kerson, T. (2006). Conducting intensive interviews using email: A serendipitous comparative opportunity. *Qualitative Social Work, 5,* 389–406.

- Merriam, S., Johnson-Bailey, J., Lee, M., Lee, Y., Ntseane, G., & Muhamed, M.

- (2001). Power and positionality: Negotiating insider/outsider status within and across. cultures. *International Journal of Lifelong Education, 20*(5), 405–416.

- Merrill, D. (2000). Instructional strategies and learning styles: Which takes precedence? In R. Reiser & J. Dempsey (Eds.), *Trends and issues in instructional technology* (pp. 33–51). Prentice Hall.

- Mikkelsen, K., & Jarche, M. (2015, October 16). *The best leaders are constant learners.* Harvard Business Review. https://hbr.org/2015/10/the-best-leaders-are-constant-learners

- Milgram, R., Dunn, R., & Price, G. (1993). *Teaching and counseling gifted and talented adolescents.* Praeger.

- Millo, Y., & Schinckus, C. (2016). A nuanced perspective on episteme and techne in finance. *International Review of Financial Analysis, 46,* 124–130.

- Mintzberg, H. (2004). *Managers not MBAs: A hard look at the soft practice of managing and management development.* Prentice Hall.

- Mintzberg, H., Lampel, J., & Ahlstrand, B. (2009). *Strategy safari: The complete guide through the wilds of strategic management.* Prentice Hall.

- Morris, M., Savani, K., & Fincher, K. (2019). Metacognition fosters cultural learning: Evidence from individual differences and situational prompts. *Journal of Personality and Social Psychology, 116*(1), 46–68.

- Morse, J. (2000). Determining sample size. *Qualitative Health Research, 10,* 3–5.

- Morse, J. (2004). Theoretical saturation. In M. Lewis-Beck, A. Bryman & T. Liao (Eds.), *The Sage encyclopedia of social science research methods* (p. 1123). Sage. http://sk.sagepub.com/reference/download/socialscience/n1011.pdf

- Morse, J. (2015). Data were saturated. *Qualitative Health Research*, *25*, 587–588.

- Morse, J., & Niehaus, L. (2009). *Mixed method design: Principles and procedures.* Left Coast Press.

- Muff, K., Kapalka, A., & Dyllick, T. (2017). The Gap Frame – Translating the SDGs into relevant national grand challenges for strategic business opportunities. *The International Journal of Management Education*, *15*, 363–383.

- Myers, I. (1990). *Gifts differing.* Consulting Psychologists Press.

- Nagel, D., Burns, V., Tilley, C., & Aubin, D. (2015). When novice researchers adopt constructivist grounded theory: Navigating less travelled paradigmatic and methodological paths in PhD dissertation work. *International Journal of Doctoral Studies*, *10*, 365–383.

- Nedopil, C., Steger, U. & Amann, W. (2011). *Complexity in organizations: Text and cases.* Palgrave.

- Nehls, K., Smith, B., & Schneider, H. (2015). Video-conferencing interviews in qualitative research. In S. Hai-Jew (Ed.). *Enhancing qualitative and mixed methods research with technology. Advances in Knowledge Acquisition, Transfer, and Management* (pp. 140–157). IGI.

- Nelson, T. O., & Narens, L. (1994). Why investigate metacognition? In J. Metcalfe & A. P. Shimamura (Eds.), *Metacognition: Knowing about knowing* (pp. 1–25). MIT.

- Newton, P., & Miah, M. (2017). Evidence-based higher education – Is the learning styles 'myth' important? *Frontiers in Psychology*, *8*(444). 10.3389/fpsyg.2017.00444

- Nikitina, T., & Lapina, I. (2017). Overview of trends and developments in business education. In *Proceedings of the 21st World Multi-Conference on Systemics, Cybernetics and Informatics* (WMSCI 2017) (Vol. 2).

- Nonaka, I., & Toyama, R. (2007). Strategic management as distributed practical wisdom (phronesis). *Industrial & Corporate Change*, *16*(3), 371–394.

- Onwuegbuzie, A., & Leech, N. (2007). A call for qualitative power analyses. *Quality & Quantity*, *41*, 105–121.

- O'Reilly, M., & Parker, N. (2012). "Unsatisfactory saturation": a critical exploration of the notion of saturated sample sizes in qualitative research. *Qualitative Research*, *13*(2): 190–197.

- Opdenakker, R. (2006). Advantages and disadvantages of four interview techniques in qualitative research. *Forum: Qualitative Social Research*, *7*(4), 34–41.

- Ormston, R., Spencer, L., Barnard, M., & Snape, D. (2014). The foundations of qualitative research. In J. Ritchie, J. Lewis, C. Nicholls & R. Ormston (Eds.), *Qualitative Research Practice: A Guide for Social Science Students and Researchers* (pp. 1–25). Sage.

- Örtenblad, A. (2001). On differences between organizational learning and learning organization. *The Learning Organization*, *8*(3), 125–133.

- Oviatt, B., & McDougall, P. (1994). Toward a theory of international new ventures. *Journal of International Business Studies*, *25*, 45–64.

- Panadero, E. (2017). Review of self-regulated learning: Six models and four directions for research. *Frontiers in Psychology*, *8*(April), 1–28.

- Pandey, S. (2017). A guide to professional doctorates in business and management. *Qualitative Research in Organizations and Management*, *12*(4), 335–337.

- Parry, K. (2003). How? And why?: Theory emergence and using grounded theory to determine levels of analysis. In F. Dansereau & F. Yammarino (Eds.), *Multi-Level Issues in Organizational Behavior and Strategy* (pp. 127–141). Emerald.

- Pashler, H., McDaniel, M., Rohrer, D., & Bjork, R. (2008). Learning styles: concepts and evidence. *Psychological Science in the Public Interest*, *9*(3), 105–119.

- Pask, G. (1988). Learning strategies, teaching strategies and conceptual learning style. In R. Schmeck (Ed.), *Learning strategies and learning styles* (pp. 83-100). Plenum Press.

- Peiperl, M., & Trevelyan, R. (1997). Predictors of performance at business school and beyond. *Journal of Management Development*, *16*(5), 354–367.

- Peng, M. (2006). Mapping a research agenda. In Butler, K. (ed.).*Finance and the search for the 'big' question in international business* (p. 5), AIB Insights.

- Perry, M., & Win, S. (2013). An Evaluation of PRME's contribution to responsibility in higher education. *The Journal of Corporate Citizenship*, *49*(March), 48–70.

- Philip, J. (1992). Management education in India: Past, present and future. *Vikalpa*, *17*(4), 19–24. https://journals.sagepub.com/doi/pdf/10.1177/0256090919920404

- Philips, J. (1996). Measuring ROI: The fifth level of evaluation. *Technical & Skills Training*, *April*, 10–13.

- Piaw, C., & Ting, L. (2014). Are school leaders born or made? Examining factors of leadership styles of Malaysian school leaders. *Procedia – Social and Behavioral Sciences, 116*, 5120–5124.

- Pintrich, P. (1995). Understanding self-regulated learning. *New Directions for Teaching and Learning, 63*, 3–12.

- Pirson, M., Goodpaster, K., & Dierksmeier, C. (2016). Human dignity and business. *Business Ethics Quarterly, 26*(4), 465–478.

- Porter, M. (2008). The five competitive forces. *Harvard Business Review, 86*(1), 79–93

- Puempin, C., & Amann, W. (2005). *Strategische Erfolgspositionen – Kernkompetenzen aufbauen und umsetzen*. Haupt.

- Rahman, A., & Manaf, N. (2017). A critical analysis of Bloom's taxonomy in teaching creative and critical thinking skills in Malaysia through English literature. *English Language Teaching, 10*(9), 245–256.

- Raja, R., & Nagasubramani, P. (2018). Impact of modern technology in education. *Journal of Applied and Advanced Research, 3*(1), 33–35.

- Ralph, N., Birks, M., & Chapman, Y. (2015). The methodological dynamism of grounded theory. International Journal of Qualitative Methods, 14, 1–6.

- Ramirez, M. (1989). Pluralistic education: A bicognitive-multicultural model. *The Clearinghouse Bulletin, 3*, 4–5.

- Reid, S. (n.d.). Online classes and how they change the nature of classes. First Monday, 14(3). https://firstmonday.org/article/view/2167/2114

- Kirschner, P. (2017). Stop propagating the learning styles myth. *Computers and Education, 106*, 166-71.

- Robinson, J. (2016). Connecting leadership and learning: Do versatile learners make connective leaders? *Higher Learning Research Communications, 6*(1), 35–51. http://www.hlrcjournal.com/index.php/HLRC/article/view/293

- Robinson, P. (2012). *Abilities to learn: Cognitive abilities*. In. N. Seel (Ed.), *Open learning environments* (pp. 17-21). Springer Academic.

- Robles, M., & Roberson, M. (2014). The state of studying and learning in business schools today: applying an expectancy theory framework. *The Journal of Research in Business Education, 56*(1), 17–31.

- Robson, C. (2002). *Real world research: A resource for social scientists and practitioner-researchers*. Blackwell Publishing.

- Rolfe, A., & Cheek, B. (2012). Learning styles. *InnovAiT*, *5*(3), 176–81.

- Rolfe, G., Freshwater, D., & Jasper, M. (2001) *Critical reflection in nursing and the helping professions: a user's guide*. Palgrave Macmillan.

- Romanelli, F., Bird, E., & Ryan, M. (2009). Learning styles: A review of theory, application, and best practices. *American Journal of Pharmaceutical Education*; *73*(1). https://www.ajpe.org/doi/pdf/10.5688/aj730109

- Rousseau, D. (1990). Assessing organizational culture: The case for multiple methods. In B. Schneider (Ed.), *Organizational climate and culture* (pp. 153–92). Jossey-Bass Publishers.

- Ruigrok, W., Amann, W., & Wagner, H. (2007). The internationalization-performance relationship at Swiss firms: A test of the S-shape and extreme degrees of internationalization? *Management International Review*, 47(3), 22–34.

- Ruigrok, W., Amann, W. & Wagner, H. (2007) The internationalization-performance relationship at Swiss firms: A test of the S-shape and extreme degrees of internationalization. *Management International Review, 47*, 349–368.

- Sadler-Smith, E. (2010). 'Learning style': frameworks and instruments. *Educational Psychology*, *17*(1–2), 51–63. https://www.tandfonline.com/doi/abs/10.1080/0144341970170103?src=recsys

- Saikia, J. (2011). *The present status of liberal commerce education and management focused business education*. https://www.scribd.com/document/48695215/The-present-status-of-Liberal-Commerce-Education-and-Management-Focused-Business-Education

- Sánchez-Prieto, J. C., Olmos-Migueláñez, S., & García-Peñalvo, F. J. (2016), Informal tools in formal contexts: development of a model to assess the acceptance of mobile technologies among teachers. *Computers in Human Behavior*, 55, 519–528.

- Salthouse, T. A. (2010). *Major issues in cognitive aging*. Oxford University Press.

- Sarangapani, P. (2014). Knowledge, curricula, and teaching methods: the case of India. *Revue internationale d'éducation de Sèvres, 67*. http://journals.openedition.org/ries/3851

- Saunders, B., Sim, J., Kingstone, T., Baker, S., Waterfield, J., Bartlam, B., & Jinks, C. (2018). Saturation in qualitative research: exploring its conceptualization and operationalization. *Quality & Quantity, 52*(4), 1893–1907.

- Schatzmann, L. (1991). Dimensional analysis: Notes on an alternative approach to the grounding of theory in qualitative research. In D. Maines (Ed.). *Social organization and social process*. Walter de Gruyter.

- Schmidt, A., & Ford, J. K. (2003). Learning within a learner control training environment: The interactive effects of goal orientation and metacognitive instruction on learning outcomes. *Personnel Psychology, 56*, 405–429.

- Schnitker, S., Emmons, R. (2013). Hegel's thesis-antithesis-synthesis model. In: Runehov A., Oviedo L. (eds) .Encyclopedia of Sciences and Religions. Springer. https://link.springer.com/referenceworkentry/10.1007%2F978-1-4020-8265-8_200183#howtocite

- Schueffel, P., Amann, W., & Herbolzheimer, E. (2011). Internationalization of new ventures: tests of growth and survival. *Multinational Business Review, 19*(4), 376–403.

- Schuh, G., Krumm, S., & Amann, W. (2013a). *Chefsache Komplexität – Worauf wir zuerst achten müssen*. Springer.

- Schuh, G., Krumm, S., & Amann, W. (2013b). Complexity management from a leadership perspective. *Complexity Management Journal, 1*(1), 4–11.

- Schwertfeger, B. (2018). IMD: 63 Prozent mehr Bewerbungen. *MBA Journal*. https://www.mba-journal.de/imd-63-prozent-mehr-bewerbungen/

- Scott, H. (2007). *The temporal integration of connected study into a structured life: A grounded theory*. [Unpublished PhD]. University of Portsmouth. http://docs.google.com/viewer?a=v&pid=sites&srcid=Z3JvdW5kZWR0aGVvcnlvbmxpbmUuY29tfHd3d3xneDoyODQ1OWIwNmJmYzRhNzVj

- Scott, S. (2004). Researching shyness: A contradiction in terms? *Qualitative Research, 4*(1), 91–105.

- Seiler, D. (2011). Age and learning style in the adult learner. *The Journal of Human Resource and Adult Learning, 7*(2), 133–138.

- Sharma, S. (2016). Achieving gender equality in India: What works, and what doesn't. https://unu.edu/publications/studys/achieving-gender-equality-in-india-what-works-and-what-doesnt.html

- Shetty, N. (2014). Management education in India: Trends, relevance and challenges ahead. *Nitte Management Review, 8*(2), 139–148. http://www.informaticsjournals.com/index.php/nmr/article/viewFile/18407/15367

- Singh, P., Singh, V., & Rani, S. (2015). Study of industry's perception towards commerce education in India. In N. Tyagi, N. Malik & S. Malik (Eds.). *2nd International Conference on Recent Innovations in Science, Engineering and Management* (p. 936). New Delhi.

- Singh, P., Thambusamy, R., & Ramly, M. (2014). Fit or unfit? Perspectives of employers and university instructors of graduates' generic skills. *Procedia – Social and Behavioral Sciences*, *123*, 315–324.

- Siriopoulos, C., & Pomonis, G. (2007). Learning style changes and their relationship to critical thinking skills. *Journal of College Teaching & Learning*, *4*(1), 45–60.

- Smeyers, P., de Ruyter, D. J., Waghid, Y., & Strand, T. (2014). Publish yet Perish: On the pitfalls of philosophy of education in an age of impact factors. *Studies in Philosophy and Education*, *33*(6), 647–666.

- Snape, D., & Spencer, L. (2003). The foundations of qualitative research. In J. Richie & J. Lewis (Eds.), *Qualitative Research Practice* (pp. 1–23). Sage.

- Sobal, J. (2001). Sample extensiveness in qualitative nutrition education research. *Journal of Nutrition Education*, *33*, 184–192.

- Spender, J.C., & Locke, R. (2011). *Confronting managerialism: How the business elite and their schools threw our lives out of balance*. Zed Books.

- Spitzeck, H., Pirson, M., Amann, W., Von Kimakowitz, E., & Khan, S. (Eds.). (2009). *Humanism in business: Perspectives on the development of a responsible business society*. Cambridge University Press.

- Stander, J., Grimmer, K., & Brink, Y. (2019). Learning styles of physiotherapists: A systematic scoping review. *BMC Medical Education*, *19*(1), 1–9.

- Stanowicz-Stanusch, A., & Amann, W. (Eds.) (2017). *Corporate Social Irresponsibility: Individual Behaviors and Organizational Practices*. IAP.

- Stanowicz-Stanusch, A., Mangia, G., Caldarelli, A., & Amann, W. (Eds.). (2017). *Organizational social irresponsibility: Tools and theoretical insights*. IAP.

- Starks, H., & Trinidad, S. (2007). Choose your method: A comparison of phenomenology, discourse analysis, and grounded theory. *Qualitative Health Research*, *17*(10), 1372–1380.

- Steger, U., Amann, W., & Maznevski, M. (Eds.) (2007). *Managing complexity in global organizations*. Wiley.

- Stephens, M. (2013). Learning to learn. *Library Journal*, *138*(11), 44.

- Stern, P. (2009). In the beginning Glaser and Strauss created grounded theory. In J. M. Morse, P. N. Stern, J. Corbin, B. Bowers, K. Charmaz, & A. Clarke (Eds.), *Developing grounded theory: The second generation* (pp. 23–34). Left Coast Press.

- Sternberg, R., Grigorenko, E., Ferrari, M., & Clinkenbeard, R. (1999). A triarchic analysis of an aptitude-treatment interaction. *European Journal of Psychological Assessment*, *15*, 1–11.

- Steup, M., & Neta, R. (2020). Epistemology. In E. Zalta (Ed.), *The Stanford encyclopedia of philosophy*. https://plato.stanford.edu/archives/sum2020/entries/epistemology/

- Strauss, V. (2013, October 16). Howard Gardner: 'Multiple intelligences' are not 'learning styles'. *Washington Post*. http://courses.educ.ubc.ca/socials/Articles/Howard%20Gardner:%20%E2%80%98Multiple%20intelligences%E2%80%99%20are%20not%20%E2%80%98learning%20styles%E2%80%99%20%7C%20The%20Answer%20Sheet.pdf

- Strauss, A., & Corbin, J. (1998). *Basics of qualitative research: Techniques and procedures for developing grounded theory* (2nd ed.). Sage.

- Strauss, A., & Corbin, J. (1990). *Basics of qualitative research: Grounded theory procedures and techniques*. Sage.

- Strieker, L., & Ross, J. (1964). An assessment of some structural properties of the Jungian personality typology. *Journal of Abnormal and Social Psychology*, *68*, 62–71.

- Suddaby, R. (2006). From the editors: What grounded theory is not. *Academy of Management Journal*, *49*(4), 633–642.

- Swedberg, L., Michelsen, H., Hammar, Ch., & Hylander, I. (2015). On-the-job training makes the difference: healthcare assistants perceived competence and responsibility in the care of patients with home mechanical ventilation. *Scandinavian Journal of Caring Sciences*, *29*(2), 369–378.

- Tashakkori, A., & Teddlie, Ch. (1998). *Mixed methodology: Combining qualitative and quantitative approaches*. Sage.

- Tempelaar, D. (2006). The role of metacognition in business education. *Industry and Higher Education*, *20*, 291–297.

- Thaker, K. (2015). Knowing, doing and being pedagogy in MBA-level management accounting classes: Some empirical evidence. *Australian Accounting Review*, *25*(3), 232–247.

- Thomas, H., Lorange, P., & Sheth, J. (2013). *The business school in the twenty-first century*. Cambridge University Press.

- Thomas, H., Thomas, L., & Wilson, A. (2013). *Promises fulfilled and unfilled in management education*. Emerald.

- Thomson, S. (2001). *Sample size and grounded theory*. https://www.researchgate.net/publication/228513695_Sample_Size_and_Grounded_Theory

- Thomson, B. & Mascazine, J. (1997). Attending to learning styles in mathematics and science classrooms. https://files.eric.ed.gov/fulltext/ED432440.pdf

- Thomson, S. (2011). Sample size and grounded theory. *Journal of Administration and Governance*, 5(1), 45–52.

- Thompson, G., & Vecchio, R. (2009). Situational leadership theory: A test of three versions. *The Leadership Quarterly*, 20(5), 837–848.

- Thornberg, R. (2006). The situated nature of preschool children's conflict strategies. *Educational Psychology*, 26(1), 109–126.

- Thornberg, R., & Charmaz, K. (2012). Grounded theory. In S. Lapan, M. Quartaroli & F. Riemer (Eds.), *Qualitative research: An introduction to methods and design* (pp. 41–67). Jossey-Bass.

- Todorov, E., Shadmehr, R., & Bizzi, E. (1997). Augmented feedback presented in a virtual environment accelerates learning of a difficult motor task. *Journal of Motor Behavior*, 29(2), 147–158.

- Tovstiga, G. (2015). *Strategy in practice*. Wiley.

- Triantafillou, E., Pomportsis, A., & Demetriadis, S. (2003). The design and the formative evaluation of an adaptive educational system based on cognitive styles. *Computers & Education*, 41(1), 87–103.

- Tripathi, S., Amann, W., & F. Kamuzora (2014). Developing responsible managers for new generation organizations: Why the existing business education system needs a humanistic shift. *Journal of Management and Leadership*, 6(1), 56–64.

- Troiano, P. (2003). College students and learning disability: Elements of self-style. *Journal of College Student Development*, 44, 404–419.

- Tuncer, F., & Ali, B. (2017). Managing schools as complex adaptive systems: A strategic perspective. *International Electronic Journal of Elementary Education*, 10(1), 11–26.

- Turner-Walker, E. (2016). *The application of metacognition to business decision making*. [Master thesis]. The Victoria University of Wellington. http://researcharchive.vuw.ac.nz/bitstream/handle/10063/5431/thesis.pdf?sequence=1

- Tyumeneva, Y., Kardanova, E., & Kuzmina, J. (2017). Grit. *European Journal of Psychological Assessment*, 1(1), 1–10.

- Uhl-Bien, M., & Marion, R. (2008). *Complexity Leadership*. Information Age Publishing.

- Valcour, M. (2016). Beating burnout. *Harvard Business Review*, *94*(11), 98–102.

- Van den Berg, H. (2015). Changes in learning styles induced by practical training. *Learning and Individual Differences*, *40*, 84–89.

- Vasileiou, K., Barnett, J., Thorpe, S., & Young, T. (2018). Characterising and justifying sample size sufficiency in interview-based studies: systematic analysis of qualitative health research over a 15-year period. *BMC Medical Research Methodology*, *18*(148). https://bmcmedresmethodol.biomedcentral.com/articles/10.1186/s12874-018-0594-7#citeas

- Viji, V., & Benedict, K. (2017a). Conceptualization: Theory and practice of Marzano's taxonomy in science teaching: An objective portrayal by the investigator. *International Journal of Research Culture Society*, *1*(8), 193–200.

- Viji, V., & Benedict, K. (2017b). Conceptualization of an Innovative Educational Taxonomy for the 21st Century Learners. https://files.eric.ed.gov/fulltext/ED578106.pdf.

- Vollstedt, M., & Rezat, S. (2019) An introduction to grounded theory with a special focus on axial coding and the coding paradigm. In G. Kaiser & N. Presmeg (Eds.), *Compendium for Early Career Researchers in Mathematics Education. ICME-13 Monographs*. Springer.

- Vroom, V., & Yetton. P. (1973). *Leadership and decision-making*. John Wiley & Sons.

- Wallen, A., Morris, B., Devine, B., & Lu, J. (2017). The MBA performance gender gap: Women respond to gender norms by reducing public assertiveness but not private effort. *Personality and Social Psychology Bulletin*, *1*, 1–21.

- Washburne, J. (1936). The definition of learning. *Journal of Educational Psychology*, *27*(8), 603–611.

- Watanabe, A. (2017). The researcher's reflexivity in qualitative interviews. *Educational Studies*, *59*, *105–116*. https://warwick.ac.uk/fac/soc/al/people/mann/interviews/watanabe_2017_the_researchers_reflexivity_in_qualitative_interviews.pdf

- Weiss, M., Razinskas, S., Backmann, J., & Hoegl, M. (2018). Authentic leadership and leaders' mental well-being: An experience sampling study. *The Leadership Quarterly*, *29*(2), 309–321.

- Wellington, J. (2000). *Educational research: Contemporary issues and practical approaches*. Continuum.

- West, B., & Blom, A. (2016). Explaining interviewer effects: A research synthesis, *Journal of Survey Statistics and Methodology*, *5*(2), 175–211.

- Whetten, D., & Cameron, K. (2002). *Developing management skills*. Prentice Hall.

- Wieland, P., Willis, J., Peters, M., & O'Toole, R. (2018). Examining the impact of modality and learning style preferences on recall of psychiatric nursing and pharmacology terms. *Nurse Education Today*, *66*, 130–134.

- Williams, K. (2009). 'Guilty knowledge': Ethical aporia emergent in the research practice of educational development practitioners. *London Review of Education*, *7*(3), 211–221.

- Willingham, D., Hughes, E., & Dobolyi, D. (2015). The scientific status of learning styles theories. *Teaching of Psychology*, *42*(3), 266–271.

- Wohlin, C. (2014). Guidelines for snowballing in systematic literature studies and a replication in software engineering. In EASE (Ed.), *Proceedings of the 18th International Conference on Evaluation and Assessment in Software Engineering*. Association for Computing Machinery. https://doi.org/10.1145/2601248.2601268

- Wright, L., & Leahey, M. (2013). *Nurses and families: A guide to family assessment and intervention*. F. A. Davis.

- Yeung, A. (2011). Student self-concept and effort: Gender and grade differences. *Educational Psychology*, *31*(6), 749–772.

- Yu, H. (2018). *Leap: how to thrive in a world where everything can be copied*. Public Affairs.

- Zahra, S., & George, G. (2002). Absorptive capacity: A review, reconceptualization, and extension. *The Academy of Management Review*, *27*(2), 185–203.

- Zajac, M. (2009). Using learning styles to personalize online learning. *Campus-Wide Information Systems*, *26*(3), 256–265.

- Zhang, L., Cao, T., & Wang, Y. (2018). The mediation role of leadership styles in integrated project collaboration: An emotional intelligence perspective. *International Journal of Project Management*, *36*(2), 317–330.

- Ziegler, M., Booth, T., & Bensch, D. (2013). Getting entangled in the nomological net: Thoughts on validity and conceptual overlap. *European Journal of Psychological Assessment*, *29*(3), 157–161.

- Zimmerman, B. (2000). Attaining self-regulation: a social cognitive perspective. In M. Boekaerts, P. Pintrich & M. Zeidner (Eds.), *Handbook of self-regulation* (pp. 13–40). Academic Press.

Table 18: Overview of the evolution of categories based on iterative comparisons of codes in the ongoing interview process

Codes from interviewee 1 and starting point for comparisons	1.1 Excusing ("The ideal situation is when faculty tailor learning. Yet, the class size of 30, 40 or 60 makes it impossible.")
Comparison with interviewee 2	1.2 Confirmed ("We try hard to satisfy our students.")
Comparison with interviewee 3	1.3 Confirmed ("Each faculty member has own style.")
Comparison with interviewee 4	1.4 Confirmed ("The school shares expectations…. Why should we bother about more, there are no incentives, no training, poor pay.")
Comparison with interviewee 5	1.5 Confirmed ("We don't talk about learning.")
Comparison with interviewee 6	1.6 Confirmed ("We are not trained for anything else…")
Comparison with interviewee 7	1.7 Confirmed ("We have a lecturing approach and no time for much more… we have many courses to teach.")
Comparison with interviewee 8	1.8 Confirmed ("Innovation - is it paid attention to?")
Comparison with interviewee 9	1.9 Confirmed ("Faculty must first learn about learning styles but in reality you choose faculty who accept the least pay… ")
Comparison with interviewee 10	1.10 Confirmed ("Corporate institutions have such high expectations, we can't fulfil.")
Comparison with interviewee 11	1.11 Confirmed ("We are plugged-in faculty … we do as told … otherwise others do it … often I feel we can do more…")

Codes from interviewee 1 and starting point for comparisons	2.1 Complying ("We have a conventional teaching approach, now exploring outcome-based learning … It is still one-sided input.")
Comparison with interviewee 2	2.2 Confirmed ("We do what the school expects us to do… lots of teaching.")
Comparison with interviewee 3	2.3 Confirmed ("On postgraduate level we are more practical.")
Comparison with interviewee 4	2.4 Confirmed ("Practical is always better.")
Comparison with interviewee 5	2.5 Confirmed ("We play our roles, it is often hectic.")
Comparison with interviewee 6	2.6 Confirmed ("Yes, sir… yes, sir, we do… yes, sir.")
Comparison with interviewee 7	2.7 Confirmed ("Practical is always better.")
Comparison with interviewee 8	2.8 Confirmed ("We lecture, no questions allowed, then the exam.")
Comparison with interviewee 9	2.9 Confirmed ("There is high turn-over… they do not invest and we do not challenge… ")
Comparison with interviewee 10	2.10 Confirmed ("We do as told, we do not have tenure… the power is clearly distributed.")
Comparison with interviewee 11	2.11 Confirmed ("I teach business law, which has a very established way of teaching it at our place.")

Codes from interviewee 1 and starting point for comparisons	3.1 Showing initial sensitivity ("Teaching should have something for all … maybe a hybrid approach can help … maybe the assignment design can help … learning is different across different people, especially the information processing.")
Comparison with interviewee 2	3.2 Confirmed ("Yes, we need to innovate … it is very traditional.")
Comparison with interviewee 3	3.3 Confirmed ("One strong style is not enough.")
Comparison with interviewee 4	3.4 Confirmed ("We need to do more.")
Comparison with interviewee 5	3.5 Confirmed ("Practical activities are good.")
Comparison with interviewee 6	3.6 Confirmed ("All learners should go through the entire cycle…")
Comparison with interviewee 7	3.7 Confirmed ("A mix is better.")
Comparison with interviewee 8	3.8 Confirmed ("Yes, we should tailor to all styles, but in reality … faculty needs to see initial positive effect.")
Comparison with interviewee 9	3.9 Confirmed ("Yes students are different.")
Comparison with interviewee 10	3.10 Confirmed ("Students are diverse.")
Comparison with interviewee 11	3.11 Confirmed ("Yes, things like gaming are coming, but…")

Codes from interviewee 1 and starting point for comparisons	4.1 Acknowledging national culture ("Power distance creates fear … whatever comes out of the mouth of a guru is considered the eternal truth … national culture matters … students are not on a first name basis with professors.")
Comparison with interviewee 2	4.2 Confirmed ("The students follow the professor.")
Comparison with interviewee 3	4.3 Confirmed ("Indian culture is there … teachers have the last word, are the key source.")
Comparison with interviewee 4	4.4 Confirmed ("The students want to know from us.")
Comparison with interviewee 5	4.5 Confirmed ("Sir…. sir…. sir…")
Comparison with interviewee 6	4.6 Confirmed ("Youth is very confused with so many influences… the past roles, the modern ones…")
Comparison with interviewee 7	4.7 Confirmed ("The professor knows best.")
Comparison with interviewee 8	4.8 Confirmed ("We do have satisfaction surveys, but students are very respectful, maybe fearful …. Students feel in their comfort zone in hierarchies … past habits are copied and pasted… we have classic hierarchies and gender differences… you perpetuate.")
Comparison with interviewee 9	4.9 Confirmed ("Family values of respect are maintained in school … you respect authority … more male authority probably.")
Comparison with interviewee 10	4.10 Confirmed ("We all respect elders, especially the students, we do not challenge people with authority and seniority like professors and we are clear on the values.")
Comparison with interviewee 11	4.11 Confirmed ("Mostly students like lectures and listening … some start to want more but that it is often premature … software and games are fun, but is it learning?")

Codes from interviewee 1 and starting point for comparisons	5.1 Acknowledging institutional culture ("The culture at our school matters.")
Comparison with interviewee 2	5.2 Confirmed ("Practical is always better.")
Comparison with interviewee 3	5.3 Confirmed ("We teach as told.")
Comparison with interviewee 4	5.4 Confirmed ("We teach so much … little time for training or innovating.")
Comparison with interviewee 5	5.5 Confirmed ("We are mostly a teaching faculty.")
Comparison with interviewee 6	5.6 Confirmed ("We deliver our courses from a pragmatist view.")
Comparison with interviewee 7	5.7 Confirmed ("We always lecture on basic concepts…")
Comparison with interviewee 8	5.8 Confirmed ("Outcome-based learning is now coming … yet still very fuzzy … one person was here who tried to change something and had to leave quickly...")
Comparison with interviewee 9	5.9 Confirmed ("Ownership matters … our private set-up makes us think very short term and on what they get out of it…")
Comparison with interviewee 10	5.10 Confirmed ("We are a private school … it is hard but we do what is expected … there is not much choice.")
Comparison with interviewee 11	5.11 Confirmed ("Lectures still dominate, very few experiments take place … new things make the professor stand out, which is not always positive among faculty or in the school in general.")

Codes from interviewee 1 and starting point for comparisons	6.1 Realising own limitations ("Some interventions can help … but this needs to be studied further.")
Comparison with interviewee 2	6.2 Implicitly confirmed
Comparison with interviewee 3	6.3 Confirmed ("Millenials don't want the basics, they want technology, it will be difficult.")
Comparison with interviewee 4	6.4 Confirmed ("We try to move away from lecturing and concepts, but…")
Comparison with interviewee 5	6.5 Confirmed ("Each course is largely the same.")
Comparison with interviewee 6	6.6 Confirmed ("There cannot be a simple answer to what is most effective … have not worked much on…")
Comparison with interviewee 7	6.7 Not confirmed
Comparison with interviewee 8	6.8 Confirmed ("Students cry in the bathroom as they cannot find internships, we need to do more…")
Comparison with interviewee 9	6.9 Confirmed ("Institutional support and faculty development are not given but much needed … faculty interest is not addressed, which limits really what we can do… ")
Comparison with interviewee 10	6.10 Confirmed ("We need to evolve… there is much to do as faculty…")
Comparison with interviewee 11	6.11 Confirmed ("We do not talk about learning to learn… we often lack the acumen, the foundations…")

Codes from interviewee 1 and starting point for comparisons	7.1 Confirming the meshing hypothesis ("Students can still learn even if uncomfortable, but not as well ... yet emphasis is less on reflection.")
Comparison with interviewee 2	7.2 Partially confirmed
Comparison with interviewee 3	7.3 Confirmed ("Postgraduate needs to be more practical ... meshing will help learn more.")
Comparison with interviewee 4	7.4 Partially confirmed ("Being practical is better... we should use more cases.")
Comparison with interviewee 5	7.5 Partially confirmed ("More practical activities are always better... we use projects...")
Comparison with interviewee 6	7.6 Confirmed ("I do a mix.")
Comparison with interviewee 7	7.7 Partially confirmed ("Professors should develop empathy.")
Comparison with interviewee 8	7.8 Confirmed ("Faculty is too busy.")
Comparison with interviewee 9	7.9 Confirmed ("High teaching load impedes us from doing more, and much needed, better things,")
Comparison with interviewee 10	7.10 Partially confirmed ("Cases are not always best ... if we ignore diversity and do not tailor, learning is less... it is still there but less.")
Comparison with interviewee 11	7.11 Partially confirmed ("Discussions make it livelier and the energy goes up, thus learning goes up.")

Codes from interviewee 1 and starting point for comparisons	8.1 Clarifying responsibilities ("Students need to learn, faculty provides input.")
Comparison with interviewee 2	8.2 Confirmed ("Students learn, that is their role.")
Comparison with interviewee 3	8.3 Confirmed ("Responsibility is with faculty as students are not mature enough.")
Comparison with interviewee 4	8.4 Confirmed ("We as professors design … students need to adapt and learn.")
Comparison with interviewee 5	8.5 Partially confirmed ("We teach in our areas, the rest you know…")
Comparison with interviewee 6	8.6 Confirmed ("The lecturer should adapt as well, not only the student…")
Comparison with interviewee 7	8.7 Confirmed ("Each student is different …. Students adapt.")
Comparison with interviewee 8	8.8 Partially confirmed ("Learning still takes place even if uncomfortable, although maybe less")
Comparison with interviewee 9	8.9 Confirmed ("We are milked as cows, not nurtured; we teach as much as possible … it is up to students to deal with it…")
Comparison with interviewee 10	8.10 Confirmed ("The professor needs to adapt … it is the right thing to do.")
Comparison with interviewee 11	8.11 Confirmed ("The faculty should decide what to do.")

Codes from interviewee 1 and starting point for comparisons	Addition 1
Comparison with interviewee 2	9.2 Showing dated teaching philosophy ("professor with actual experience is superior"… "has to have research too"… "active learning is always better")
Comparison with interviewee 3	9.3 Confirmed ("The responsibility is with faculty as students are not mature enough.")
Comparison with interviewee 4	9.4 Confirmed ("We lecture, yet cases are better.")
Comparison with interviewee 5	9.5 Confirmed ("A mix should be better.")
Comparison with interviewee 6	9.6 Confirmed ("I rely on my practical knowledge…Lecture comes first, then a case.")
Comparison with interviewee 7	9.7 Confirmed ("Basic concepts always have lecture, then discussion.")
Comparison with interviewee 8	9.8 Confirmed ("Faculty should tailor to all needs.")
Comparison with interviewee 9	9.9 Confirmed ("Faculty teaches…")
Comparison with interviewee 10	9.10 Confirmed ("I still lecture a lot… it is good for learning.")
Comparison with interviewee 11	9.11 Confirmed ("The lecture still shares most content most clearly")

Codes from interviewee 1 and starting point for comparisons	Addition 2
Comparison with interviewee 2	
Comparison with interviewee 3	
Comparison with interviewee 4	
Comparison with interviewee 5	10.5 Limiting the learner ("Some have more versatility but that depends on IQ.")
Comparison with interviewee 6	10.6 Not confirmed ("Learners do all … can do all.")
Comparison with interviewee 7	10.7 Confirmed ("I don't know if learners are born or made … students are immature.")
Comparison with interviewee 8	10.8 Confirmed ("Maturity makes all the difference … there isn't a lot.")
Comparison with interviewee 9	10.9 Confirmed ("The student has no voice.")
Comparison with interviewee 10	10.10 Confirmed ("Not all can adapt.")
Comparison with interviewee 11	10.11 Confirmed ("Students are not ready to listen to practical things … they need to learn and listen to more concepts first.")

Codes from interviewee 1 and starting point for comparisons	Addition 3
Comparison with interviewee 2	
Comparison with interviewee 3	
Comparison with interviewee 4	
Comparison with interviewee 5	
Comparison with interviewee 6	
Comparison with interviewee 7	
Comparison with interviewee 8	11.8 Idealising ("Tailor to all needs … a private school status can help trigger action… ")
Comparison with interviewee 9	11.9 Implicitly confirmed ("Faculty must learn about learning styles and surveys from students can help us improve.")
Comparison with interviewee 10	11.10 Confirmed ("We need to talk more about how to learn to learn.")
Comparison with interviewee 11	11.11 Confirmed ("I could do more … I probably would feel better if I did more for the students … in the future I aspire to do more.")

About the author

Prof. Dr.oec. DEdPsy D.Litt. (hon.) Wolfgang Amann graduated from the University of St.Gallen in Switzerland with a doctorate in international strategy. He is also a graduate of key faculty development programs, such as Harvard University's Institute for Management and Leadership in Education, IESE's IFP, IMD's ITP, the EFMD International Deans Program, CEEMAN's IMTA and added a doctorate in educational psychology later on. Next to being active in top management consulting and serving on boards, he has been designing and delivering executive education seminars and advising senior leaders for more than 22 years. He previously was executive academic director of the Goethe Business School, dean of the Complexity Management Academy, director of the MBA program family at the University of St.Gallen and founder of the EBS University, a law school and a supply chain school.

He was repeatedly honored for delivering the best CEMS course amongst all courses offered in the global CEMS network of top business schools. Two of his CEMS courses on strategy as well as globalisation have repeatedly won best course awards at the University of St.Gallen. Together with the colleagues at HEC Paris in Qatar, he won further awards, such as the Enterprise Agility & Entrepreneur of the Year 2015 Award, and the Educational Institute of the Year Award 2016. He currently serves as professor of strategy and leadership as well as the academic director of degree, certificate, open enrolment and custom programs of HEC Paris in Qatar. In his free time, he travels the world for marathon and Ironman races.

www.ingramcontent.com/pod-product-compliance
Lightning Source LLC
Chambersburg PA
CBHW080603170426
43196CB00017B/2887